The First-Year Experience in American Higher Education

{ AN ANNOTATED BIBLIOGRAPHY 4TH EDITION }

Andrew K. Koch, Editor-in-Chief

Stephanie M. Foote, Sara E. Hinkle, Jennifer Keup, and Matthew D. Pistilli, Editors

National Resource Center for The First-Year Experience® and Students in Transition, University of South Carolina, 2007

ACPA American College Personnel Association

Cite as:

Koch, A. K., Foote, S. M., Hinkle, S. E., Keup, J., & Pistilli, M. D. (Eds). (2007). *The first-year experience in American higher education: An annotated bibliography* (4th ed.). Columbia, SC: University of South Carolina, National Resource Center for The First-Year Experience and Students in Transition.

ISBN 978-1-889-27158-3

Additional copies of this monograph may be obtained from the National Resource Center for The First-Year Experience and Students in Transition, University of South Carolina, 1728 College Street, Columbia, SC 29208, Telephone (803) 777-6029, Fax (803) 777-4699.

Special gratitude is expressed to Jean M. Henscheid, Fellow, Tracy L. Skipper, Editorial Projects Coordinator, and Patricia Willingham, Editor, for copyediting; to Dottie Weigel for creating the index and proofing; to Barbara F. Tobolowsky, Associate Director, for proofing; and to Erin M. Morris, Graphic Artist, for layout and design; all at the National Resource Center for The First-Year Experience and Students in Transition.

Library of Congress Cataloging-in-Publication Data

The first-year experience in American higher education : an annotated bibliography / Andrew K. Koch ... [et al.], editors. -- 4th ed.
    p. cm. -- (The first-year experience monograph series ; no. 3)
 Includes bibliographical references and index.
 ISBN 978-1-889271-58-3
 1. College freshmen--United States--Bibliography. 2. College student orientation--United States--Bibliography. I. Koch, Andrew K. (Andrew Karl)
II. National Resource Center for the First-Year Experience & Students in Transition (University of South Carolina).
Z5814.S88F57 2007
[LB2343.32]
016.3781'980973--dc22
                    2007032940

*For Aidan and Shane Keup, Hudson and Hunter Koch, and Gwendolyn Reese Pistilli—
five future first-year students who make our work more purposeful than we ever could have
imagined before they graced our lives.*

{ CONTENTS }

Foreword 1

Introduction 3

I. The First-Year Student 7

Student Needs and Development Issues.................................9
    Student Behavior and Characteristics.................................9
    Student Development Theory and Life Tasks 13
    Health and Wellness... 14
    Spirituality... 20

Diverse Student Populations... 21
    Race, Gender, and Sexual Orientation 21
    Commuter Students.. 29
    Students with Disabilities... 31
    First-Generation and Low-Income Students.................... 31

II. Creating Successful Transitions to the First College Year 35

Precollegiate Experiences and Programs 37
    Precollege and Summer Bridge Programs....................... 37
    Shaping Students' Expectations of College..................... 39
    Admissions 42

Orientation Programs... 45

III. Promoting First-Year Student Success 49

Curricular Interventions Comprising The First-Year Experience........................... 51
    Curriculum and Teaching... 51
    First-Year Seminars 53
    General Information on First-Year Curricular Interventions 56
    Learning Communities... 58
    Library and Information Literacy.................................... 68
    Service-Learning.. 69
    Supplemental Instruction and Other Forms of Academic Support.................... 70

Support Services and Programs.. 73
    Academic and Career Advising.. 73
    Programs Designed to Support Social and Academic Adjustment.................... 77

Involvement in Campus Life and Living Environments 82

Technology 86

Agents of Socialization and Support in the First Year 89
    Faculty as First-Year Student Advocates 89
    Academic Advisors and Other Professional Staff 93
    Parents and Family Members 95
    Peer Influence, Interaction, and Training 99

IV. Other Aspects of the First-Year Experience 105

Access to College 107

The First-Year Experience at Two-Year Institutions 111

The First-Year Experience at Specific Types of Four-Year Colleges & Universities 113

V. Transforming the First-Year Experience 117

Critical Competencies and Attitudes in the First Year of College 119

Promising Institutional Practices in the First-Year Experience 124

Retention and Success of First-Year Students 128

Reports with Implications for the First-Year Experience 135

Assessment and Evaluation 139

About the Editors 149

Index 151

Issues surrounding student access and persistence in the first college year have received increasing attention in recent years. This increased awareness stems from changes in the higher education landscape, including demands from regional accrediting agencies for greater accountability. Also, institutional budget officers and policy makers and others who care about first-year students and their diverse abilities expect assessment and data-driven decision making. Whatever the reasons that led you to pick up this annotated bibliography on the first-year experience in higher education, we know you will be thankful for having so much research described in an organized fashion.

This publication is the result of a collaborative effort between a well-known national research center, the National Resource Center for The First-Year Experience and Students in Transition, and a practitioner-oriented international association, the American College Personnel Association – College Student Educators International (ACPA). This effort illustrates the connections made between research and practice that are needed in higher education today more than ever. Both organizations agree that the collaboration between researchers and practitioners should continue and expand as we explore what we still need to know to make the first college year even more effective.

Edited by a team of higher educators actively engaged in the first-year experience movement, this volume illustrates the collaborative and synergistic nature of research and practice. We hope that it will assist practitioners and researchers alike who need ready access to information about first-year students and the factors, strategies, and practices that influence their success. More important, we hope that the dissemination of this information will influence administrative practice. This is truly an effort designed to allow research to inform practice and, in turn, to allow practice to generate new research questions.

We sincerely hope that as you read this annotated bibliography you will be well informed and enlightened and that you will become even more curious about the needs of first-year students on your own campus.

Vasti Torres
ACPA President
Associate Professor of Higher Education and Student Affairs
Indiana University

Mary Stuart Hunter
Assistant Vice Provost and Executive Director
National Resource Center for The First-Year Experience and Students in Transition
University of South Carolina

{ INTRODUCTION }

This annotated bibliography is about research, and we define the term *research* broadly to include both quantitative and qualitative studies as well as summative and reflective essays on practice. As such, this annotated bibliography is also about practice. Ideally, it is about research and practice at the same time; for we, the editors of this publication, believe that when functioning optimally, research informs practice and practice informs research. To take things a step further, we do not believe in a bifurcation of research and practice. Rather, we believe in their flexible hybridity, that the liminal space where research and practice intersect is the place where innovation and improvement occur. This monograph exists to inform and inspire first-year experience practitioners and scholars who operate in that liminal space.

Our primary goal for this publication is to communicate information to our readers about the sources that we feel are the major contributions to the body of scholarship on the first-year experience published since 2000—the year in which the last edition of this monograph was produced. But we also have higher-order applications in mind. We ask our readers to take into account that our definition of the term communicate does not imply passive listening, or reading, on their part. Rather, it calls for action.

Drawing on the philosophy of John Dewey as shared in his seminal work on aesthetics, *Art as Experience*, we feel that "communication is the process of creating participation" (1934, p. 248)—active participation. Consequently, we hope that this monograph will provide information that can be synthesized and applied to enhance the first-year experience, thereby continuing the important work that has been a major focus of higher education particularly during the last three to four decades. In essence, our broad purpose for writing this work is to help its readers apply the lessons of the past to the present, so that they can positively shape the future.

This work is structured around a five-part framework. Each of the five parts is further divided into subsections to allow closer and, thus, richer examination. We hope that configuring the current edition of the monograph in this way will provide the reader with a logical structure for accessing and applying its content. And we hope that you will be able to use the information as we present it to facilitate change in practices and approaches for scholarly research and assessment associated with the first year of college.

Part I of this monograph, titled "The First-Year Student," includes annotations that provide insight into the behavior, characteristics, and many ways of categorizing our newest students. The section is composed of two subsections: (a) one focused on the needs of and developmental issues faced by first-year students and (b) the other addressing the rich diversity (i.e., race, gender, sexual orientation, disability status) associated with today's first-year students and what this diversity means to student learning and success.

Part II includes annotations for sources that describe methods institutions use to create successful transition experiences for their first-year students. The first subsection highlights sources that deal with precollege programs and experiences, including articles addressing recruitment and admission of first-year students. These sources are included in keeping with the belief that the manner in which an institution recruits its students can directly impact later success. The annotations found in the second subsection focus on orientation programming for both students and parents.

Part III, titled "Promoting First-Year Student Success," examines curricular and cocurricular and support-related components of the college experience intended to enhance student learning and success during the first year of college. It does so through five subsections, each of which examines a different approach to achieving first-year student success. These subsections include (a) Curricular Interventions Comprising the First-Year Experience, (b) Support Services and Programs, (c) Involvement in Campus Life and Living Environments, (d) Technology, and (e) Agents of Socialization and Support in the First Year.

Part IV covers college access and includes a collection of sources on the first-year experience at two-year colleges. It also references research associated with the first year at various types of four-year colleges and universities, including tribal colleges, research universities, and historically Black colleges and universities.

Part V focuses on content that explicitly addresses transformation of the first-year experience and related student and institutional transformations. Here, we include five subsections, each looking at a different aspect of institutional and/or student transformations that occur as a result of attention paid to the first-year experience. These subsections include (a) Critical Student Competencies and Attitudes in the First Year of College, (b) Promising Institutional Practices in the First-Year Experience, (c) Retention and Success of First-Year Students, (d) Reports with Implications for the First-Year Experience, and (e) Assessment and Evaluation.

We begin each part of this monograph with an introductory overview. These overviews, respectively and collectively, provide answers to four key questions: (a) How does the material in this section update material found in the previous edition of the publication? (b) When compared to the last edition of this publication, what subsections and/or headings have we altered or amalgamated for reasons of presentation and/or interpretation? (c) What topical headings or subsections have we added? (d) What is missing—either by design or because major research has not been conducted in this area since 2000? One additional note—on occasion, we repeat some of the annotations. This is done because a few of the sources we reviewed and included in this publication fit into more than one category. Thus, the complete annotation of some sources will appear in more than one section.

Few if any publications come to fruition without the support and contributions of an intricate web of persons—a web that extends well beyond those individuals listed on the cover. This monograph is no exception. Because of this, we, the editors, wish to acknowledge and thank our extensive network of supporters.

This monograph would not exist if it were not for the backing, tolerance, and good nature of the staff of the National Resource Center for The First-Year Experience and Students in Transition. Stuart Hunter must be credited for employing her vision, grace, and skill to bring together this writing team. Tracy Skipper, our coach, is to be lauded as much for her timely reminders as for the prescient suggestions she dispensed to the "Wolfgang list"—our discussion group name—throughout the writing process. We also thank Jean Henscheid for her sage editorial review, and Inge Lewis and Barbara Tobolowsky for their earnest succor and helpful hints about sources and structure.

We move from thanking our supporters in our intellectual home, the National Resource Center, to showing appreciation for the people who aided us in our actual places of residence—our spouses. We are deeply indebted to Peter Keup, Sara Stein Koch, Kelly Pistilli, and Jason Plafcan. Without their steadfast encouragement and enduring patience, this monograph would never have seen the light of day—at least not during this decade.

If our families helped to clear our schedules and sustain our spirits so we could complete this project, then librarians made sure we had the material on which to focus our energized attention. In particular, we extend our gratitude to Brigitte Smith, interlibrary loan supervisor at the University of South Carolina Aiken, as well as the interlibrary loan staffs at New York University, the Humanities and Social Sciences Library at Purdue University, and the University of California at Los Angeles. The respective and collective assistance of these librarians allowed us to span the body of literature on the first-year experience without needing to span the globe.

Finally, we wish to thank Greg Roberts and Jacqueline Skinner Jackson of the American College Personnel Association (ACPA) and the members of the ACPA's Commission on Admissions, Orientation, and the First-Year Experience. Their respective and collective support and sponsorship of this effort have significantly added to the publication's depth and breadth.

While we share with and owe our successes to the aforementioned persons, we take full responsibility for any errors of interpretation or sins of omission.

PART I

The First-Year Student

INTRODUCTORY OVERVIEW

This first part of this monograph includes sources that shed light on the behaviors, characteristics, and various categorizations that help professionals across all areas of higher education understand and support today's first-year students. The section contains two subsections. The first subsection, titled Student Needs and Development Issues, is divided into four topical headings: (a) Student Behavior and Characteristics, (b) Student Development Theory and Life Tasks, (c) Health and Wellness, and (d) Spirituality. The second subsection is described below.

Updates and Additions

The sources in this part of the monograph expand on and update those provided in the third edition, including the earlier edition's sections on Health Topics and Issues; Student Behavior, Characteristics, and Development; and Student Subpopulations. In addition to updating and supplementing previous material, it also includes content on Millennial students—included under the Student Behavior and Characteristics heading—and a new heading on spirituality. These additions reflect the growing attention paid to generational studies and the increasing tendency of students to turn to religion in their search for meaning and purpose.

The second subsection, Diverse Student Populations, includes references and annotations on sources that address the rich diversity found on today's campuses. For clarity, we divided the content of this subsection into four topical headings, each reflecting categories commonly used in the academy. These headings include (a) Race, Gender, and Sexual Orientation, (b) Commuter Students, (c) Students with Disabilities, and (d) First-Generation and Low-Income Students. We must note that these "neat" categories are, in reality, anything but neat because students often fit into more than one category. Despite this limitation, the sources in this subsection can serve as a good start for professionals interested in practice and research associated with the diversity of first-year students.

Omissions and/or Missing Components

A few topics appearing in the third edition are omitted from this revision. The earlier edition included a heading for honors students, which is not included here. Given the increasing attention institutions are giving to high-ability students, we were surprised and disappointed to find that little had been written on this topic since 2000.

In addition, our spirituality section is relatively brief. Unlike the dearth of sources we found on honors students, we did discover enough on spirituality in the first year of college to include it in this new edition.

STUDENT NEEDS AND DEVELOPMENT ISSUES

Student Behavior and Characteristics

Astin, A. W., Oseguera, L., Sax, L. J., & Korn, W. S. (2002). *The American freshman: Thirty-five year trends*. Los Angeles: Higher Education Research Institute, UCLA.

This monograph is the fourth in a series of reports published by the Higher Education Research Institute (HERI) of trend data from the annual administration of the Cooperative Institutional Research Program (CIRP) Freshman Survey. Initially drawing on the key findings highlighted in the previous trend report, the authors identify survey items for which trends have continued over the past five years (e.g., grade inflation, academic disengagement, increasing volunteerism, political disengagement, declining social activism) as well as items for which trends have reversed (e.g., less concern about finances, more liberal socio-political views, less interest in medical careers). The report continues with more specific analysis of trends related to students' family background (e.g., increases in parents' level of education, family income, and students from divorced families) and gender differences in educational aspirations, career plans, and personal views that favor women and resulted in gender convergence. Further, this report highlights the paradoxical trends of increases in students' grades, academic expectations, post-graduate aspirations, and college applications and decreases in nearly all measures of academic and intellectual engagement. Finally, an analysis of students' reported interest in particular majors and careers reveal that students have moved from an interest in liberal arts fields to more professional fields such as education, nursing, and allied health. Three appendices provide a complete list of weighted national normative responses to CIRP Freshman Survey items from 1966 to 2001 for women, men, and all students at baccalaureate institutions.

KEY WORDS: national data sets, student characteristics, student trends.

Bauer, K. W., & Liang, Q. (2003). The effect of personality and precollege characteristics on first-year activities and academic performance. *Journal of College Student Development, 44*(3), 277-290.

The authors investigate how student personality traits and precollege characteristics (e.g., gender and predicted grade index) impact academic performance through involvement in curricular and cocurricular activities. They surveyed 265 first-year college students from select majors at a doctoral-extensive institution. The participants completed the NEO Five-Factor Inventory, the Watson-Glaser Critical Thinking Appraisal, and the College Student Experiences Questionnaire during the spring semester. The researchers discovered that personality and precollege characteristics have an effect on students' quality of effort, critical thinking, and first-year academic performance. For example, students with a high neurotic score on the NEO Five-Factor Inventory put less effort toward academic activities. Further, high levels of extraversion—as measured by the same tool—negatively impacts grade point average. The authors suggest that knowledge of student personality traits could help faculty, academic advisors, and tutors to direct students toward appropriate learning-centered activities. For example, students who are less open to new experiences might need greater encouragement to study abroad.

KEY WORDS: academic success, assessment measures, involvement, STEM disciplines, student characteristics.

Brooks, D. (2001, April). The organization kid. *The Atlantic Monthly*, 40-54.

Drawn primarily from recent observations of students at Princeton University coupled with citations of current national statistics and studies, this article attempts to characterize the "elite" students of the 21st century and compares them with previous cohorts of college students. The outcome of this examination is the description of students "at the top of the meritocratic ladder" (p. 42) as extremely intelligent, enthusiastically involved, group-oriented, respectful of authority, extraordinarily driven, and regulated academically and personally to the degree that the author assigns them the moniker, "The Organization Kid." The same set of observations, however, also prompts the author to describe these students as lacking in true intellectual curiosity, possessing few socio-political passions, and more focused on achievement and appearance than true personal depth. The article also discusses the impact of social trends and national policies in the past few decades on these students' personal development from infancy through adolescence as well as their educational experiences as potential origins for the "Organization Kids" in colleges today.
KEY WORD: Millennial students.

Coomes, M. D., & DeBard, R. (Eds.). (2004). *Serving the millennial generation* (New Directions for Student Services, No. 106). San Francisco: Jossey-Bass.

Drawing on the writing of several authors and research on generations, this book captures aspects of generational similarities and differences to provide a framework for discussion of the current student population, the potential impact this group may have on the student affairs profession, and strategies to serve these students. The first chapters provide a foundation for understanding the significance of generations in the context of higher education and help the reader see the relationship between their generation and Millennial students and understand the historical context of each. For example, the authors demonstrate how popular culture fosters common attributes of the current student population. Further, the authors compare values of various generations, particularly those to which faculty and staff may belong and describe how understanding these values may help in development of the Millennial generation. The authors also relate generational characteristics to issues of teaching and learning, as well as understanding and appreciating diversity. The final chapter relates generational characteristics to specific needs of Millennial students and suggests changes in educational practice necessary to meet those needs.
KEY WORDS: Millennial students, student affairs practice.

Crissman Ishler, J. L. (2005). Today's first-year students. In M. L. Upcraft, J. N. Gardner, & B. O. Barefoot (Eds.), *Challenging & supporting the first-year student: A handbook for improving the first year of college* (pp. 15-26). San Francisco: Jossey-Bass.

This chapter contextualizes the first-year experience of students in the 21st century by providing an updated portrait of today's entering college students both demographically and with respect to their personal characteristics. Drawing from multiple national data sources, the author identifies the first-year student population of the new millennium as skewing older and with a larger percentage of women than previous generations, more racially and ethnically diverse than ever before (with historically under-represented minority groups experiencing the largest rates of recent growth), and with more varied enrollment statuses and retention patterns than past cohorts of students (e.g., increases among part-time students, stop-outs, and Americans studying at international institutions). Further, there has been a recent shift in the most prevalent disabilities among entering college students from physical disabilities to learning disabilities. In addition to these demographic trends, several risk factors have emerged or broadened over the past few decades. These include an increase in the number of students who come from divorced and single-parent families, the rise in emotional and mental health disorders, and greater financial concerns due to the rising cost of higher education and decreasing financial aid

options. The author contends that these demographic and personality characteristic changes have altered the work environment of higher education researchers and practitioners and illustrate that the stereotypical profile of an entering college student ("Joe College") is no longer valid.
KEY WORDS: diversity, Millennial students, student characteristics.

Gordon, V. N., & Steele, G. E. (2003). Undecided first-year students: A 25-year longitudinal study. *Journal of The First Year Experience & Students in Transition, 15*(1), 19-38.
This study, conducted over 25 years, identified common characteristics and needs of students entering an institution as undecided students. The participants were surveyed during orientation, with more than 19,800 students participating in the survey over the 25 years that data were collected. The survey indicated little change in the students (e.g., expectations, motivation) entering the institution undecided during the 25 years. Specifically, the investigators found similar reasons for attending college (e.g., training for an occupation, opportunity to become an educated person), as well as some common levels of indecision among students in the sample. Further, the study indicated that students in the sample had various levels of indecision, with 22% expressing complete indecision. Rather, many more students expressed difficulty choosing one idea or another, and thus, entered the institution undecided. Finally, although many of the undecided students in the sample indicated some level of knowledge about a major or career, 80% had some level of anxiety.
KEY WORDS: assessment, motivation, student expectations, undecided students.

Horn, L., Peter, K., & Rooney, K. (2002). *Profile of undergraduates in U.S. postsecondary institutions: 1999-2000* **(NCES 2002-168). U.S. Department of Education, National Center for Education Statistics. Washington, DC: U.S. Government Printing Office.**
This report includes demographic information for students belonging to the first phase of the Millennial generation, those entering institutions of higher education between 1999 and 2000. Drawing from data collected from close to 16.5 million students, it specifies the racial, economic, and academic backgrounds of these students, as well as institutional choice, academic programs, and admission status. The report provides a comprehensive impression of many of the attributes that make this student population unique.
KEY WORDS: national data sets sets, Millennial students, student characteristics.

Howe, N., & Strauss, W. (2000). *Millennials rising: The next great generation.* **New York: Vintage Books.**
Often cited as the key source for characterizations of the current cohort of entering college students and the text that spawned the most commonly used name for this generation (the "Millennials"), the authors draw upon sources that range from scholarly research to pop culture to depict the generation of youth coming of age in America at the turn of the century and explore the demographic, political, economic, familial, educational, and cultural forces that helped forge it. The authors posit that, unlike previous generations (Generation X and the Baby Boomers before them), Millennials are an optimistic, high-achieving, civic-minded, and moral group who hold the promise of true greatness. However, the flip side of each of these good qualities also can be observed among this cohort of youth, including the capacity to follow rather than lead, homogeneity of thought, excessive collectivism, and a disregard for a meaningful inner life. As Millennials are now entering college, the expectations and characteristics of these students are influencing the first-year experience movement, and higher education is facing the charge of guiding this generation to meet their full potential.
KEY WORDS: Millennial students, student characteristics.

Keeling, S. (2003). Advising the millennial generation. *The Journal of the National Academic Advising Association, 23*(1), 30-36.

The author provides information about the Millennial generation, compares this generation with others in recent history, and includes considerations for academic advisors as they work with Millennial students. Common characteristics of this generation include the desire to work in teams, increasing diversity, and awareness of diversity. This group may also be considered more protected than previous generations. The article includes additional considerations related to the generation with implications for academic advisors: increased expectations, pressure to exceed in all aspects of the college experience (academic and cocurricular), and a greater level of parental/familial involvement. Finally, the author provides suggestions for advisors working with this student population, specifically encouraging them to exercise creativity.
KEY WORDS: academic advising, Millennial students, student characteristics.

National Center for Education Statistics. (2005). *The condition of education, 2005* **(NCES 2005-094). Washington, DC: U.S. Government Printing Office.**

This congressionally mandated report provides current information on 40 indicators of success in the American education system from elementary school through higher education, including enrollment trends, student achievement, school environment, dropout rates, degree attainment, financial support, and outcomes of education. Findings from the report with implications for the first year of college include stable high school completion rates overall but a decline in dropout rates among White, African American, and Hispanic high school students, which diversifies the pool of applicants for American colleges and universities. Similarly, the report identifies that the rate of enrollment in postsecondary education after graduation from high school has remained constant but also reveals a variation in enrollment among specific sub-populations of high school graduates. Specifically, an increasing number of students are enrolling in college immediately after completing high school. However, African Americans and Hispanics are enrolling at a much lower rate than White high school graduates and more often enroll in two-year colleges than baccalaureate institutions. Further, women outpace men in higher education enrollment, a trend that is expected to continue well into the future.
KEY WORDS: enrollment data, national data sets, transition to college, two-year institutions.

Newton, F. B. (2000, November-December). The new student. *About Campus, 6*, 8-15.

The author offers characteristics of the Millennial generation using interview data collected from approximately 200 students over a two-year time period. Common characteristics include a stronger inclination toward activities involving groups; greater knowledge of technology and greater access to information; more work experience (generally part-time work); greater tendency to exhibit a lack of focus on school work and to possess career goals without understanding what achieving these goals requires; and possession of an awareness of campus rules and regulations, which they often ignore. The author offers suggestions to faculty and staff for working with Millennial students.
KEY WORDS: Millennial students, student characteristics.

Pryor, J. H., Hurtado, S., Saenz, V. B., Lindholm, J. A., Korn, W. S., & Mahoney, K. M. (2005). *The American freshman: National norms for fall 2005.* **Los Angeles: Higher Education Research Institute, UCLA.**

This monograph is the 40th annual report of data collected through the annual administration of the Cooperative Institutional Research Program (CIRP) Freshman Survey. This report is based on the responses of more than 260,000 students at 385 baccalaureate-granting colleges and universities across the country, which were weighted to reflect the responses of the 1.3 million first-time, full-time, first-year students entering four-year institutions in 2005. These data reveal an increased sense of social concern and civic responsibility, as well as record-high rates of high school service and expected rates of volunteerism in college. Further, after many years of significant decline, the responses of this cohort of students represent a rebound in political interest and commitment to the levels reported by first-year students in 1994. Other significant findings include a continued decline in beer drinking, slightly lower levels of religious participation, a significant upward shift in the percentage of students who report discussing religion, and a decline in support for national military spending. The authors also highlight the results of sub-group analyses, which reveal gender differences in reasons for attending college as well as greater financial concern and different motivations for pursuing an undergraduate degree for first-generation college students as compared to their peers. Three appendices provide a complete list of weighted national normative responses to the 2005 CIRP Freshman Survey items for women, men, and all students at baccalaureate institutions.

KEY WORDS: national data sets, student characteristics, student trends.

U. S. Census Bureau. (2005). *School enrollment: Social and economic characteristics of students: October, 2003.* Washington, DC: U.S. Department of Commerce.

Drawing from data obtained in the October 2003 Current Population Survey (CPS) conducted by the U. S. Census Bureau, this report highlights school enrollment trends of students from nursery school through graduate school as well as the social and economic characteristics of the diverse student population participating in the American education system. Findings with implications for higher education in general and the first year of college in particular include a greater representation of minority populations among high school students, which will increase the racial/ethnic diversity of the pool of college applicants. Greater high school drop-out rates among African American and Hispanic students and students from lower-income families threaten the potential for gains in diversity at the college level. The report also summarizes changes in college enrollments, which increased by more than one million students in a decade. Numbers of traditional-aged students (i.e., 18-24 year olds) continue to grow while the college enrollment of students over the age of 25 has remained relatively constant since 1980. These data also indicate that women continue to outnumber men among college students, two thirds of all college students are enrolled full-time, two thirds of all undergraduates attend four-year institutions, and 60% of college students work at least part-time during college. These data provide a national context for understanding general college enrollment patterns and for identifying potential areas of need among first-year students.

KEY WORDS: enrollment data, national data sets, transition to college.

Student Development Theory and Life Tasks

Pascarella, E. T., & Terenzini, P. T. (2005). *How college affects students: A third decade of research.* San Francisco: Jossey-Bass

This book provides an examination of the myriad factors that contribute to the effects higher education has on student development and change and updates the first edition of the book published in 1991. In the first chapter, the authors present six key questions and identify and define important terms used throughout. Most of the chapter describes how the literature about students has changed in the years since the first edition, changes that prompted the new edition. The second chapter summarizes several student development theories, identifies commonalities among the theories, and provides several models of college impact (e.g., Astin's I-E-O model) on students. The third chapter focuses on changes related to learning. Specifically, this chapter explores how the college experience impacts the development of academic skills and knowledge of subject matter and includes examples of instructional techniques and learning opportunities (e.g., Supplemental Instruction, learning communities). Chapter 4 examines the development of general skills and cognitive abilities such as critical thinking and decision making. Chapter 5 explores the psychosocial changes and development students often experience, including personal changes in identity and academic and social concepts, and changes in the ways students view others. Chapters 6 and 7 provide discussion of changes in attitudes, values, and moral development among college students. Chapter 8 examines the relationship between education and socioeconomic status, as well as the accessibility of higher education to various groups of students, and chapters 9 and 10 provide insight on the career/economic and personal (e.g., health and wellness, connection to community) gains associated with earning a college degree. Drawing on information presented in chapters 9 through 10, chapter 11 summarizes how students are affected by the college experience, and leads the reader to the final chapter detailing implications for practice and research.

KEY WORDS: college outcomes, student characteristics, student development theory.

Skipper, T. L. (2005). *Student development in the first college year: A primer for college educators.* **Columbia, SC: University of South Carolina, National Resource Center for The First-Year Experience and Students in Transition.**

This book provides a comprehensive overview of student development theory, focusing specifically on those theories that are most relevant to students in their first year of college. The author explores several types of theories, including psychosocial theory, cognitive development, and models of student retention. In addition to examples in each theoretical category, the author and two colleagues provide examples of practical application of the theories in a composition class, in residence hall-based learning environments, and in learning communities. These examples are intended to illustrate the interrelationship between theory and practice. The book concludes with a discussion of theory-based assessment and measurement of student learning and describes the importance of understanding student development.

KEY WORDS: assessment, student development theory.

Health and Wellness

Bergen-Cico, D. (2000). Patterns of substance abuse and attrition among first-year students. *Journal of The First-Year Experience and Students in Transition, 12*(1), 61-75.

Participants in this study were students enrolled at a single institution during 1997-98 who required some level of intervention (institutional or other) for substance abuse. Their experiences were used to create profiles of substance abusing students. Of the 255 students involved in the study, 40% were in their first year of college. Findings from the study revealed that alcohol was abused by 79% of the group. The second largest category of abuse was a combination of alcohol and various types of drugs, including use of alcohol and prescribed medication. The study indicated that first-year students who abused drugs may be less likely to persist in college and revealed a prevalence of drug abuse among first-year students. The author offers suggestions for programmatic interventions to discourage drug use among students.

KEY WORDS: intervention strategies, retention, student support, substance abuse.

Bray, S. R., & Born, H. A. (2004). Transition to university and vigorous physical activity: Implications for health and psychological well-being. *Journal of American College Health, 52*(4), 181-188.

With a sample of 145 first-year students at a liberal arts university in Canada, this study investigated students' patterns of vigorous physical activity during the transition from high school to college, as well as the relationship between activity levels and psychological well-being. Student self-reports of their activity levels during the last two months of high school and the first two months of college show a significant decline in vigorous physical activity. Two thirds of the students reported they were involved in adequate levels of vigorous activity during high school as compared to only 44% who met similar standards during the first eight weeks of college. Students who remained active during their transition to college reported lower levels of tension and fatigue and higher levels of vigor compared to those who were insufficiently active. While the small sample size requires additional follow-up, this study provides empirical support for programs that encourage physical activity among students in general and particularly among students experiencing their initial transition to college.

KEY WORDS: mental health, physical health, transition to college.

Charles, C., Dinwiddie, G., & Massey, D. (2004). The continuing consequences of segregation: Family stress and college academic performance. *Social Science Quarterly, 85*(5), 1353-1373.

Drawing on data collected from the National Longitudinal Survey of Freshmen (NLSF) about first-year students entering 28 selective colleges and universities, this study sought to explore the relationship between segregated living environments of African American students and grade point average. Further, the data were used to consider the relationship between living environment and family stress and the ongoing effects that stress has on students. The sample yielded approximately 4,000 diverse students who participated in initial and follow-up interviews in the second semester of their first year of college and again in the sophomore year. Findings from the study indicated that among the first-year populations surveyed (African Americans, Asian Americans, Latinos, and Whites), African American students experienced greater levels of familial stress that persisted even when they were removed from the segregated neighborhoods. The effects of segregation and family stress were found to have a negative impact on the academic performance of African American students.

KEY WORDS: academic performance, assessment, living environments, stress, students of color.

Gold, J. M., Miller, M., & Rutholz, J. (2001). Grief experiences of first-year women students in the transition to college: Implication for individual and systematic interventions. *Journal of The First-Year Experience & Students in Transition, 13*(2), 37-54.

This study examined "disenfranchised grieving," or the normal grieving that often accompanies life transition, among women in their first semester of college. The researchers surveyed 289 first-year female students enrolled at a large southeastern university. At the sixth and seventh weeks of the fall semester, participants completed an adapted Grief Experiences Questionnaire and a demographic survey. Their grade point average (GPA) and enrollment status were also collected at the conclusion of the spring semester. The researchers discovered that in-state students who had not visited home had a more severe grief reaction. High grievers had lower fall GPAs and persistence rates. Student ethnicity did not have a significant effect on grief experiences. The authors suggest types of residence hall programming and immediate individual or group counseling in order to help women cope with grief experiences and promote their persistence and success.

KEY WORDS: female students, grief experiences, persistence, transition to college.

Kitzrow, M. A. (2003). The mental health needs of today's college students: Challenges and recommendations. *NASPA Journal, 41*(1), 167-181.

This article provides a review of literature from 1985 to 2002 on the changing mental health needs of today's college students. The primary theme from this body of work is that a larger proportion of recent and current cohorts of college students are dealing with significant, and often more severe, psychological problems and emotional health issues than in previous decades. While some of these issues emerge during college, more students are entering college with at least moderate, if not severe, symptoms of psychological distress. Not surprisingly, there have been commensurate increases in the demand for college counseling staff and services in the first year and beyond. However, there has not been a corresponding increase in human and fiscal resources in campus counseling centers, which has created one of the largest challenges for student affairs professionals and student support programs. Since mental health problems are associated with lower levels of social integration, academic performance, and retention, statistics on mental and emotional health needs are of great concern to higher education professionals. The article ends with a series of recommendations, including educating students, staff, administrators, and faculty about available services, the importance of removing the stigma of seeking assistance for psychological and emotional health issues, and making mental health needs a priority for everyone in academe, not just student affairs or counseling professionals.
KEY WORDS: counseling services, mental health.

Lenz, B. K. (2004). Tobacco, depression, and lifestyle choices in the pivotal early college years. *Journal of American College Health, 52*(5), 213-219.

The author explores the correlates of tobacco use among 18- and 19-year-old students at a midwestern university in order to help create "anticipatory guidance" strategies for students during their first college year when they are beginning to make lifestyle and health choices for themselves. The study employed descriptive, univariate, and multivariate analyses on the responses of 203 first- and second-year students at one university to the 2001 College Health Survey. One third of students in the sample reported using tobacco at least once a month in the past year. Findings also indicated that tobacco use was associated with marijuana and alcohol use, exposure to a smoking environment, purging and use of diet pills, and decreasing levels of fitness since high school. The largest relationship among all variables under consideration was between tobacco use and diagnosis and treatment of depression. These results are intended to inform tobacco prevention programs as well as to understand how tobacco use may be symptomatic of other health issues (e.g., depression, eating disorders) among new students.
KEY WORDS: mental health, physical health, substance use.

Lowery, S. E., Robinson-Kurpius, S. E., Befort, C., Blanks, E. H., Sollenberger, S., Foley Nicpon, M., et al. (2005). Body image, self-esteem, and health-related behaviors among male and female first-year college students. *Journal of College Student Development, 46*(6), 612-623.

This study examined self-esteem issues of first-year students within the context of body image, exercise, and other health-related behaviors with particular emphasis on gender differences. Participants were 433 first-year students (62% women and 38%) men enrolled in a first-year seminar who completed a survey midway through their first semester at a large, southwestern, research university. Consistent with previous research, the results of the survey indicated that men have a more positive body image than women do. Further, body image has a much stronger relationship with self-esteem for women than for men. Analyses of the effects of exercise patterns on body image and self-esteem showed that they had no effect on body image for either gender. Similarly, there was no self-esteem difference between those first-year women who exercised and those who did not. While exercise does not appear to provide a means of enhancing body image overall or self-esteem among first-year female students, other health-related behaviors (e.g., stress management, eating behaviors, substance use) were positively related to self-esteem for both men and women. Results of the study can be used to inform creation and operation of effective interventions for body-image problems among first-year students, particularly women and to inform operation of general health programs for first-year students.

KEY WORDS: gender differences, physical health, self-image.

Perrine, R. M. (2001). College stress and persistence as a function of attachment and support. *Journal of the First-Year Experience & Students in Transition, 13*(1), 7-22.

The purpose of this study was to measure the relationship between stress and persistence among first-year students, with a focus on social support and attachment. Using a sample of 171 first-year students at a university in the Southeast with an enrollment of approximately 16,000, the researcher measured attachment styles, perceived stress, and social support. Attachment data were collected during the second week of classes and again during the sixth week. The findings from the study indicated that persistence was affected by attachment style. Specifically, students with a fearful attachment were less likely to persist. Further, these students also reported greater levels of stress and less overall satisfaction with support. Additional findings from the study indicated a relationship between gender and perceived support and self-reported stress.

KEY WORDS: attachment, persistence, social support, stress.

Pritchard, M. E., & Wilson, G. S. (2003). Using emotional and social factors to predict student success. *Journal of College Student Development, 44*(1), 18-28.

While demographic and retention variables have been the primary focus of previous studies on college students' academic success and persistence, the current study sought to identify potential relationships between student emotional and social health and grade point average and retention. While the sample included undergraduates at all levels of study at a private, midwestern university, 50% of the sample were first-year students. Data from first-year students were not included in the analyses that predicted GPA, but results showed that aspects of students' emotional health, such as self-esteem, fatigue, and coping tactics, had a significant impact on the intent to drop out of school. However, the combined influence of social health measures (e.g., introversion/extroversion, alcohol behaviors, involvement in campus organizations) did not have a significant effect on the intent to leave college. Based on these findings, it appears that providing students with the skills to "deal successfully with the multitude of emotional stresses encountered in college life" (p. 25) is perhaps more important for persistence than attention to social health issues and should be a priority of student support programs in the first year and beyond.

KEY WORDS: mental health, persistence, social support, student success.

Racette, S. B., Deusinger, S. S., Strube, M. J., Highsteing, G. R., & Deusinger, R. H. (2005). Weight changes, exercise, and dietary patterns during freshman and sophomore years of college. *Journal of American College Health, 53*(6), 245-251.

The goals of this study were to assess the weight, height, body mass index (BMI), and exercise and dietary habits of 764 first-year students at college entry and to assess the changes in these dimensions during the first two years at Washington College in St. Louis, Missouri. The study revealed that 76% of new students were considered normal weight; 70% regularly participated in strength, aerobic, and/or stretching activities; 30% consumed five or more fruits and vegetables daily; and more than 40% ate fried foods and high-fat fast foods at least three times per week. A one-year follow-up was conducted with just over one third of the sample. Follow-up data showed an average weight gain of nine pounds,

a decline in aerobic exercise, an increase in stretching activities, a decrease in the consumption of fried foods, and no change in the consumption of fruits and vegetables and fast food from the first to second year of college. However, analyses indicated no significant association between weight gain and changes in exercise and/or dietary habits. Overall, these data help identify the need for early counseling and intervention among first-year students with respect to exercise and dietary habits in order to forge a foundation of good health and wellness.
KEY WORDS: physical health.

Reifman, A., & Watson, W. K. (2003). Binge drinking during the first semester of college: Continuation and desistance from high school patterns. *Journal of American College Health,* *52*(2), 73-81.

This research sought to identify psychosocial factors that predict binge drinking in the first semester of college. A sample of 274 new students at Texas Tech University completed a survey and social network grid near the end of their first term, which provided a measure of the dependent variable for the study, binge drinking in college, as well as data for several independent variables. Descriptive statistics indicated that binge drinking patterns remained consistent from high school to college for approximately 75% of the sample. Logistic regression and chi-square analyses were conducted separately for high school binge drinkers and for high school non-binge drinkers. Drinking patterns among students' social networks and the importance students placed on partying as an element of the collegiate lifestyle were significant predictors for both sub-samples. Three other measures were unique predictors for the high school non-binge drinkers: (a) being female, (b) expectancies of social and physical pleasure from alcohol, and (c) the perception of approval of drinking among friends. Participating in the Greek system was not a significant predictor of first-term binge drinking for either group in this study. The authors note the implications of these findings for intervention strategies in high school and college.
KEY WORD: substance abuse.

Sax, L. S., Bryant, A. N., & Gilmartin, S. K. (2004). A longitudinal investigation of emotional health among male and female first-year college students. *Journal of The First-Year Experience* *& Students in Transition, 16*(2), 39-65.

This study explored changes in the emotional health of men and women during their first college year and identified college experiences that were associated with changes in emotional health for male and female first-year students to help inform first-year counseling and support services. Using weighted national data collected from the 2000 CIRP Freshman Survey and 2001 Your First College Year (YFCY) survey, the researchers used cross-tabulations to examine changes in two measures of psychological well-being during the first year: (a) self-rated emotional health and (b) frequency of depression. These items also comprised part of a composite dependent variable for regression analyses, which were run separately for men and women to tease out potential gender differences in the variables that contribute to emotional health during the first year. Findings revealed that women rate themselves lower than men with respect to emotional health and report more frequent depression at college entry. During the first year, men and women decline in self-rated emotional health at similar rates, but men experienced a larger increase in instances of depression, thereby narrowing the gender gap between men and women on this measure of psychological well-being. Further, while there are many similarities in the college experiences that predict emotional health for men and women, particularly those related to peer relationships, the most significant gender difference emerged in the importance of family relationships to the emotional health of first-year women.
KEY WORDS: gender differences, mental health.

Schwitzer, A. M., & Rodriguez, L. E. (2002). Understanding and responding to eating disorders among college women during the first-college year. *Journal of The First-Year Experience & Students in Transition, 14*(1), 41-64.

The study, conducted over six years examined eating disorders among 130 female college students involved in an intervention program administered by a university counseling center. Data were collected from two self-reported assessments and analyzed through a process that identified common themes, including family background/history and psychological issues. Additionally, several issues related to college adjustment emerged from the study. Findings from the study suggested that women with eating disorders often exhibit perfectionist behaviors extending beyond eating habits to their academic experience. Further, the study indicated that the need for perfectionism might cause them stress, possibly resulting in academic difficulty during the college transition and first year of college. Finally, data collected from the study suggested the need for education about eating disorders, possibly early in the college experience (e.g., during orientation, in first-year seminars).
KEY WORDS: eating disorders, intervention strategies, mental health, physical health.

Sessa, F. M. (2005). The influence of perceived parenting on substance use during the transition to college: A comparison of male residential and commuter students. *Journal of College Student Development, 46*(1), 62-74.

This study offers a comparison of the experiences of commuter and residential students by focusing on the influence of the perceived parent-child relationship on the use of alcohol and marijuana. The researcher collected survey data from 50 residential and 57 commuter male college students who were an average of 18.5 years old and were attending two different baccalaureate-granting institutions in the same general region of a mid-Atlantic state. Demographic comparisons of the two student groups revealed no statistically significant differences. Results of descriptive analyses and MANOVAs yielded three main findings. First, residential and commuter first-year men had different patterns of substance use. Residential students used alcohol more frequently than commuter students, while commuter students reported more frequent use of marijuana than their residential peers. Second, residential and commuter first-year students in the sample have different relationships with their parents. Specifically, residential students in the study felt that their parents monitored their behavior more than commuter students did and that their parents were less encouraging of their independence. Finally, these results indicate that the effect of perceived parenting on substance use is significant for commuter college students but not for residential first-year male students in this study. This study highlights the importance of recognizing the diversity of first-year student experiences, particularly with respect to patterns of substance use and parental influence. These findings can be used to inform orientation and first-year intervention programs for both students and parents.
KEY WORDS: commuter students, parental involvement, substance abuse.

Struthers, C. W., Perry, R. P., & Menec, V. H. (2000). An examination of the relationship among academic stress, coping, motivation, and performance in college. *Research in Higher Education, 41*(5), 581-592.

This study explored the relationship between academic stress, motivation, and performance. The Student Coping Instrument (SCOPE), as well as measures of motivation and academic stress, were used to survey 203 participants at the beginning of the academic year. The grades for the participants were also recorded at the end of the semester. Findings from the study indicated that the level of academic stress impacted grades and that motivation and coping styles can further influence academic performance. In addition, the researchers found that stronger academic motivation has a positive effect on grades (confirming their hypothesis in the process). Implications for practice include helping students develop better coping skills and encouraging participation in courses emphasizing skill development (e.g., study skills, time and personal management).

KEY WORDS: assessment measures, coping with stress, motivation, stress.

Zajacova, A., Lynch, S. M., & Espenshade, T. J. (2005). Self-efficacy, stress, and academic success in college. *Research in Higher Education, 46*(6), 677-706.

Using data from a sample of 107 students in their first semester of college, this study explored the relationship between academic self-efficacy, stress, and academic performance. All students in the sample had entered the institution in the spring semester with an average age of 20.7 for the group. This age was consistent with the average age of all students who entered the institution in the spring the year the study was conducted. The study was conducted using a survey administered during the second-to-last week of an orientation seminar that included measures of stress and self-efficacy. The measures of self-efficacy were drawn from multiple existing instruments. Information on grades, number of credits, and other registration data were obtained for the sample one year after initial enrollment. Findings from the study indicated a negative correlation between self-efficacy and stress and suggested that the student's sense of academic self-efficacy is the strongest predictor of academic performance (measured by grade point average). In this study, stress was found to have little impact on grade point average but did have a marginal impact on persistence.

KEY WORDS: academic success, effect of stress, self-efficacy.

Spirituality

Bryant, A. N., Choi, J. Y., & Yasuno, M. (2003). Understanding the religious and spiritual dimensions of students' lives in the first year of college. *Journal of College Student Development, 44*(6), 723-745.

This study sought to examine spiritual and religious changes among students during the first year of college, the potential relationship between spirituality and religiosity for first-year students, and the personal and collegiate characteristics and experiences that contribute to this aspect of students' development during their transition to college. The authors conducted both descriptive and multivariate analyses on a sample of 3,680 students at 50 colleges and universities across the country who had completed both the 2000 CIRP Freshman Survey and the 2001 Your First College Year (YFCY) survey. Descriptive statistics show a decline in students' spiritual self-concept and religious involvement but an increase in commitment to integrating spirituality into their lives. Further, these analyses indicate that spirituality and religiosity are highly correlated constructs among first-year students. Although students' degree of spirituality or religiosity at college entry (the pretest) is the strongest indicator of commitment to these ideals at the end of the first year of college, the results of regression analyses show that high institutional selectivity, being politically conservative, and measures of family cohesiveness also are positive predictors of both spirituality and religiosity during the first year. Further, this research identifies other variables that are unique predictors for spirituality (e.g., no religious affiliation, being White, time spent surfing the Internet) and for religiosity (e.g., high school grade point average, attending a Protestant four-year college, participation in community service, partying in college).

KEY WORDS: spirituality, student development.

Higher Education Research Institute. (2005). *The spiritual life of college students: A national study of college students' search for meaning and purpose.* Los Angeles, CA: Author.

This report is a summary of the findings from a national administration of a two-page addendum to the Cooperative Institutional Research Program (CIRP) Freshman Survey in 2004. The survey addendum, titled College Student Beliefs and Values (CSBV), focused on students' perspectives and practices with respect to religion and spirituality and was administered at 236 institutions of different sizes, types, and controls across the country. Overall, these data indicate that college students not only have high levels of spiritual interest and involvement and religious commitment but also possess high degrees of religious tolerance and acceptance. Factor analyses of the 2004 CSBV and CIRP Freshman Survey data yield 12 dimensions of spirituality and religiousness that frame the discussion of these national findings. They include spirituality, spiritual quest, equanimity, religious commitment, engagement, skepticism, struggle, religious/social conservatism, charitable involvement, compassionate self-concept, ecumenical world view, and ethic of caring. Further, the data show significant relationships between these 12 dimensions and political orientation, socio-political attitudes, psychological and physical well-being, and religious preference.

KEY WORDS: spirituality, student characteristics.

{ DIVERSE STUDENT POPULATIONS }

Race, Gender, and Sexual Orientation

Bryson, S., Smith, R., & Vineyard, G. (2002). Relationship of race, academic and nonacademic information in predicting the first-year success of selected admissions first-year students. *Journal of The First-Year Experience & Students in Transition, 14*(1), 65-80.

The purpose of this study was to predict the first-year grades of conditionally admitted African American and White students by examining race; traditional academic variables such as high school rank, ACT scores, and grade point average (GPA); and nonacademic dimensions of the student experience as assessed by the Bryson Instrument for Noncognitive Assessment (BINA). The students, who did not meet regular admissions criteria at a comprehensive, predominantly White institution (PWI) participated in a special program while enrolled in general studies courses required of all entering students. The program included study skills courses and other supportive elements, such as counseling, tutoring, and mentoring. The results indicate BINA scores accounted for 2% of the variance for the first-year grades. The research provides evidence that different processes are involved in academic success for African American and White students at PWIs. Specifically, high school GPA was found to be the best predictor of first-year GPA for African American students, while high school rank was the best predictor for White students. There were also racial differences among the noncognitive predictors. For African American students, the only significant predictor of academic success was self-esteem; for White students, self-appraisal was the only significant predictor. The authors suggest that admissions professionals should reconsider using a single formula for institutional entry and consider a more holistic method tailored to the needs of individual students.

KEY WORDS: academic success, academic support, admissions standards, assessment measures, self-image, students of color.

Charles, C., Dinwiddie, G., & Massey, D. (2004). The continuing consequences of segregation: Family stress and college academic performance. *Social Science Quarterly, 85*(5), 1353-1373.
Drawing on data collected from the National Longitudinal Survey of Freshmen (NLSF) about first-year students entering 28 selective colleges and universities, this study sought to explore the relationship between segregated living environments of African American students and grade point average. Further, the data were used to consider the relationship between living environment and family stress and the ongoing effects that stress has on students. The sample yielded approximately 4,000 diverse students who participated in initial and follow-up interviews in the second semester of their first-year of college and again in the sophomore year. Findings from the study indicated that out of the first-year populations surveyed (African Americans, Asian Americans, Latinos, and Whites), African American students experienced greater levels of familial stress that persisted even when they were removed from the segregated neighborhoods. The effects of segregation and family stress were found to have a negative impact on academic performance of African American students.

KEY WORDS: academic performance, assessment, living environments, stress, students of color.

First-year experience to help students succeed. (2005, Spring). *Tribal College*, 41-44.
This article offers an overview of a first-year seminar at the Lummi campus of Northwest Indian College (NWIC). The program is described as a cohort experience, one of the first at a tribal college, focusing on building community through experiential projects and incorporating opportunities to learn more about the perspectives of Native American peoples. Additionally, the FYE course also contains content specific to the seasons. For example, during the winter, students are encouraged to reflect and consider Native American history and communication. Finally, the course also encourages connection to the campus and local community through service-oriented activities and the incorporation of guest speakers from the Native American community.

KEY WORDS: first-year seminars, Native American students, tribal colleges.

Furr, S. R., & Elling, T. W. (2002). African American students in a predominately White university: Factors associated with retention. *College Student Journal, 36*(2), 188-203.
Drawing on data collected through a campus climate survey administered at a southeastern university to 183 African American students in the first semester of their first year of college and retention data for that group over a period of seven semesters, this study sought to explore factors contributing to first-year student retention. Findings from the study revealed higher grade point averages among students who returned for the second semester compared to the GPAs of students who did not return. Similar findings persisted for returners and non-returners throughout the seven semesters of the study. Several other factors prevailed among students who did not persist during the period in which the study was conducted, including financial aid/family income, noninvolvement in campus activities, work (20 hours or more per week), and credit hours earned. The authors warn that these should be considered risk factors for student attrition and that educational practices should be designed accordingly.

KEY WORDS: academic performance, African American students, retention.

Hernandez, J. C., & Lopez, M. A. (2004). Leaking pipeline: Issues impacting Latino college student retention. *Journal of College Student Retention: Research, Theory, & Practice, 6*(1), 37-60.

In light of the fact that Latinos comprise more than 10% of the nation's population—the nation's largest minority group—this article provides a necessary review of literature associated with postsecondary success among Latino students. Particular attention is paid to the personal, environmental, involvement, and socio-cultural factors demonstrated by the literature to have an influence on students from this population. Recommendations for assisting Latino students are offered, including approaches appropriate for the first year of college.

KEY WORDS: Latino students, students of color, retention, retention theory.

Hrabowski, F. A. (2005). Fostering first-year success of underrepresented minorities. In M. L. Upcraft, J. N. Gardner, & B. O. Barefoot (Eds.), *Challenging & supporting the first-year student: A handbook for improving the first year of college* (pp. 125-140). San Francisco: Jossey-Bass.

The author of this chapter shares best practices for working with first-year minority students and identifies factors that may impact the success of these students. The chapter begins with a display of data on increases in minority populations in higher education, which has prompted an increased interest in writing and researching issues related to these students. The author joins others in calling for the creation of programs that support student achievement (both minority and non-minority students), combat stereotypes, and raise expectations for and among students. The author offers examples of practices that provide support and demonstrate commitment to first-year minority students, including purposeful recruitment and collaboration with local high schools and surrounding communities. These practices can specifically ensure that students and their families feel a strong connection to the institution. The author suggests that after students enroll, faculty, staff, and senior-level administrators should interact with and encourage these students particularly through their first year. Orientation, academic advising, formation of study groups, mentoring programs, and service opportunities are cited as key out-of-class opportunities to connect students to each other, the institution and the community as well as enrich their academic experience.

KEY WORDS: academic success, mentoring, retention, students of color.

Hurtado, S., & Carter, D. F. (1997). Effects of college transition and perceptions of the campus racial climate on Latino students' sense of belonging. *Sociology of Education, 70*(4), 324-345.

This study taps into and tests Tinto's theoretical model for student departure to determine the extent to which Latino students' pre-entry characteristics and experiences during their first and second years of college affect their sense of belonging in the third college year. The findings indicate that out-of-class discussion of course content with other students, involvement in religious and social organizations, and structured first-year experience programs all had positive effects on Latino students' sense of belonging, while perceptions of a hostile racial climate had a deleterious impact on the sense of belonging by the third college year. These outcomes suggest that greater attention be paid to creating an increased sense of integration into campus life for Latino students, particularly through appropriate sequencing of college experiences.

KEY WORDS: campus climate, Latino students, students of color, retention, retention theory.

Jones, W. T. (2005). The realities of diversity and the campus climate for first-year students. In M. L. Upcraft, J. N. Gardner, & B. O. Barefoot (Eds.), *Challenging & supporting the first-year student: A handbook for improving the first year of college* (pp. 141-154). San Francisco: Jossey-Bass.

This chapter examines campus climate and attitudes about diversity and access to higher education for diverse student populations and explores opportunities for institutional transformation to promote and assess diversity efforts. The author begins with an exploration of common first-year student attitudes about diversity, indicating the potential for frustration among students who are seeking opportunities to identify with similar peer groups through involvement in clubs and organizations. Furthermore, the author indicates that first-year students of color are often surprised by features of institutional climate when they arrive on campus. For example, throughout the admissions process, they may believe the campus is diverse and celebratory of differences; however, when they arrive as students, they may find the campus to be different from what they had expected. The author indicates this realization is often compounded by communication difficulties between minority and non-minority students and differential treatment based on social class. For some minority students from lower socioeconomic levels, their academic preparedness may be lower than that of majority students. The author notes that minority students face challenges in the classroom with curriculum that has not been adapted to meet the needs of diverse students. To create institutional transformation, the author suggests exploration of methods of prejudice reduction and assessment of campus diversity efforts. The chapter concludes with a set of recommendations, including diversifying the student body and faculty and staff and creating a plan for increasing diversity. These efforts are focused on improving the level of institutional commitment to diversity and involve all campus constituents and various aspects of the campus climate and culture.
KEY WORDS: academic preparation, campus climate, diversity, socioeconomic status, student development.

Laar, C. V., Levin, S., Sinclair, S., & Sidanius, J. (2005). The effect of university roommate contact on ethnic attitudes and behavior. *Journal of Experimental Social Psychology, 41*(4), 329-345.
This study examined the influence of living with an African American, Asian American, Latino, or White roommate on the affective, cognitive, and behavioral indicators of prejudice among university students. Roommate contact for more than 2,000 students was examined in two ways: (a) by examining prejudice as a function of living with randomly assigned roommates during the first year of college and (b) by examining the impact of voluntary second- and third-year contact with a roommate on the prejudicial views held by students during the fourth year of study. The findings reveal that, overall, students randomly assigned to live with students from other races at the start of the first year of college displayed less prejudice by the end of the year. In addition, students who voluntarily continued to interact with roommates from different races during their second and third years of college also showed decreases in prejudice. One notable exception that emerged involved random assignment to an Asian American roommate during the first year of college and voluntary interaction with Asian American roommates in subsequent years of study. Both of these conditions resulted in the increase of prejudicial attitudes, particularly toward African American and Latino students. The study carries implications for residence life practitioners and other educators interested in decreasing prejudice and enhancing student success during and after the first year of college.
KEY WORDS: diversity education, prejudice, residence life.

Longerbeam, S. D., & Sedlacek, W. E. (2006). Attitudes toward diversity and living-learning outcomes among first- and second-year college students. *NASPA Journal, 43*(1), 40-55.
This article offers findings from a study that compared diversity attitudes of first- and second-year students who participated in a civic-related living-learning program (CIVICUS) and a group of students who did not participate in the program. Data were collected from the two groups using the Miville-Guzman University Diversity Scale (M-GUDS-S), which was administered a total of three times (at orientation, at the end of the first semester of the first year, and during the sophomore year). Two administrations of the survey took place in courses in the CIVICUS program or in introductory

sociology courses. Analysis of data indicated no significant difference in attitudes about diversity between the two groups. However, the findings did indicate some change in behaviors related to issues of diversity; specifically, some improvement in behaviors was noted. The study also suggested that diversity awareness and appreciation may need to be cultivated over time. This, the authors suggest, is a limitation of a study that attempts to measure impacts of programs like CIVICUS during or shortly after the students' participation.

KEY WORDS: assessment measures, diversity, residential learning communities.

Longerbeam, S. D., Sedlacek, W. E., & Alatorre, H. M. (2004). In their own voices: Latino student retention. *NASPA Journal, 41*(3), 538-550.

Drawing on data collected from 2,991 students (175 of those students were Latino), the researchers in this study sought to measure Latino student retention through the administration of the University New Student Census (UNSC). The survey was administered to first-year students during orientation to measure "student perceptions, attitudes, expectations, and interests" (p. 543). Findings from the study revealed several differences between Latino and non-Latino students, including a prevailing concern among the Latinos about financing their education. This concern for finances is a factor in student attrition, with greater numbers of Latino students reporting that they would leave an institution for financial reasons. Latino students who participated in the study also indicated that a perceived lack of academic ability would be a factor in their decision to leave. In addition to differences in financial concerns and perception of academic abilities, there were also marked differences in acceptance for diversity between Latinos and non-Latinos. Latinos who participated in this study indicated some level of acceptance for diverse peoples by reporting that they had a close friend of a different race, whereas non-Latinos indicated that most of their close friends were of the same race. The researchers in this study suggested that factors for attrition are different between Latinos and non-Latinos and that these differences be considered when developing programs to support different student populations.

KEY WORDS: Latino students, retention, student expectations.

Malaney, G. D., & Berger, J. B. (2005). Assessing how diversity affects students' interest in social change. *Journal of College Student Retention: Research, Theory & Practice, 6*(4), 443-460.

Authors of this article suggest that as colleges and universities take steps to diversify student populations and prepare all students to contribute to a diverse society, they must first understand how diversification efforts may affect campus climate, undergraduate peer relations, and retention of both minority and majority students. The authors suggest that failing to do so could mean that well-intentioned efforts do more harm than good. To explore this issue, the authors examined how pre-entry characteristics, precollege environments, and precollege activities influenced three outcomes: (a) social change self-efficacy, (b) social action engagement, and (c) social leadership skills. These outcomes serve as potential indicators of new undergraduate students' readiness to positively engage with diversity. Data were collected from 10 public universities as part of a 2001 national study, with results indicating that students who are more engaged with diversity prior to college are more likely to perceive themselves as ready to engage proactively with diversity as college students. This finding suggests that increasing student diversity on campus without focusing attention on the students' prior historical, psychological, and behavioral experiences and issues may create conflict and adversely impact the educational experience of all students. The authors suggest that educators, particularly those working with first-year students, should be aware of the developmental readiness of their students to engage with diversity before they launch diversity-related initiatives.

KEY WORDS: diversity.

Ness, J. E. (2002). Crossing the finish line: American Indian completers and non-completers in a tribal college. *Tribal College, 13*(4), 36-40.

This qualitative study examined the reasons why American Indian students either completed or did not complete their collegiate programs of study. Thirteen interview participants suggested various societal, programmatic, organizational, and/or personal factors that influenced their decision to finish or abandon their higher education efforts. In addition to providing lists of retention risk factors and characteristics of degree completers germane to Native Americans, the article provides suggestions on policies and directions for future research that merit consideration for faculty and staff seeking ways to enhance the success of American Indian students both during and after the first year of college.
KEY WORDS: Native American students, research studies, retention, tribal colleges.

Packard, B. W., Walsh, L., & Seidenberg, S. (2004). Will that be one mentor or two? A cross-sectional study of women's mentoring during college. *Mentoring & Tutoring: Partnership in Learning, 12*(1), 71-85.

The researchers conducted this study to determine whether the structural model underlying the mentoring of college women is dyadic in nature, as it is in adolescence and school settings, or networking in nature, as it is in adulthood and workplace settings. The data were collected though mentoring surveys conducted with two cohorts of traditional-aged college women—one in its first year and the other in its fourth year of college. The findings reveal that first-year college women were more likely to seek and experience mentoring in the form of a dyadic relationship with one mentor and this mentor often came in the form of a family member or a recent high-school teacher. Fourth-year college women were more likely to seek and experience mentoring in the form of a network of multiple mentors, which included family, peers, and college faculty. Fourth-year students reported being challenged more by their mentors than first-year students did, but they found this challenge supportive in nature. The authors conclude the article by describing the study's implications for designing developmentally appropriate mentoring initiatives for college women.
KEY WORDS: mentoring, retention, female students.

Rendón, L. I., García, M., & Person, D. (Eds.). (2004). *Transforming the first year of college for students of color* (Monograph No. 38). Columbia, SC: University of South Carolina, National Resource Center for The First-Year Experience and Students in Transition.

This monograph, a collaboration among several authors, offers a foundation for understanding the transition to college for students of color and suggests methods for improving that experience. The authors represent diverse voices and backgrounds and use current and predictive statistics throughout each chapter to support the need for transformation in the experience of a wide variety of students of color, including African Americans, Latinos, Asian/Pacific Americans, American Indians/Alaska Natives, and multiracial/biracial students. The chapters are organized into sections that present several overarching concepts: identifying the student population, supporting students inside and outside the classroom through creating more inclusive learning environments, providing mechanisms for academic and social support for students of color, working with various populations, improving intergroup relationships, and applying information to future improvements. The monograph's first section begins with narratives from first-year students of color, each illustrating specific experiences that relate to the chapter content. Chapter summaries are provided throughout the volume, with student voices used to illustrate key concepts.
KEY WORDS: academic support, intergroup relations, students of color, transition to college.

Sanlo, R. (2005). Lesbian, gay, and bisexual college students: Risk, resiliency, and retention. *Journal of College Student Retention: Research, Theory & Practice, 6*(1), 97-110.

This article explores the lives of lesbian, gay, and bisexual (LGB) students—also known as sexual minority students—to help readers comprehend how the students' language, behavior, and sources of stress influence their academic achievement and success in college. The article is a review of the literature, yet the author stresses the relative absence of research on the academic transition, retention, and ultimate graduation of sexual minority students. Discrimination and coping, health effects/outcomes, and resiliency are three themes that the author suggests for future exploration in an effort to help improve understanding of issues related to this student population. The article is of interest to practitioners and researchers concerned with the success of LGB students during the first year of college and beyond.
KEY WORDS: Lesbian/Gay/Bisexual/Transgendered Students

Schwartz, R. A., & Washington, C. M. (2002). Predicting academic performance and retention among African American freshmen men. *NASPA Journal, 39,* 355-370.

This study sought to identify patterns of academic performance and retention among 229 African American first-year students at Bethel College (a small, private historically Black college located in the South). In the study, several variables (e.g., high school grades, class rank, and SAT scores) were observed for predictive value when coupled with the results of two measures: the Noncognitive Questionnaire Revised (NCQ-R) and the Student Adjustment to College Questionnaire (SACQ). The two questionnaires were used to measure noncognitive variables such as college expectations, self-esteem, and social and institutional adjustment. In addition, researchers also considered the academic performance of the students in the sample during their first year of college using the following dependent variables: (a) grade point average earned in the first semester, (b) academic status (probation), and (c) persistence to the second semester. Findings from the study indicated that high school class rank and grades were most predictive of academic success in the first year of college. Further, when considering retention, the data collected indicated a correlation between high school class rank and social adjustment in college. Finally, the findings also suggested that academic achievement could be predicted by measuring institutional attachment.
KEY WORDS: academic performance, African American students, assessment measures, college adjustment, self-esteem, student expectations.

Torres, V. (2004). Familial influences on the identity development of Latino first-year students. *Journal of College Student Development 45*(4), 457-468.

This article expands upon previous work in the area of "situating identity" by exploring the impact of a construct called "Generation in the United States and Familial Influences" in the expression and development of ethnic identity of Latino first-year students. The study used theoretical sampling as part of a constructivist grounded theory methodology to select 83 self-identified Latino first-year students at seven institutions to participate in interviews. Analyses of data collected from these participants identified three new issues to consider within the "Familial Influence and Generational Status in the U.S." construct. First, specific contexts (e.g., living near the Mexican-American border) may cause a student to choose a self-identifier that confounds their country of origin (i.e., the United States or Mexico) with their cultural heritage (e.g., Hispanic, Latino, Chicano), which makes it challenging to understand fully a student's contextual experiences. Second, first-year students from Latino enclaves, particularly women, may appear acculturated to the United States but actually experience a variety of cultural conflicts with the college environment. Finally, students who come from mixed backgrounds or who are adopted by White parents are blending into the overall environment of their colleges but may have ethnic/racial identity issues that are not being fully addressed. This article provides information on the variety of cultural and familial influences for first-year Latino students so that college faculty, staff, and administrators may support these students and their families in their transition to college. *KEY WORDS: Latino students, racial/ethnic identity development.*

Tsao, T. M. (2005). Open admissions, controversies, and CUNY: Digging into social history through a first-year composition course. *The History Teacher, 38*(4), 469-482.
This article traces the development and delivery of a first-year composition course taught at LaGuardia Community College (NY) that used the topic of open admissions as a vehicle for teaching the composition course's content. Using both primary and secondary documents, students analyzed the history of open admissions in the CUNY system in their class assignments and discussions. Based on what they had learned, students expressed deep concern about the relationship between race and educational opportunity—particularly their own opportunities. They also reported a deeper value for the educational opportunities that were available to them.
KEY WORDS: access to higher education, English Composition, race/ethnicity.

Wasburn, M. H., & Miller, S. G. (2004). Retaining undergraduate women in science, engineering, and technology: A survey of a student organization. *Journal of College Student Retention: Research, Theory & Practice, 6*(2), 155-168.
This article summarizes efforts at Purdue University–West Lafayette (IN) to determine the need for and support given to women enrolled in the institution's School of Technology. Approximately 15% of the school's students were women, and no changes in this demographic statistic had occurred in the five years prior to the study. The authors employed a modified version of the WEPAN Pilot Climate Survey—a tool created to measure engineering students' perceptions of the educational climate at their respective institutions—to glean insight into the perspectives of the women majoring in technology-based programs of study. Outcomes of the study were used to formulate and implement support strategies designed to attract and retain women in technology. Several common first-year student support initiatives (i.e., mentoring programs and learning communities) were created as a result.
KEY WORDS: assessment measures, campus climate, female students, retention, STEM disciplines.

Weissman, J., Bulakowski, C., & Jumisko, M. (1998). A study of White, Black, and Hispanic students' transition to a community college. *Community College Review, 26*(2), 19-42.
This study draws on data collected from 71 first-year students at the College of Lake County (IL) who participated in focus group sessions, organized by race, with the intent to better understand their college transition. Academic information about the students who participated in the focus group was obtained from survey data collected in the fall, as well as institutional records. These data were considered in the study, in addition to the focus group data collected in the fall and spring. Findings from the study indicated marked differences among racial groups (White, African American, and Hispanic). Some of the most significant differences between the groups included college goals and expectations. African American and Hispanic students indicated college attendance helped fulfill their desire to be a role model for family members and others in their community. The focus group data also suggested that White students had higher academic aspirations, often articulating a desire to earn more advanced degrees, a desire not as commonly reported among African American and Hispanic students. Additionally, expectations of what the college experience would be like varied from group to group, with the White and Hispanic students indicating that college was more like high school—easier than they had anticipated. Conversely, most of the African American students commented on the difficulty of college overall. Finally, perceptions of the institution differed by racial groups, with African American

and Hispanic students indicating that they felt uncomfortable, to some extent, with conversations in the classroom surrounding racism. They also reported experiencing a level of isolation and loneliness on campus. To combat this, the researchers suggested that more diverse faculty and staff be recruited, in addition to creating mechanisms to help students of color feel greater support on campus.
KEY WORDS: academic aspirations, African American students, focus groups, Latino students, students of color, transition to college.

White, J. W. (2005). Sociolinguistic challenges to minority collegiate success: Entering the discourse community of the college. *Journal of College Student Retention: Research, Theory & Practice, 6*(4), 369-393.
This article examines the relationship between knowledge about language used by colleges and universities and student academic success. Based on intensive interviews conducted with four students at the University of Colorado at Boulder, the authors assert that first-generation and minority students need to be "academically literate" in order to succeed (p. 377). In other words, they need to know the institutional community's jargon. Not knowing or failing to acquire this language can lead to a sense of alienation and attrition. Suggestions for teaching academic literacy and related cultural identity formation issues are also discussed.
KEY WORDS: access to higher education, first-generation students, students of color.

Zurita, M. (2005). Stopping out and persisting: Experiences of Latino undergraduates. *Journal of College Student Retention: Research, Theory & Practice, 6*(3), 301-324.
This qualitative study explores the experiences of 10 Latino undergraduate students—five who completed degrees and five who did not—at a large, midwestern, public university. Analysis of interview data indicated similarities and differences between the two groups. Both the students who persisted and those who left described similar home environments, perceptions of being academically unprepared, and a sense of being socially isolated. Students who finished their degrees reported more favorable experiences with the home-to-school transition and their first contacts with the university, mastery of academic challenges and possession of a set of clear education and career goals. These goals were not held by nonreturning students. The authors offer recommendations for supporting Latino students and suggestions for future research.
KEY WORDS: Latino students, students of color, retention.

Commuter Students

Clark, M. R. (2005). Negotiating the freshman year: Challenges and strategies among first-year students. *Journal of College Student Development, 46*(3), 296-316.
The primary aim of this study was to explore and expand upon the concept of student strategies as a means for understanding how new students transition to college. The researcher conducted a series of 10 individual interviews with eight traditional-aged first-year students during the second semester of their first year at a public, four-year, commuter college located in a major eastern city. Analyses of these data suggest that students' transition to college includes "an active process of strategizing" (p. 302). Further analysis revealed that challenges to the process of transition for first-year students and the related strategies that the students devised to cope with these challenges could be categorized into

four broad themes: (a) overcoming an obstacle, (b) seizing an opportunity, (c) adapting to a change, or (d) pursuing a goal. However, the researcher noted that similar challenges did not necessarily yield similar strategies among the students in this study, but instead reflected other, often interconnected, influences such as the students' perceptions of their own personal responsibility, available resources, and available options as well as personal characteristics such as persistence and confidence. By acknowledging these strategies and recognizing their influences, it is possible for campus personnel and programs that serve first-year students to help them recognize these challenges during their transition to college, clarify appropriate college role responsibilities, and enhance their strategies for success.

KEY WORDS: college adjustment, commuter students, locus of control, student success.

Jacoby, B., & Garland, J. (2004). Strategies for enhancing commuter student success. *Journal of College Student Retention: Research, Theory & Practice, 6*(1), 61-79.
This article explores how practitioners can use what is known about commuter students to create and manage initiatives that enhance the success and retention of students from this diverse subpopulation. Included in the article is a discussion of the complex differences between commuter students and their common needs. The authors provide several theoretical frameworks that have proven useful when working with and understanding commuter students, and they conclude by presenting an organizational model that combines these theories with specific strategies designed to promote and enhance the success of commuting students. Specific emphasis is placed on interventions that occur immediately prior to and during the first year of college.

KEY WORDS: commuter students, student success.

Sessa, F. M. (2005). The influence of perceived parenting on substance use during the transition to college: A comparison of male residential and commuter students. *Journal of College Student Development, 46*(1), 62-74.
This study offers a comparison of the experiences of commuter and residential students by focusing on the influence of the perceived parent-child relationship on the use of alcohol and marijuana. The researcher collected survey data from 50 residential and 57 commuter male college students who were an average of 18.5 years old and attending two different baccalaureate-granting institutions in the same general region of a mid-Atlantic state. Demographic comparisons of the two student groups revealed no statistically significant differences. Results of descriptive analyses and MANOVAs yielded three main findings. First, residential and commuter first-year men had different patterns of substance use. Residential students used alcohol more frequently than commuter students, while commuter students reported more frequent use of marijuana than their residential peers. Second, residential and commuter first-year students in the sample have different relationships with their parents. Specifically, residential students in the study felt that their parents monitored their behavior more than commuter students did and that their parents were less encouraging of their independence. Finally, these results indicate that the effect of perceived parenting on substance use is significant for commuter college students but not for residential first-year male students in this study. This study highlights the importance of recognizing the diversity of first-year student experiences, particularly with respect to patterns of substance use and parental influence. These findings can be used to inform orientation and first-year intervention programs for both students and parents.

KEY WORDS: commuter students, parental involvement, substance abuse.

Students with Disabilities

Belch, H. A. (2005). **Retention and students with disabilities.** *Journal of College Student Retention: Research, Theory & Practice, 6*(1), 3-22.
This article identifies factors affecting the success and retention of students with disabilities, with a specific emphasis on issues related to the transition from secondary to postsecondary environments. Key elements associated with the success of students with disabilities in college are highlighted, and successful strategies and practices for assisting students from this subpopulation are discussed, including initiatives at the Universities of Georgia, Minnesota, and Washington.
KEY WORDS: students with disabilities, retention, retention theory.

Smith, S. G., English, R., & Vasek, D. (2002). **Student and parent involvement in the transition process for college freshmen with learning disabilities.** *College Student Journal, 36*(4), 491-504.
This study involved 60 first-year students with learning disabilities at Baylor University and measured the level of involvement of parents and students in the transition to higher education using the High School and Beyond survey (HS&B) from the National Education Longitudinal Study (NELS). Findings from the study indicated that most of the students in the sample came from families with parents who had achieved some level of higher education and that most of the students felt they lacked a sense of self-advocacy and direction. Further, data collected in the study suggested that many students in the sample relied on their parents for help with course selection and decisions about school activities. The researchers indicated a need to move from this self-reported parent-advocacy to a greater level of self-advocacy on the part of the students. Finally, instruction in a number of skills, including communication and cooperation was suggested to help encourage the transfer of decision-making from the parents and family members to the first-year students.
KEY WORDS: assessment measures, learning disabilities, parental involvement, self-advocacy.

First-Generation and Low-Income Students

Elkins, S. A., Braxton, J. M., & James, G. W. (2000). **Tinto's separation stage and its influence on first-semester college student persistence.** *Research in Higher Education, 41*(2), 251-268.
This study explores the persistence of first-year students at a public, four-year institution. As a framework, the researchers used Tinto's construct of separation from his interactionalist theory of student departure. The Cooperative Institutional Research Program's Student Information Form was used to collect background information on the participants. The First Semester Collegiate Experiences Survey, which includes items derived from Tinto's notion of separation, was administered at the midpoint of the fall semester. Enrollment data were collected from the 411 respondents who completed both surveys. The researchers learned that support from family and friends in students' previous communities was the biggest factor in students' decisions to attend and remain in college. Members of racial/ethnic minority groups, students with lower levels of high school achievement, and those with lower income parents received less support. For students who did not receive this support, their ability to reject the attitudes and values of their past communities led to greater persistence. The researchers concluded that first-semester students who are able to successfully negotiate the separation stage are more likely to persist to their second semester. They also asserted that Tinto's construct of separation has construct validity. The authors recommended that higher education professionals work to involve family members

in assisting students with negotiating the separation process. They suggested systematic communication with parents, as well as programs that bring prospective students and their families to campus, especially for first-generation college students. Finally, they stressed the importance of providing both social and academic support to students, including residence hall and student activities initiatives and early warning systems that use absenteeism or low grades as a catalyst for outreach.

KEY WORDS: parental involvement, retention theory, social support.

Grant-Vallone, E., Reid, K., Umali, C., & Pohlert, E. (2003-4). An analysis of the effects of self-esteem, social support, and participation in student support services on students' adjustment and commitment to college. *Journal of College Student Retention: Research, Theory, & Practice, 5*(3), 255-274.

The researchers surveyed 118 college students to assess the relationship between self-esteem, family support, peer support, and program use, academic and social support, and college commitment. The students were participants in one of the following support programs geared toward low-income and first-generation students: Educational Opportunity Program (EOP), Academic Support Program for Intellectual Rewards (A.S.P.I.R.E.), and Faculty Mentoring Program (FMP). The authors found that students with higher self-esteem and peer support reported better academic and social adjustment. Students who used the university support programs more frequently also tended to report higher levels of social adjustment. In addition, students who felt more involved in campus life and were better adjusted academically were more likely to report that they were committed to the university and the goal of a college degree. The researchers concluded that such support programs promote adjustment for economically disadvantaged and underrepresented students. They stressed the value of encouraging student involvement in campus activities and programs. The authors also suggested that since the support programs impacted social but not academic adjustment, more could be done to develop academic adjustment.

KEY WORDS: college adjustment, first-generation students, student services.

Somers, P., Woodhouse, S., & Cofer, J. (2004). Pushing the boulder uphill: The persistence of first-generation college students. *NASPA Journal, 41*(3), 418-435.

The researchers identified several factors, including background, achievement, aspirations, college experience, financial aid, and price that they perceived had an impact on the persistence of first-year college students. Drawing on data collected through the National Postsecondary Student Aid Survey of 1995-96 (NPSAS: 96), the researchers were able to assemble a sample of 8,290 first-generation students and 15,972 students who were not first generation. The findings from the study indicated several points associated with each of the aforementioned factors. Data collected about background suggested that first-generation students were at greatest risk of not persisting when several variables (e.g., age and income) were present. The data also indicated that aspiration and achievement variables were also linked to persistence levels of first-generation students. Additionally, there were variables related to college experience that impacted persistence as well, including living on campus, course load, work, and grade point average. A final factor, price variables, yielded some persistence data for first-generation students. Increases in tuition negatively impacted the retention of students in the study; however, financial aid, grants, and work study increased the level of persistence in this group. Findings from the study indicated several differences between first-generation and other college students and revealed varying levels of influence of each of the factors. The researchers suggested that there is a greater need for programs to educate first-generation students and their parents early on (e.g., in middle school) about the college experience—from the financial commitment to advantages associated with earning a degree. Finally, they emphasized a need to continue support for first-generation students by working closely with high school faculty and guidance counselors, providing admissions and financial aid information, and offering students opportunities to participate in summer transition programs.

KEY WORDS: academic performance, first-generation students, persistence.

PART II

Creating Successful Transitions to the First College Year

{ INTRODUCTORY OVERVIEW }

Part II includes annotations that address methods used by colleges and universities to successfully admit and transition their students into the first year of college. The first subsection in Part II, Precollegiate Experiences and Programs, focuses on sources that deal with precollege academic experiences, the recruitment and admission of first-year students, and other efforts—with the exception of orientation—that prepare students for and shape their pre-enrollment expectations of college. The second subsection, addresses orientation programming for students, parents, and families.

Updates and Additions

The content we include in the Orientation Programs subsection is primarily an update to the comparably named section of the third edition. The Precollegiate Experience and Programs subsection is an amalgamation of two separate sections included in the previous edition—the Precollege and Summer Bridge Programs sections. We believe this change provides readers with greater access to content that logically fits together.

The Precollegiate Experience and Programs subsection does not include general content pertaining to admissions and recruitment. Rather, we have included sources that specifically address admissions practices directly impacting success in the first year of college. Specifically, the admissions-related content we annotated deals with approaches for evaluating and/or shaping prospective students' expectations, perceptions, and/or skills during the recruitment process in an effort to increase the probability of a good fit between the institution and the student. The phrase "recruiting to retain" is key here.

Omissions and/or Missing Components

When we created our outline for this part of the bibliography, we intended to include content on concurrent enrollment programs through which students take courses at their high schools that bear the credit of a college or university. We also hoped to include a number of annotations on transfer orientation programs—particularly transfer programs for students who come to college with fewer than 30 credits. We believed this addition was important because these students tend to exhibit behaviors and require support similar to those of new first-year students. Unfortunately, our search yielded no sources that demonstrated how interventions for these populations are used to enhance success during the first year of college. We invite practitioners, researchers, and program evaluators to work toward filling this gap in published works on these topics.

{ PRECOLLEGIATE EXPERIENCES AND PROGRAMS }

Precollege and Summer Bridge Programs

Glennen, R. E., Martin, D. J., & Walden, H. (2000). Summer honors academy: A descriptive analysis and suggestions for advising academically talented students. *NACADA Journal, 20*(2), 38-45.

Academically talented students are often overlooked in advising for college because their superior academic performance often masks a real need for counseling about expectations and the transition experience. To provide more insight into the characteristics and needs of this population, the authors examined 504 former participants in the Regents Honors Academies, a summer honors program for academically talented high school students held on college campuses in Kansas between 1987 and 1998. An analysis of personal background characteristics revealed that honors academy participants were more often women, were from advantaged backgrounds, worked part-time in college, and were active in extracurricular activities in addition to their intellectual pursuits. Results of a survey also indicated that nearly all of the respondents who were college-aged had enrolled in postsecondary education and 80% attended an institution in Kansas. Previous participants identified the academy's greatest benefit as its ability to expose students to the college experience while they were still in high school. Previous participants also reported that they appreciated the academy for providing them with intellectual stimulation, a social network of students at other high schools, and training in time management skills. The authors conclude that the summer academy is successful in assisting academically talented students in their transition to college.

KEY WORDS: academic success, honors programs, summer bridge programs.

Logan, C. R., Salisbury-Glennon, J., & Spence, L. D. (2000). The learning edge academic program: Toward a community of learners. *Journal of The First-Year Experience & Students in Transition, 12*(1), 77-104.

This article examines the impact of the Learning Edge Academic Program (LEAP) on the academic and social adjustment of first-year college students. LEAP is an optional six-week summer academic program open to all first-semester students at a large research institution. Students in the program were housed together and received mentoring from an upperclass undergraduate while taking two courses required for graduation. The two courses were linked by content and assignments, were scheduled over a blocked time period, and encouraged the use of small "learning teams" composed of four to five students. Training for using technological and library resources was part of the courses. To assess the program's impact, 84 of the 100 LEAP students completed the University Experiences Scale (included as an appendix in the article). A control group of 48 students also completed the self-report. LEAP participants were significantly more likely to report positive classroom experiences, support within and outside the classroom, and comfort using technology. Retention rates for LEAP students were 99% after two semesters, compared with a 94.2% retention rate for all students who entered the same year. Suggestions for improving the effectiveness of the program are presented.

KEY WORDS: assessment measures, clustered/linked courses, college adjustment, retention, summer bridge programs, technology.

McLure, G. T., & Child, R. L. (1999). Upward Bound students compared to other college-bound students: Profiles of nonacademic characteristics and academic achievement. *The Journal of Negro Education, 67*(4), 346-363.

The authors of this article conducted descriptive statistical analysis on ACT admissions data from 1998 to create profiles of 2,538 Upward Bound students and compared them to similar profiles that they developed for 997,069 non-Upward Bound students. These comparisons indicated that both groups were generally similar with respect to demographics, educational aspirations, and core course-taking patterns. However, Upward Bound students scored lower than the control group on several measures of academic performance, including the number of college preparatory courses completed in high school, expected grade point average at the end of the first year of college, and average ACT score. Also, Upward Bound students were disproportionately in the lowest financial bracket and scored higher on measures of financial concern, such as the expectation to apply for financial aid and to work during the first college year. Despite these challenges, other comparisons indicate that Upward Bound students respond positively to the program. They are more confident in their choice of a major and are more comfortable expressing a need for student support services during their first year. These patterns of similarity and differences help identify particular areas of risk and advantage among incoming students who participated in Upward Bound programs.
KEY WORDS: access to higher education, diversity, financial aid, student success.

Paul, E. L., Manetas, M., Grady, K., & Vivona, J., (2001). The transitions program: A precollege advising and orientation workshop for students and parents. *The Journal of the National Academic Advising Association 21*(1 & 2), 76-87.

This article describes The College of New Jersey's Transitions Program, which is designed to help students and parents form realistic expectations about the college experience and develop effective coping strategies for the college transition. The authors provide a theoretical and empirical rationale for the program and a detailed description. The College offers this program during its Expectations Week in late June, when students take placement exams, register for fall classes, obtain ID cards, and meet their academic advisors and faculty members. During the Transitions Program, students and parents complete a brief questionnaire about their expectations of college. Staff and faculty facilitators use the questionnaires as a catalyst for discussion during separate parent and student sessions. The dialogue about expectations and adjustment is extended into the semester for students through a one-credit first-year seminar course, workshops, and residence hall programs. Follow-up surveys revealed that students who attended the Transitions Program were significantly better adjusted socially than those who did not. Academic and emotional adjustment were also better for participants, though not at a statistically significant level. The authors assert that the following components of the program contribute to its success: timing of the workshop, involvement of parents, collaboration between staff and faculty, provision of coping tools for parents and students, and establishment of a framework for ongoing advising. Parent and student handouts used during the program are provided in the appendix.
KEY WORDS: college adjustment, orientation, outreach programs, parental involvement, student expectations.

Perna, L. W. (2002). Precollege outreach programs: Characteristics of programs serving historically underrepresented groups of students. *Journal of College Student Development, 43*(1), 64-83.

Using descriptive data drawn from the National Survey of Outreach Programs, this study examines the characteristics of outreach programs that focus on low-income, historically underrepresented, first-generation, and low-performing students. In particular, the author analyzes the goals and services of

1,100 outreach programs to determine the degree to which they address the five most critical predictors of college enrollment: goal of college attendance, participation in college tours, visits or fairs, goal of rigorous course-taking, parental involvement, and beginning program services by the eighth grade. While nearly all outreach programs include some of these components, only 25-30% of these programs address all five of these predictors. This paper provides critical contextual information for understanding the pathways and preparation of first-year students who participate in outreach programs.

KEY WORDS: diversity, first-generation students, outreach programs, students of color.

Wolf-Wendel, L. E., Tuttle, K., & Keller-Wolff, C. M. (1999). Assessment of a freshman summer transition program in an open-admissions institution. *Journal of The First-Year Experience & Students in Transition, 11*(2), 7-32.

The article offers the history, context, description, and assessment of Kansas University's Freshman Summer Institute. The optional program, which is open to all entering students, includes two, four-week residential programs serving at least 70 students in each session. Students earn five hours of academic credit during the program by enrolling in a faculty-taught, discipline-based course and an orientation course focused on campus resources, life/study skills, and major and career exploration. Outcomes assessment from the first three years of the program compared the participants' grade point averages (GPA) and retention rates against a matched control group. Qualitative data were also collected through focus groups. Though participation in the program did not significantly impact GPA or retention, there was a significant increase in a sense of academic and social self-efficacy among less academically prepared students. The qualitative data revealed that the program served to ease the students' transition to college in several respects, including academic transition, social transition, transition to adulthood, and logistical transition. The authors offer a number of theory-based explanations for the disparity between the quantitative and qualitative findings.

KEY WORDS: college adjustment, self-efficacy, summer bridge programs, retention.

Shaping Students' Expectations of College

Helland, P. A., Stallings, H. J., & Braxton, J. M. (2001-2). The fulfillment of expectations for college and student departure decisions. *Journal of College Student Retention: Research, Theory & Practice, 3*(4), 381-396.

The researchers posited that the more information students have about a college or university, the higher that institution's "image potency" will be, and the greater the likelihood that the students' experiences will match expectations for the college of choice. During the 1995-96 academic year, the authors administered three surveys: (a) the Student Information Form (SIF), (b) the Early Collegiate Experiences Survey (ECES), and (c) the Freshman Year Survey (FYS). Respondents were 718 first-time, full-time, first-year students of traditional college age enrolled at a highly selective, private Research I university. The researchers found that the fulfillment of social expectations had a direct positive impact on social integration and institutional commitment, and an indirect positive impact on intent to re-enroll. They stressed the importance of accurately depicting campus social climate through college catalogues, viewbooks, and presentations to high school guidance counselors and prospective students, which allows students to form more accurate expectations of that institution. In addition, the authors suggest that institutions encourage and facilitate campus visits for prospective students to help them further develop a realistic set of expectations for campus life. The researchers recommend further examination of the relationship between image potency and the formation of college expectations and the process through which institutional images are formed.

KEY WORDS: assessment measures, institutional identity, retention, student expectations.

Hicks, T. (2003). First-generation and non-first-generation precollege students' expectations and perceptions about attending college. *Journal of College Orientation and Transition, 11*(1), 5-17.

This study examined the perceptions and expectations that first-generation and non-first-generation college students have about college. The participants included first-year college students attending one of two 2001 summer programs at a four-year public research and doctoral degree-granting institution in the mid-Atlantic region. Among the sample of 197 students, 112 were first-generation students and 85 were non-first-generation students. The participants completed the PEEK (Perceptions, Expectations, Emotions, and Knowledge) questionnaire as a pre- and posttest during the first day and last week of the summer program. Results revealed that both first-generation and non-first-generation students did not initially express a need to seek outside help to succeed in college; both groups of students believed that instructors would teach them study skills as part of class. In addition, at the beginning of the program, more students in both groups perceived they would be responsible for their own learning. By the end of the program, more students perceived they would not make it through college. Students in both groups thought they would be less involved in college than they were in high school, and first-generation students expressed more concern about making new friends than non-first genera-tion students. The results suggest that educators should be mindful of new student perceptions when designing transition and support services and recognize that first-generation and non-first-generation students may have different needs.

KEY WORDS: assessment measures, first-generation students, student expectations.

Jackson, L. M., Pancer, S. M., Pratt, M. W., & Hunsberger, B. E. (2000). Great expectations: The relation between expectancies and adjustment during the transition to university. *Journal of Applied Social Psychology, 30*(10), 2100-2125.

The researchers conducted a longitudinal study to examine the nature of student expectations about college attendance and its impact on their subsequent adjustment to college. The participants completed questionnaires at five points in time: One was completed just prior to matriculation, and the rest dur-ing their first, second, and fourth years of study. The authors identified four expectation clusters: (a) optimistic, (b) prepared, (c) fearful, and (d) complacent. The prepared group had the highest college adjustment and study persistence rates; those students with fearful expectations demonstrated poorer adjustment and were more likely to drop out of the study. Students with optimistic or complacent expectations were neither better nor more poorly adjusted. This research suggests that the "Freshman Myth" (Stern, 1966), the presence of overly idealistic expectations that can lead to maladjustment, was not ubiquitous. The authors assert that those in the prepared expectations group fared best because they had developed better coping skills and had a greater sense of personal agency. They suggest that helping those with fearful expectations develop active coping strategies and techniques for managing personal challenges could promote adjustment to college.

KEY WORDS: college adjustment, "Freshman Myth," student expectations.

Miller, T. E., Bender, B. E., & Schuh, J. H. (2005). *Promoting reasonable expectations: Aligning student and institutional views of the college experience.* **San Francisco: Jossey-Bass.**

A team of faculty, administrators, leaders of national educational organizations, and higher education scholars explore the many dimensions of new student expectations of college, expectation fulfillment or disillusionment, and the relationships between expectations and numerous college experiences and outcomes. Examples include an examination of expectations as defined by key demographic and background characteristics, the influence of institutional type and environmental characteristics on student expectations and experiences, and the nature and impact of students' expectations about campus services, educational experiences, cost and financial aid, and life after college. The authors suggest that student expectations are a critical component of the relationships forged between first-year students and the institution and provide the foundation for student-institutional compatibility. Throughout the text, authors connect research and assessment findings to strategies and practices that help enhance the transition experiences of new students and the overall success of undergraduates.

KEY WORDS college adjustment, student success.

Schilling, K. M., & Schilling, K. L. (1999, May/June). Increasing expectations for student effort. *About Campus, 4*, 4-10.

This piece underscores the importance of setting high expectations for students early in their college careers. The authors report on a multi-institution project in which students at seven colleges and universities completed the College Student Expectations Questionnaire (CSXQ) upon matriculation and again at the end of their first year. The goal was to assess how students' entering expectations for college compared with their actual experiences. They discovered that students expected that they would devote less time to their studies than faculty asserted they must in order to be successful. Furthermore, at the end of their first year, students reported that they actually worked less than they expected to work in college. Students' expectations also fell short in terms of the types of learning activities in which they engaged. For example, students reported memorizing formulas more often than using higher-order thinking skills, which was counter to what they expected. Despite this less-than-expected meaningful time spent on academics, national statistics suggest that student grade point averages are on the rise. The authors assert that institutions must do more to close the gap between student and faculty expectations as well as student expectations and their actual experiences. They recommend (a) sending a systematic message about academic rigor from both academic and student affairs; (b) creating a student "job description" that specifies what behaviors are needed to produce desired college outcomes; and (c) heightening the intellectual challenge of courses, as opposed to simply grading harder.

KEY WORDS: academic success, involvement, student expectations.

Schilling, K. M., & Schilling, K. L. (2005). Expectations and performance. In M. L. Upcraft, J. N. Gardner, B. O. & Barefoot (Eds.), *Challenging and supporting the first-year student: A handbook for improving the first year of college* (pp. 108-123). San Francisco: Jossey-Bass.

This chapter evaluates the nature and significance of expectations in higher education, particularly those held by incoming first-year students. The authors review previous findings on expectancy theory and the "Freshman Myth" and suggest strategies for learning about expectations on individual campuses, using both qualitative and quantitative approaches. In one such assessment at Miami University, the authors found that students' responses to a five-minute free writing exercise at orientation tended to focus on academic, personal, and social expectations about college. Follow-up assessments indicated that there were many discrepancies between students' expectations as stated during orientation and actual first-year experiences, particularly with respect to time spent on academics versus other activities. Further, longitudinal assessments of student behavior indicated that the patterns of time allocation established during the first year persisted throughout the students' time at college, thereby making new student expectations and their subsequent first-year experiences of critical importance for long-term student success. The authors suggest that coupling student expectations data with data from an audit of cultural cues and clear expectations from faculty allows the institution to more effectively assist first-year students in their transition to college.

KEY WORDS: college adjustment, "Freshman Myth," student expectations, student success.

Smith, J. S., & Wertlieb, E. C. (2005). Do first-year college students' expectations align with their first-year experiences? *NASPA Journal, 42*(2), 153-174.

Drawing on expectancy-value theory and ecological theory, this study investigated the alignment between academic and social expectations and first-year experiences of college students. The researchers also explored the potential relationships between expectations, experiences, and academic achievement. By administering a survey to 31 new prebusiness students at a four-year, public university at three points in time (two weeks after college entry, mid-way through the first year, and at the end of the spring semester), the researchers found that students' first-year experiences do not live up to their precollege expectations. The findings indicated more significant gaps between the students' social expectations and their actual social experiences. Differences between expectations of academic experiences and actual academic experiences were not as large as those associated with the social aspects of college. The authors share methodological and practical implications of this work and identify the disparity between expectations and experiences as symptomatic of an overall disconnect between high school and college that educators in both realms must work together to address.

KEY WORDS: academic achievement, "Freshman Myth."

Wallace, D., Abel, R., & Ropers-Huilman, B. (2000). Clearing a path for success: Deconstructing borders through undergraduate mentoring. *The Review of Higher Education, 24*(1), 87-102.

The primary goal of this article is to examine students' interpretations of formal mentoring programs offered in three TRIO programs aimed at promoting access of first-generation, low-income, disabled, and historically underrepresented students to higher education. The article depicts students' strategies for success and retention in the first year and beyond. The study described in the article used critical theory to analyze student comments about their formal mentoring relationships with one or more TRIO staff members. Qualitative data were collected through individual interviews with 20 students participating in the three TRIO programs. Analyses of the interview data indicated that formal mentoring relationships forged prior to college positively influenced students' decisions to attend and enroll in college. Further, these formal mentoring relationships were an important resource in students' initial integration and adjustment to college. These relationships were made particularly important because students served by the TRIO programs did not establish informal mentoring relationships with faculty during their transition to college. The authors conclude that formal mentoring relationships can have a positive effect on TRIO students' access to higher education and their transition to college.

KEY WORDS: access to higher education, diversity, mentoring students of color.

Admissions

Bryson, S., Smith, R., & Vineyard, G. (2002). Relationship of race, academic and nonacademic information in predicting the first-year success of selected admissions first-year students. *Journal of The First-Year Experience & Students in Transition, 14*(1), 65-80.

The purpose of this study was to predict the first-year grades of conditionally admitted African American and White students by examining race; traditional academic variables such as high school rank, ACT scores, and grade point average (GPA); and nonacademic dimensions of the student experience as assessed by the Bryson Instrument for Noncognitive Assessment (BINA). The students, who did not meet regular admissions criteria at a comprehensive, predominantly White institution (PWI) participated in a special program while enrolled in general studies courses required of all entering students. The program included study skills courses and other supportive elements, such as counseling, tutoring, and mentoring. The results indicate BINA scores accounted for 2% of the variance for the first-year grades. The research provides evidence that different processes are involved in academic success for African American and White students at PWIs. Specifically, high school GPA was found to be the best predictor of first-year GPA for African American students, while high school rank was the best predictor for White students. There were also racial differences among the noncognitive predictors. For African American students, the only significant predictor of academic success was self-esteem; for White students, self-appraisal was the only significant predictor. The authors suggest that admissions professionals should reconsider using a single formula for institutional entry and consider a more holistic method tailored to the needs of individual students.
KEY WORDS: academic support, academic success, assessment measures, admissions standards, self-image, students of color.

Freer-Weiss, D. (2004-5). Community college freshmen: Last in, first out? *Journal of College Student Retention: Research, Theory and Practice, 6*(2), 137-154.

This study sought to discover the characteristics of late-admission, first-time, first-year students who enrolled at an open-access institution. The author examined the relationship between students' date of admission and their subsequent academic success and persistence. Guided by Tinto's (1987) theoretical framework, the researcher examined students' pre-entry attributes, academic abilities, and goals from closed admission files at a two-year metropolitan regional campus. The investigator discovered that students who apply late have different characteristics from those who apply early. For example, students who apply late are less academically successful and are less likely to re-enroll for the next term. The author concluded that a strong relationship exists between a high-risk student profile, late application, and attrition. She suggests that admissions policies be reconsidered to ensure that the needs of all students are met. Earlier admissions dates might provide more time to offer services, such as orientation and advising, that would optimize student success and promote their persistence.
KEY WORDS: academic success, admissions standards, at-risk students, two-year institutions.

King, T. M., & Wessel, R. D. (2004). Impact of admitted student programs on matriculation and retention. *Journal of College Orientation and Transition, 11*(2), 5-12.

This study explored the impact of an admitted college student program on matriculation and persistence to the second semester at a midwestern, public, mid-size, doctoral-intensive institution. The admitted student program included an overnight residence hall stay, attending a university class, and meeting current students. The participants were 7,384 admitted students, who were divided into four sub-groups: (a) 378 attended an admitted student program; (b) 2,206 attended an on-campus admissions program; (c) 4,571 did not attend a special program; and (d) 229 attended both an admitted student program and an on-campus admissions program. The researchers learned that 73% of students who participated in the admitted student program matriculated, 59% of students who attended on on-campus admissions program matriculated, and 43% of students who attended neither program matriculated. In addition, 94% of students who attended the admitted student program persisted to second semester, 93% who attended an on-campus admissions program persisted, and students who attended neither program persisted at a rate of 77.5%. The researchers suggest that institutions should consider offering and strongly encouraging student participation in admitted student programs to increase matriculation rates and promote student persistence.

KEY WORDS: enrollment, orientation, persistence, pre-enrollment programs.

Reingold, D. (2004). How to humanize the college admission game. *Journal of College Admission, 184*, 18-22.

In this era of competitive college admissions, particularly at selective institutions, the author explores the general procedures as well as the benefits and detriments of four different admissions policies: early decision, early action, rolling admissions, and early notification. The author is particularly critical of early decision programs and the negative implications of this admissions approach. He also includes an in-depth profile of early notification systems as the newest admissions strategy. The author identifies specific financial aid strategies used to entice students to attend and the steep competition among institutions for "desirable" students as two of the most significant problems associated with student recruitment practice today. This article illustrates the types of decisions that institutions and students are forced to make as part of the admissions process and highlights the implications on the fit between institution and student, the students' first-year experiences, and their overall college success.

KEY WORDS: early notification programs, selective admissions.

St. John, E. P., Hu, S., Simmons, A. B., & Musoba, G. D. (2001). Aptitude vs. merit: What matters in persistence. *The Review of Higher Education, 24*(2), 131-152.

Given the ongoing legal debate about the use of racial preferences in college admissions, higher education scholars and practitioners are considering new measures to use in the admissions process that promote both fairness and diversity. One such measure is the merit-aware index, which represents the difference between an individual's SAT score and the average standardized test score for their school. The index provides a means of evaluating individual merit within the context of high school quality. The authors cite previous research that shows that the merit-aware index led to the consideration and yield of a higher percentage of African American applicants than previous admissions methods. In this article, the authors expand on the evaluation of this method of admissions to consider how well the merit-aware index predicts new student success as measured by first-year persistence rates. Logistical regression analyses were conducted on data from a sample of 2,500 in-state first-year students who attended public higher education institutions in Indiana. Results of these analyses show that the merit-aware index predicts college persistence as well as the SAT currently does. As such, the authors conclude that the merit-aware index is a promising new admissions practice that has the potential to improve ethnic diversity while maintaining first-year college persistence rates.

KEY WORDS: diversity, persistence, selective admissions, students of color.

Tam, M. S., & Sukhatme, U. (2004). How to make better college admission decisions: Considering high school quality. *Journal of College Admission, 183*, 12-16.

The authors of this article explored the effectiveness of combining a measure of high school quality (i.e., average ACT score of the high school) with the previously used measure of high school percentile rank in admissions decisions to improve the predictive power of admissions decisions at the University of Illinois at Chicago. Using data from a cohort of 2,529 students entering the university in 1994, the researchers compared the students' six-year degree completion rate with the importance of four admissions variables: (a) high school percentile rank, (b) ACT score, (c) the average ACT score of the high school, and (d) a new combined variable. Results indicated that the new combined variable was the most powerful predictor of six-year graduation rate, followed by average high school ACT score and individual ACT score. Personal high school percentile rank showed the weakest relationship with graduation rates. Based on these findings, the authors recommend that both the student's rank in the high school and the measure of high school quality be used in admissions decisions. The authors suggest that these findings, and improved enrollment management decisions they support, are particularly important in an era of increasingly selective admissions standards, limited educational resources, and greater demands for educational accountability.

KEY WORDS: admissions standards, graduation rates.

{ ORIENTATION PROGRAMS }

Busby, R. R., Gammel, H. L., & Jeffcoat, N. K. (2002). Grades, graduation, and orientation: A longitudinal study of how new student programs relate to grade point averages and graduation. *Journal of College Orientation and Transition, 10*(1), 45-57.

This study examined the impact of an orientation program at Stephen F. Austin State University (TX) using a longitudinal assessment of students' first-semester grade point averages (GPA) and graduation rates. Research participants included first-year students at the university from 1986-1994. Results indicated that students who attended orientation had a significantly higher GPA (2.11) than those who did not attend orientation (1.73). This pattern persisted when orientation attendees were matched with those who did not attend based on gender and standardized test scores. Furthermore, students who attended orientation persisted at a significantly higher rate than those who did not attend. Results suggest that the orientation program at this institution positively impacts student success, as measured by first semester GPA and retention rates.

KEY WORDS: assessment, orientation, student success.

Crissman Ishler, J. L., & Upcraft, M. L. (2001). Assessing first-year programs. In J. H. Schuh, & M. L. Upcraft (Eds.), *Assessment practice in student affairs: An applications manual* **(pp. 261-274). San Francisco: Jossey-Bass.**

This chapter presents a comprehensive model for assessing first-year programs. The model includes the assessment of first-year students' backgrounds, needs, satisfaction with a specific first-year program, and gains resulting from program participation. The model also identifies the importance of considering the scope and cost-effectiveness of any first-year assessment effort. The authors use the model to work through 11 steps of an assessment example measuring new student orientation attendance and student satisfaction.

KEY WORDS: assessment, orientation, student affairs practice.

Dadonna, M. F., & Cooper, D. L. (2002). Comparison of freshmen perceived needs prior to and after participation in an orientation program. *NASPA Journal, 39*(4), 300-318.

The purpose of this research was to compare the perceived needs of first-year college students before and after their participation in a week-long orientation program. Participants were 77 first-semester students at a two-year private liberal arts college in the Southeast. The researchers administered the Freshman Survey, designed for the purposes of this study, during the first day of orientation and during the second week of school. The survey includes items related to personal/emotional, social, academic, and career needs. The results revealed that the students' pre- and post-orientation needs were focused on academic and career areas, such as course scheduling, selecting a major, and sources of academic information. Women expressed higher pre-orientation needs than men on personal/emotional, social, and career issues. African American students indicated greater social and academic pre-orientation needs than Asian/Pacific Islander students, which were also higher than White students. The authors recommend that orientation programs should balance academic and social components, while addressing the most pressing needs early in the program. Educators should also be sensitive to the needs of different types of students.

KEY WORDS: gender differences, orientation, student needs, students of color.

Donnelly, D. L, & Borland, K. W., Jr. (2002). Undeclared students' patterns of declaration: Practical and political implications for orientation and transition programs. *Journal of College Orientation and Transition, 10*(1), 5-13.

This research presented patterns of student major declaration over a two-year period at a northwestern university. The 449 participants were first-year students who had participated in a summer orientation program and completed a general studies seminar course in fall 1998. They completed an in-class survey during the first and last weeks of the semester. For two years, the researchers examined transcripts of the study population in order to assess enrollment and major declaration patterns. The findings revealed that 63.5% of students declared their major in either their second or third semester of study, and 93.5% declared with less than 46 credits earned. Students who declared a major had higher retention rates than those who did not; 80% of the students who left the institution during the study had not decided on a major. The researchers stress the importance of having accurate data about undeclared students so that appropriate orientation and academic advising initiatives can be designed to assist them in making decisions about their academic major.

KEY WORDS: academic advising, orientation, retention, undecided students.

Fabich, M. (Ed.). (2004). *Orientation planning manual.* **Flint, MI: National Orientation Directors Association.**

This manual includes 10 articles that address the design and implementation of first-year college student orientation programs. Topics included are (a) the connection of orientation and student retention; (b) staff selection and training; (c) developing programs for special populations, transfer students, and families; (d) orientation for two-year institutions; (e) use of technology; and (f) assessment. Half of the volume is composed of appendices, which provide practical resources for orientation planning and implementation. For example, the manual offers an orientation leader job description, application, training syllabus, training schedule, and contract; sample orientation schedules for use at two-year colleges and for working with special populations, transfer students, and families; sample assessment questions; as well as Council for the Advancement of Standards and National Orientation Directors Association standards for orientation programs.

KEY WORDS: CAS standards, diversity, orientation, technology, two-year institutions.

Haulmark, M., & Williams, P. (2004). **Designing orientation for a new audience and learning environment: Moving the college experience course online.** *Journal of College Orientation and Transition, 11*(2), 19-25.

This article describes the development, implementation, and review of an online College Experience (CE) class at Rogers State University (RSU) in Claremore, Oklahoma. The one-credit course, which focuses on critical skills for academic success, is required of all incoming RSU first-year students. The authors document the process of moving the course to an online format and examine the effect that the new format had on course content. In developing the course, the faculty and instructional design team created a general profile of online learners, based on RSU data and scholarly writing on the topic. They used this profile to develop course components, including technical skills, strategies for learning online, time management, learning styles and critical thinking, tests taking, stress management, and reading and writing skills. The 39 students enrolled in the online CE were surveyed in the eighth week of the 12-week course, and 29 responded (74.36%). Based on analysis of the data collected, the design team concluded that the preliminary assumptions about the student profile of online learners were correct and that the content choices were appropriate. They identified the following as issues for further examination: the number of credit hours awarded, topics and activities that impact the success of adult learners, gender-specific content (women comprise the majority enrolled in RSU online courses), and faculty preparation to meet the needs of adult learners.
KEY WORDS: adult learners, first-year seminars, online learning, orientation, technology.

Keppler, K., Mullendore, R. H., & Carey, A. (Eds.): (2005). *Partnering with the parents of today's college students.* **Washington, DC: National Association of Student Personnel Administrators.**

This volume contains seven articles describing methods for fostering collaboration between educators and parents to promote student success. Topics include the changing demographics and diversity in higher education, parent orientation programs, legal issues, and managing parent expectations. The book provides an annotated bibliography of parent and administrator resources, and the appendices offer practical information to educators, such as model parent programs, activities, and related materials.
KEY WORDS: orientation, parental involvement.

Miller, M. T., Dyer, B. G., & Nadler, D. P. (2002). **New student satisfaction with an orientation program: Creating effective learning transitions.** *Journal of College Orientation and Transition, 10*(1), 51-57.

This study examined an orientation program at a highly selective urban research institution of 10,000 students located in the Southeast. The research goals were to determine how successful the program was in meeting Council for the Advancement of Standards (CAS) guidelines and to identify themes in participant responses. Data were collected during the fall 2000 orientation program using a survey designed by a research team. Of the 1,300 students who received the survey, 1,048 (80%) of them returned it. Results revealed that each of the 20 CAS objectives was met and that the participants had a positive response to the program. All students agreed or strongly agreed to each of 20 affirmative statements about the program. The two main clusters of student responses were focused on how to make decisions and on meeting their immediate needs (e.g., fitting in, belonging, making friends). While the orientation program met its goals, the researchers suggest that students may experience information overload from the heavily scheduled four-day program. The authors recommend use of an ongoing orientation program that would allow educators to highlight important information at relevant points during the academic year.
KEY WORDS: CAS standards, orientation, transition to college.

Nadler, D. P., Miller, M. T., & Dyer, B. G. (2004). Longitudinal analysis of standards used to evaluate new student orientation at a case institution. *Journal of College Orientation and Transition, 11*(2), 36-41.

This seven-year study examined an orientation program's level of compliance with guidelines established by the Council for the Advancement of Standards (CAS). The setting was a highly selective urban research institution of 10,000 students located in the Southeast. Demographic data were collected on program participants as well as data from a survey of 20 items from the CAS guidelines for new student orientation. Data from 7,250 surveys were analyzed with an average of 1,035 surveys completed by new students each year of the study. Four survey items consistently rated higher than others over the seven years: (a) "[Orientation] assisted me in developing positive new relationships with other new students"; (b) "[Orientation] provided information concerning academic policies, procedures, requirements, and programs"; (c) "[Orientation] promoted awareness of non-classroom opportunities"; and (d) "[Orientation] provided appropriate information on personal safety and security." The institution used these results to design workshops for orientation staff and to prompt discussions on necessary programmatic changes. The study particularly highlighted the importance of involving faculty in orientation. The researchers recommend that other institutions consider CAS guidelines for design and evaluation of their programs.

KEY WORDS: CAS standards, longitudinal assessment, orientation.

Twale, D. J., & Schaller, M. A. (2003). Mandatory computer purchases and student preparedness: Implications for new student orientation. *Journal of College Orientation and Transition, 10*(2), 60-69.

The purposes of this study were to assess the level of technical preparedness and competence of incoming students participating in a mandatory personal computer purchase program and to examine any differences in these skills based on gender, race, year in college, and discipline. Participants (167 the first year and 169 the second year) were first-year students at a private, religious, midwestern university who completed a questionnaire during the fall semester. Data revealed that students indicated gains over time in ability to use hardware and software, regardless of their level of technical competence at entry. Researchers also learned that while men indicated greater usage of software applications, the Internet, and the Web, women indicated a greater willingness to ask for assistance with technology. The authors assert that as incoming students in general become more technologically competent at entry, institutions might focus more on logistical and ethical issues associated with computer technologies as they orient new students.

KEY WORDS: orientation, technology.

PART III

Promoting First-Year Student Success

{INTRODUCTORY OVERVIEW}

The third part of this monograph includes annotations on curricular and cocurricular approaches as well as resources used to enhance the first-year experience. The longest section of the monograph, it includes five subsections, each examining a different aspect of the approaches used by institutions to achieve first-year student success. These subsections include (a) Curricular Interventions Comprising the First-Year Experience, (b) Support Services and Programs, (c) Involvement in Campus Life and Living Environments (d) Technology, and (e) Agents of Socialization and Support in the First Year.

Updates and Additions

The annotations on curriculum and teaching, first-year seminars, learning communities, and Supplemental Instruction and other forms of academic support included in the first subsection of Part III are chiefly updates to similar annotations offered in the previous edition of this monograph. For this edition, they are included under one heading, Curricular Interventions Comprising the First-Year Experience. This change was made because curricular efforts like these are often intertwined. For example, learning communities can include first-year seminars in their course clusters, and first-year seminars can include academic support components. Bringing together potentially linked initiatives is intended to help the reader find and use this content. Also, two new topical headings have been added: (a) library and information literacy and (b) service-learning. These inclusions reflect the increasing prevalence of these curricular approaches in the first college year.

The annotations in the subsection Involvement in Campus Life and Living Environments, span an array of campus life topics (e.g., athletics, residence life, student activities). This content both updates and expands the Residence Life section of the third edition. Our penchant for this connected and expanded approach is also evident in the Agents of Socialization and Support subsection. Here, we include annotations on sources that address how faculty and staff, parents and family members, and peers impact student success during the first year of college.

The subsection Technology includes annotations for sources published about this topic since 2000 and serves as an update to the identically named section in the previous edition.

Omissions and/or Missing Components

Unfortunately, unlike service-learning, not all of the curricular approaches that postsecondary institutions use with their first-year students were present in published works. With the attention that summer reading programs have received over the past six years in national publications such as the *Chronicle of Higher Education, USA Today,* and *Time Magazine,* we thought we would find ample research on the impact that these efforts have had on first-year students. We were wrong. Our search efforts yielded nothing. This is clearly a gap in research on the first-year experience—one we hope to see addressed by practitioners and scholars in the near future.

CURRICULAR INTERVENTIONS COMPRISING THE FIRST-YEAR EXPERIENCE

Curriculum and Teaching

Braxton, J. M., Milem, J. F., & Sullivan, A. S. (2000). The influence of active learning on the college student departure process. *The Journal of Higher Education, 71*(5), 569-590.

Drawing on data collected from 718 first-year students through the administration of the Student Information Form (SIF), the Early Collegiate Experience Survey (ECES), and the Freshman Year Survey (FYE), this study sought to measure student persistence and retention and to identify common factors impacting both. The instruments were administered throughout the first year, beginning at orientation and continuing through the first and second semesters. Six measures emerged from data analysis including institutional commitment, aspects of active learning, and departure decisions, as well as all characteristics described in Tinto's *Leaving College: Rethinking the Causes and Cures of Student Attrition* (1993). Additional composite measures were identified to gauge levels of active learning. Findings from this study indicated a connection between active learning and persistence. Additionally, the researchers found an influence of social integration on persistence; interaction with faculty and active learning were found to play a strong role in social integration. The influence of teaching, and the effects of various teaching pedagogies (e.g., lecture) and relationship to student learning are additional areas that researchers in this study suggested for further examination.
KEY WORDS: active learning, assessment, persistence, retention.

Dahlgren, D. J., Wille, D. E., Finkel, D. G., & Burger, T. (2005). Do active learning techniques enhance learning and increase persistence of first-year psychology students? *Journal of The First-Year Experience & Students in Transition, 17*(1), 49-65.

In order to examine the impact of active-learning techniques on academic performance, student evaluations of teaching, and persistence, the authors collected data from a sample of 231 undergraduates (75% of whom were first-year students) enrolled in four sections of an introductory psychology class. Two sections were taught by faculty who used active-learning strategies, and two were taught by faculty who lectured. While students were not randomly assigned, all four sections were relatively balanced in terms of student abilities and personal characteristics and all four instructors had previously received equally positive evaluations for their teaching in the introductory psychology course. The result of MANOVAs, one-way ANOVAs, and chi-square analyses indicated that active-learning strategies enhanced students' perceived involvement (as articulated on the teaching evaluations) and class completion rates in the course. However, student grades on the first three exams were statistically equal in both conditions, and the active-learning group scored lower on the fourth exam in the class. While the authors posit that this effect may be partially explained by the higher course persistence rates (i.e., "weaker" students were retained throughout the course, thereby decreasing the overall academic performance of the class), the study indicated that exam grades were not enhanced by active learning strategies.
KEY WORDS: academic performance, active learning, persistence.

Erickson, B. L., & Strommer, D. W. (2005). Inside the first-year classroom: Challenges and constraints. In M. L. Upcraft, J. N. Gardner, & B. O. Barefoot (Eds.), *Challenging and supporting the first-year student: A handbook for improving the first year of college* (pp. 241-256). San Francisco: Jossey-Bass.

This chapter considers issues specific to teaching first-year college students, such as academic preparation, motivations for learning, learning styles, and stages of intellectual development. The authors offer pedagogical recommendations for teaching in the first year and provide a summary of findings from recent research on basic learning processes. This research has identified a continuum of student approaches to learning ranging from surface learning to deep learning and describes several optimal conditions that foster deep learning among students, including helping students discover intrinsic motivation, connecting abstractions to concrete activity, and promoting interaction with one another. The chapter also describes five teaching methods especially effective in teaching first-year students: (a) small group discussions, (b) writing-to-learn activities, (c) case studies and scenarios, (d) problem-based learning, and (e) experiential learning. Implementation strategies for each method are highlighted. Practical recommendations for pedagogical practices in the first year conclude the chapter. *KEY WORDS: learning, teaching strategies.*

Junco, R. (2005). Technology and today's first-year students. In M. L. Upcraft, J. N. Gardner, & B. O. Barefoot (Eds.), *Challenging and supporting the first-year student: A handbook for improving the first year of college* (pp. 221-238). San Francisco: Jossey-Bass.

The author of this chapter provides an overview of the relationship between networked technologies and first-year students. The following is discussed: (a) research associated with the use and impact of technology, (b) examples of technology in the classroom experience, (c) the gap between student and faculty experience with technology, and (d) recommendations for uses of technologies with first-year students. The chapter begins with examples of the types of technologies used most often by first-year students (e.g., instant messaging, cell phones, e-mail, Internet) and considers how and why students use these technologies. The author examines research that indicates differences in technology use among students by socioeconomic status and gender and suggests that appropriate uses of technologies can enhance the educational experience of first-year students. The chapter also offers negative and positive examples of technology use in and out of the classroom (with an emphasis on the impact on academic performance). The experience gap between students and faculty is also highlighted as a consideration as use of technologies becomes ubiquitous. For example, both students and faculty tend to use e-mail, but many faculty members do not have the same level of Internet experience as their students and, consequently, might not be as comfortable using the Internet in the classroom. The author recommends future uses of networked technologies with first-year students, suggests standardizing the types of technologies used on a campus, and recommends introducing these technologies early in the college experience. *KEY WORDS: technology and teaching.*

Smith, B. L., & McCann, J. (Eds.). (2001). *Reinventing ourselves: Interdisciplinary education, collaborative learning, and experimentation in higher education.* Boston: Anker Publishing Company, Inc.

This book describes the reinvention of teaching and learning practices among members of a diverse group of faculty and staff working in higher education and offers examples of the members' innovation and creativity. Chapters are organized into three sections: (a) Historical Perspectives and Institutional Examples, (b) Powerful Pedagogies, and (c) Taking Stock and Looking Ahead. Part I offers a history of innovation and examples from colleges and universities that pioneered innovative educational practices and pedagogical transformation. All of the institutions described, from the well established to the new, exhibit a high level of commitment to enhancing undergraduate education. Part II of the book examines the learning communities movement, offers examples of integration of service-learning and learning communities, and describes the relationship between liberal education and learning communities at one institution. Drawing on additional institutional examples, the second half of this section focuses attention on interdisciplinary education. The final section acknowledges previous accomplishments and provides a vision for the future, with an emphasis again on interdisciplinary education. Several examples of new, innovative directions being taken by colleges and universities are offered.

KEY WORDS: interdisciplinary education, learning, learning communities, service-learning, teaching strategies.

First-Year Seminars

Cavote, S. E., & Kopera-Frye, K. (2004). Subject-based first-year experience courses: Questions about program effectiveness. *Journal of The First-Year Experience & Students in Transition, 16*(2), 85-102.

This study investigated the relationship between participation in first-year seminars integrated into introductory academic major courses and student academic performance and persistence. Data were collected from a sample of 381 students who completed an academic subject-based, first-year experience course at the University of Nevada, Reno and a control group of 332 students who did not complete a first-year experience course. The researchers conducted two analyses of covariance (ANCOVAs) to detect differences between the two groups on (a) grade point averages in both terms of their first year and in the first term of their second year and (b) retention rates through the first year and first-to-second-year persistence rates. These analyses did not yield any group differences and, thus, indicate that these academic subject-based, first-year experience courses were not related to student grades or persistence over a two-year period. The authors offer a number of potential explanations for these results including methodological and analytical limitations of the study but conclude that caution is warranted when considering institution-wide implementation of first-year seminars that are linked to students' academic discipline.

KEY WORDS: academic success, first-year seminars, retention.

Dooris, M. J., & Blood, I. M. (2001). Implementing and assessing first-year seminars. *Assessment Update, 13*(4), 1-2, 12-13.

The authors review the implementation and assessment of an institution-wide, first-year seminar at The Pennsylvania State University considered the hallmark of a new general education curriculum. The design of the new program curriculum reflected input from alumni, students, and analysis of student registration data as well as a review of the literature and existing best practices. The new first-year seminar became a campus-wide requirement, although individual colleges, departments, and campuses were given considerable autonomy with regard to course content and structure. Although this variation created some challenges to assessing the program, the faculty senate and central administration were committed to understanding the program's effects. A general education assessment interest group was formed to assess use, impact, and outcomes of the first-year seminars during their inaugural year. Information on course offerings and enrollment patterns comprised the bulk of the utilization study, while faculty and student focus groups and student surveys gauged the impact and outcomes of the courses. Overall, the assessments yielded data in favor of the program and identified specific areas of positive impact (e.g., small class sizes and longer duration of the course). This case study provides an example of how assessment can be used in planning, implementing, and evaluating a new first-year program.

KEY WORDS: assessment, first-year seminars, general education.

Henscheid, J. M. (Ed.) (2004). *Integrating the first-year experience: The role of learning communities in first-year seminars* **(Monograph No. 39). Columbia, SC: University of South Carolina, National Resource Center for The First-Year Experience and Students in Transition.**

This edited collection focuses on the theoretical and practical intersection of two of the most commonly used curricular interventions for first-year students: learning communities and first-year seminars. The monograph begins with an analysis of the learning outcomes associated with stand-alone first-year seminars as compared to those linked with learning communities. This research, conducted through The First-Year Initiative Benchmarking Survey, indicates that linked courses are associated with greater perceived gains on numerous learning outcomes. The bulk of the monograph is devoted to case studies of 16 institutions that offer learning communities with embedded first-year seminars. Each institution was selected for its excellence in these program offerings, but also with an eye toward providing examples from a diverse set of institutions, as well as the generalizability of the approach, assessment, and outcomes associated with learning communities and first-year seminars. Each case study provides a brief history, description and rationale for the program, details on administration of the programs, and a summary of processes and outcomes of learning assessments and program evaluations. With these examples, the monograph provides several models for institutions to consider when developing or improving their own first-year programs.

KEY WORDS: assessment, case studies, first-year seminars, learning communities.

Hunter, S. M., & Linder, C. W. (2005). First-year seminars. In M. L. Upcraft, J. N. Gardner, & B. O. Barefoot (Eds.), *Challenging & supporting the first-year student: A handbook for improving the first year of college* **(pp. 275-291). San Francisco: Jossey-Bass.**

The authors of this chapter provide a definition and rationale for first-year seminars, as well as a brief history of this common curricular intervention. They also offer a typology of first-year seminars that includes extended orientation seminars, academic seminars, professional and discipline-linked seminars, and basic skills seminars. The authors discuss research gathered from the triennial administration of the National Survey on First-Year Seminars by the National Resource Center for The First-Year Experience and Students in Transition. This survey collects data on characteristics of these seminars including (a) instructional practices, (b) amount of course credit, (c) course content, (d) linkages with learning communities, (e) residence life programming, and (f) service-learning. These data offer insights into recent trends for first-year seminars, including an increasing use of these programs, shifts toward the inclusion of more traditional academic content, a slight increase in the number of institutions requiring students to complete the seminar, and an increase in the number of institutions offering the seminar for academic credit. Findings from this survey help provide a national context for institutional development and administration of the first-year seminar.

KEY WORDS: first-year seminars, national survey findings.

Keup, J. R., & Barefoot, B. O. (2005). Learning how to be a successful student: Exploring the impact of first-year seminars on student outcomes. *Journal of The First-Year Experience & Students in Transition, 17***(1), 1-37.**

Drawing on longitudinal data collected through the 2000 Freshman Survey and 2001 Your First College Year (YFCY) survey sponsored by the Cooperative Institutional Research Program (CIRP), the authors explore the relationship between first-year seminar participation and academic engagement, social experiences, and adjustment during the first college year. Results of descriptive analyses show a statistically significant relationship between first-year seminar participation and interaction with professors, academic interactions with other students, class attendance, cocurricular involvement, and developing close friendships. Results of multivariate analyses indicate a direct relationship between seminar participation and students' feelings of success with establishing a network of friends on campus and an indirect relationship between seminar participation and students' feelings of success at establishing meaningful connections with faculty. Similar regression analysis did not yield a statistically significant relationship between first-year seminar participation and students' feelings of success at using campus services. The results of this research conducted on national data provide insight into the types of first-year experiences and outcomes that are enhanced by participation in first-year seminars. This can provide a framework and context for first-year seminar development, improvement, and assessment.

KEY WORDS: *cocurricular involvement, college adjustment, engagement, first-year seminars.*

Schnell, C. A., & Doetkott, C. (2002-3). First year seminars produce long-term impact. *Journal of College Student Retention: Research, Theory & Practice, 4*(4), 377- 391.

Drawing on retention data for 1,853 students (half enrolled in the first-year seminar and half not enrolled), this study sought to examine the long-term effects of participation in a first-year seminar. Demographic and academic data were collected from the two groups of participants, including high school class rank, ACT scores, and major. These data were used to match members of the two groups, thus creating a better comparison between students with similar characteristics and attributes. Retention for all students in the study was tracked for four years, and during the years of the study, students who had enrolled in the seminar were retained at greater numbers than those who did not.

KEY WORDS: *first-year seminars, retention.*

Starke, M. C., Harth, M., & Sirianni, F. (2001). Retention, bonding, and academic achievement: Success of a first-year seminar. *Journal of The First-Year Experience & Students in Transition, 13*(2), 7-36.

Drawing on persistence and academic achievement data from students who participated in a first-year seminar at Ramapo College over a seven-year period, this study sought to explore the college experience of students who enrolled in the seminar compared to those who did not. With the exception of the first semester following participation in the seminar, findings from the study indicated that students who enrolled in the course persisted at greater levels than those who did not. Further, retention of students of color also increased as did the graduation rates among all students who enrolled in the first-year seminar during the time of the study. In addition to increased levels of persistence, students who took the seminar consistently earned higher grade point averages than their peers who did not take the course. Additionally, students who participated in the course reported a greater connection to the institution and faculty and indicated a stronger propensity to be involved in campus activities.

KEY WORDS: *academic success, first-year seminars, retention, students of color.*

Thomson, J. S., & Stringer, S. B. (2000). First-year seminar: Using technology to explore professional issues and opportunities across locations. *Journal of General Education, 49*(1), 66-73.

The purpose of this study was to identify ways to enhance the first-year seminar at The Pennsylvania State University using a variety of means, including integration of computer technologies into the seminar. Students enrolled in the course in fall 1996 were surveyed about computer use and what they hoped to learn, with 142 students enrolled in the seminar completing the survey. The study's findings revealed a range of computer and other technological knowledge among the students and variations in accessibility to these technologies. Fifty-seven percent of students in the sample reported owning a computer, more than 50% reported daily computer use, either to access the Internet/ World Wide Web or to complete class assignments. Results from the study informed creation of web-based resources for students and faculty to be used as enhancements to teaching and learning.

KEY WORDS: first-year seminars, technology and teaching.

Tobolowsky, B. T. (2005). *The 2003 National Survey on First-Year Seminars: Continuing innovations in the college curriculum* **(Monograph No. 41). Columbia, SC: University of South Carolina, National Resource Center for The First-Year Experience and Students in Transition.**

This monograph shares the findings of the sixth National Survey on First-Year Seminars conducted by the National Resource Center for The First-Year Experience and Students in Transition. A brief history of first-year seminars in general as well as findings from previous surveys set the context for a broad overview of survey findings on seminar characteristics, instructional approaches, course content, and student outcomes of seminars, which are reported overall and disaggregated by institutional characteristics and seminar types. In addition to a summary of findings, the author provides detailed analyses of survey data in chapters dedicated to comparisons of seminars at two- and four-year institutions, teaching in first-year seminars, assessment of seminar outcomes, and new developments in first-year seminars such as online offerings, inclusion of service-learning, and the integration of learning communities and first-year seminars. The chapter closes with an evaluation of first-year seminar trends that have emerged from the six surveys. These data provide a national context for developing, refining, or assessing institutional first-year seminar programs.

KEY WORDS: first-year seminars, learning communities, service-learning, two-year institutions.

Tobolowsky, B. T., Cox, B. E., & Wagner, M. T. (Eds.) (2005). *Exploring the evidence: Reporting research on first-year seminars, volume III* **(Monograph No. 42). Columbia, SC: University of South Carolina, National Resource Center for The First-Year Experience and Students in Transition.**

This is the third volume in a series of monographs that highlight findings from institutional assessments of first-year seminar characteristics and outcomes. The volume contains 39 case studies of first-year seminars at colleges and universities representing various institutional sizes, regions of the country, and seminar types. The majority of the studies include evidence of the relationship between enrollment in the seminar and retention, grade point average, student satisfaction and engagement, and student achievement of course goals. However, two primary changes in the landscape of research on this topic are the widespread inclusion of the seminar in learning communities and the changing nature of seminar assessment, which now includes a number of national instruments to evaluate first-year seminars and the general first-year experience. These studies are intended to serve as resources for establishing, improving, and sustaining first-year seminars.

KEY WORDS: assessment, first-year seminars, learning communities.

General Information on First-Year Curricular Interventions

Barefoot, B. O. (2000, January/February). The first-year experience: Are we making it any better? *About Campus, 4,* **12-18.**

Beginning with a brief summary of the history of the first-year experience movement, this article provides a broad view of the first year in American colleges and universities. The author highlights successful first-year initiatives and identifies institutions that have used innovative practices to boost first-year retention, increase student involvement and satisfaction, enhance student intellectualism, and reduce behavior problems. The article also identifies six common themes and objectives that guide the development and delivery of many first-year programs, including increasing interaction between students and faculty, increasing student involvement on campus, linking the curriculum and the co-curriculum, and increasing the academic engagement and success of all students, particularly those who are academically underprepared. The article ends with a focus on how improvements in the first year of college can continue, with identification of previous initiatives that proved unsuccessful, and with a list of new challenges shaping future efforts to improve the first college year.

KEY WORDS: engagement, student success.

Cutright, M. (2002, September/October). What are research universities doing for first-year students? *About Campus, 7,* **16-20.**

This study used qualitative data collected by the Policy Center on the First Year of College from more than 75 research universities as part of the project Strengthening First-Year Student Learning at Doctoral/Research-Extensive Universities. The project aimed to determine successful first-year initiatives at these types of institutions. The author identified seven themes common to first-year programs at research universities: (a) the proliferation of first-year programs, (b) first-year initiatives housed in a discipline or college, (c) integration of multiple strategies to support first-year programs, (d) learning communities as a cornerstone of first-year efforts, (e) a re-examination of teaching and learning, (f) strong academic and student affairs partnerships, and (g) intentional assessment and evaluation. These themes and the article's description of best practices provide the foundation for launching or examining first-year programs at research universities.

KEY WORDS: learning communities, research universities.

Hunter, M. S. (2006, Summer). Fostering student learning and success through first-year programs. *Peer Review 8*(3), **4-7.**

This article offers readers a look into what scholars know about learning and describes how that information can best be used to help first-year students succeed. The author also outlines a brief history of first-year programming, noting that the first year of college, rather than being "grade 13" is a major transitional period requiring specialized attention. The author suggests that student success and learning, not retention, should be the primary focus of efforts in support of first-year students and describes how campuses might consider defining that success. Examples of initiatives illustrate how several institutions have translated their definitions into actions to help first-year students. The author also posits that work with first-year students is a campus-wide responsibility and offers a list of resources administrators, faculty, and staff may access to support this work.

KEY WORDS: learning, retention, student success.

Keup, J. R. (2005). The impact of curricular interventions on intended second year re-enrollment. *Journal of College Student Retention: Research, Theory & Practice, 17*(1-2), **61-89.**

This article investigates the relationship between three first-year curricular interventions—first-year seminars, service-learning, and learning communities—and first-to-second-year retention. Using national data collected through the 2002 Freshman Survey and 2003 Your First College Year (YFCY) Survey administered by the Cooperative Institutional Research Program (CIRP), the researcher identified numerous positive relationships between these three interventions and integrative first-year experiences as defined by Tinto's Model of Student Departure. Results of logistic regression provide additional information about the potential impact of these three first-year programs on students' intention to re-enroll for a second year at the same institution. These results suggest that first-year courses with a service-learning component have a positive indirect impact on first-year retention. The results of this research also indicated that student participation in both first-year seminars and learning communities was the largest positive predictor of re-enrollment for these students. This study advances the theoretical and practical concept of packaging these curricular programs as part of a comprehensive first-year experience.

KEY WORDS: first-year seminars, learning communities, national survey findings, retention, service-learning.

Mandel, R. G., & Evans, K. (2003, March/April). First choice: Creating innovative academic options for first-year students. *About Campus, 8,* 23-26.

This article chronicles the nearly 20-year process of institutionalizing a successful first-year experience at the State University of New York (SUNY) at Oswego and offers one example of an institutional effort to develop a comprehensive and integrated first-year experience. Early efforts to establish a first-year seminar at the institution were challenged by suspicions regarding its academic rigor, its relegation to student affairs with little support from faculty, and difficulties with marketing the opportunity to students. Several institutional transitions led to increased receptivity to this and other first-year programming efforts. Specifically, concerns about retention, momentum, an assessment of student advising, and enhanced interest in self-evaluation were key issues that primed the campus for a renewed focus on first-year student success. As a result, the campus established a first-year advisory council, which developed an institutional philosophy on the importance of first-year programs, established criteria for programs to be included in a comprehensive first-year experience, integrated the existing first-year programs, and developed new courses and services. The intent of these combined efforts was to offer a first-year academic experience to 85% of new students. The article ends with lessons learned during this process, such as the value of collaboration between academic and student affairs, the significance of academic support, and the importance of assessment in the evolution of first-year programming.

KEY WORDS: academic affairs and student affairs collaboration, assessment, comprehensive first-year initiatives.

Learning Communities

Bailey, T. R., & Alfonso, M. (2005, January). *Paths to persistence: An analysis of research on program effectiveness at community colleges* (New Agenda Series, Vol. 6, No. 1). Indianapolis, IN: Lumina Foundation for Education.

The authors of this report issued by the Lumina Foundation for Education completed a critical analysis on the effectiveness of community colleges' practices in four areas: (a) advising, counseling, mentoring and orientation programs; (b) learning communities; (c) developmental education and other services for academically underprepared students; and (d) campus-wide reform. Key findings suggest that learning communities generally have a strong positive correlation with student retention and graduation. The researchers note that no one form of developmental education, counseling, or advising programs is best at increasing students' ability to succeed in college. All are important to student success. The authors present several suggestions for improving research on community colleges and offer six strategies for fostering a research culture on these campuses.

KEY WORDS: research studies, retention, two-year institutions.

Baker, L. A., Meyer, K. R., & Hunt, S. K. (2005). First-year students' perceptions of power and use of persuasive techniques: A comparison of learning community versus traditional classes. *Journal of The First-Year Experience & Students in Transition, 17*(2), 23-48.

Using survey data drawn from 309 undergraduates (96% of whom were first-year students) at a large midwestern university, the authors examined the key differences in persuasive communication strategies used by students overall, as well as patterns of communication by gender and learning community enrollment. The researchers developed and administered a survey to gauge students' use of 19 Behavior Alternation Techniques (BATs) and Behavior Alternation Messages (BAMs) in their interactions with the course instructor. Results of MANOVAs showed large differences in communications strategies by gender: Men use a wider array of BATs and more aggressive tactics than women, while women are more likely to draw upon emotional displays in their persuasive techniques and messages than men. Other study findings indicate that there is no difference in the communication strategies between students who are enrolled in learning communities and those who are not. These findings may help dispel the myth that a negative outcome of learning communities is more collusive and group-based communication strategies developing among students. Further, these findings can be used to help train new instructors and teaching assistants to identify different types of persuasive communication strategies and to capitalize on them to empower first-year students in their classrooms.
KEY WORDS: gender differences, learning communities, student-faculty interactions.

Barrows, S., & Goodfellow, M. (2005). Learning effects on first-year student success in a general chemistry course. *Journal of The First-Year Experience & Students in Transition, 17*(2), 11-22.

This study explores the relationship between learning community participation and academic performance of first-year students in a general chemistry course at the Schuylkill Campus of The Pennsylvania State University. The students in this study enrolled in a required first-year seminar course with an emphasis on science or technology along with an introductory general chemistry course. In addition to providing additional access to faculty teaching these courses, the learning communities program offered first-year students the support of peer leaders, students in their sophomore year who had taken both first-year seminar and general chemistry and earned an A in each course. The researchers used another section of the general chemistry course as a control group. To measure the learning effects, pre- and posttests were administered to both the sample and control groups, and the researchers gathered additional information about the two groups (e.g., SAT scores, high school grade point average, and science evaluation index). After the students completed the first-year seminar and chemistry course, those grades were considered along with the other data collected for the study. Findings indicated little difference between the grade point average of either group during the first semester, with no significant difference in performance (of either group) in the chemistry course. Over time, academic differences between the sample and control group emerged, and more students in the learning community continued beyond the general chemistry course to take additional chemistry courses (in a three-course sequence). The sample group also persisted at a greater rate than students in the control group.
KEY WORDS: academic performance, first-year seminars, learning communities, STEM disciplines.

Blackhurst, A. E., Akey, L. D., & Bobilya, A. J. (2003). A qualitative investigation of student outcomes in a residential learning community. *Journal of The First-Year Experience & Students in Transition, 15*(2), 35-59.

The authors conducted a qualitative exploration of students' perceptions of learning community outcomes and the relationship between students' stated experiences in a learning community and the measurable outcomes associated with those experiences. The study complements findings from numerous quantitative studies on this subject. Analysis of data from interviews conducted with 20 first-year student members of a learning community yielded seven themes characterizing students' perceptions of their experience. Students perceived that participation in the learning community (a) eased the transition to college, (b) facilitated social integration, (c) helped develop personal relationships with faculty, (d) facilitated in-class learning, (e) created a positive living-learning environment, and (f) worked against peer norms of individualism and competitiveness. Students also perceived that the outcomes of their participation in the learning community could not be attributed solely to self-fulfilling expectations. These themes provide the foundation for marketing efforts to attract new students to the learning community program as well as for information to help faculty better understand the potential impact of the learning community experience.

KEY WORDS: assessment, college adjustment, learning communities, residential learning communities.

Commander, N. E., Valeri-Gold, M., & Darnell, K. (2004). The strategic thinking and learning community: An innovative model for providing academic assistance. *Journal of The First-Year Experience & Students in Transition, 16*(1), 61-76.

Georgia State University instituted several learning communities to facilitate the engagement and retention of first-year students at the institution. This article shares the process and results of a study conducted on a learning community with the theme "Strategic Thinking and Learning" (STL). While STL was structured similarly to the other first-year learning communities at the university, the unique feature of STL was that it offered academic assistance to new students as it built community among first-year students. Results of a one-way analysis of variance (ANOVA) conducted on 134 students enrolled in an introductory psychology class (20 were enrolled in a learning community, and 35 students served as a control group) indicated that students in STL earned significantly higher grades in the course than did students in any other learning community and in the control group. These results support the development and delivery of thematic first-year seminars that support both community building and academic assistance for first-year students.

KEY WORDS: academic success, academic support, learning communities.

Crissman Ishler, J. L. (2001). Clustered and nonclustered first-year seminars: New students' first-semester experiences. *Journal of The First-Year Experience & Students in Transition, 13*(1), 69-88.

This study examined the effects of clustered courses on the experience of first-year students at one institution. For the purpose of the study, the researcher compared the first-semester experience of students in clustered (students taking both first-year seminar and English together) and nonclustered (students only taking first-year seminar) courses. The researcher used a phenomenological approach to guide development of data collection procedures for four focus groups (two of clustered students and two of nonclustered students). All focus groups were conducted in November, with a total of 13 clustered students and 26 nonclustered students. Findings revealed an overall satisfaction among members of both groups with their first-year experience, although students in the clustered group expressed a more positive view of the first-year seminar than their nonclustered peers. Comments from students in nonclustered sections of the first-year seminar, in some cases, indicated an overall dissatisfaction with the course. Similarly, when asked about skills learned in the course, the clustered students agreed on the academic value of skills they were acquiring; whereas, views among nonclustered students were divided. Students in both groups were strongly satisfied with the level of support and bonding that occurred with their peers and instructors. Overall, the findings of this study suggested a greater level of academic satisfaction among first-year students in clustered courses, compared to those in nonclustered courses.

KEY WORDS: clustered/linked courses, first-year seminars, learning communities.

Dillon, J. (2003). Bringing counseling to the classroom and the residence hall: The university learning community. *Journal of Humanistic Counseling Education and Development, 42*(2), 194-208.

This article describes a first-year student learning community program at the State University of West Georgia involving partnerships among counselors, faculty, and residence life staff. The learning communities, organized around the theme "making decisions," include psychological, social, and academic components. During the first two years of the program, the author collected qualitative and quantitative data on 48 students to determine the relationship among learning communities, student development, and academic success. In assessing the psychological component, the author discovered a relationship among the following: (a) participation in the program and ease of transition to college, (b) students' feelings of acceptance and being valued, (c) increased alcohol awareness, and (d) improved eating habits. Assessment of the social elements revealed that students reported greater sensitivity to the role of race, learning styles, and the importance of serving the community; students also reported an improvement in ethical decision making. Learning community participants had higher grade point averages and persistence rates than those who did not participate. In addition, students reported increased academic excitement, increased faculty interaction, and competence in decision making. The author asserts that the learning communities appeared successful in promoting development and success among new students.

KEY WORDS: academic support, residential learning communities, retention, student-faculty interaction, student success.

Franklin, K. K. (2000). Shared and connected learning in a freshman learning community. *Journal of The First-Year Experience & Students in Transition, 12*(2), 33-60.

Drawing on data collected from learning communities offered at the University of Little Rock (AR) that linked introductory courses in anthropology, writing, and speech, the researcher explored the academic experience of 24 first-year learning community students. The student experience in the learning communities was measured with (a) an attitude survey (administered before and after participation in the community), (b) focus group sessions held at the beginning of the semester, (c) a course portfolio, and (d) a reflective journal. Findings from the study indicated that the students who participated in the learning community had higher ACT scores than nonparticipants and also exhibited an interest in connecting knowledge and learning from one course to another. The learning community experience appeared to fulfill that desire for the participants and provide them with an opportunity to make connections among their courses. Other aspects of the program highlighted by the students as positive included opportunities for shared learning, collaboration, and group work with peers; some level of connection with peers; and study groups and other learning opportunities that took place informally within the peer groups. The data indicated a consensus among students that shared learning was the most important aspect of participating in the learning community.

KEY WORDS: learning communities.

Golde, C. M., & Pribbenow, D. A. (2000). Understanding faculty involvement in residential learning communities. *Journal of College Student Development, 41*(1), 27-40.

Drawing on data collected from interviews with 15 faculty members who had been involved in residential learning communities at a large university, this study gathered information about the faculty experience in the program and their motivation for involvement. Data were collected on initial and ongoing involvement of the faculty in the communities. Faculty participants indicated that they had become involved in the communities out of a concern for undergraduate students and out of an interest in learning more about this student population. Further, faculty participants indicated that the communities provided an opportunity for them to engage in various forms of instruction and to be more inventive in the classroom. Interviewees commented on the general appeal of the concept of residential learning communities, and while they were interested in the idea, there was some concern about the time commitment. Faculty members expressed an initial concern that they may not be welcomed into the community by students, but most indicated that they continued to participate because of the relationships they were able to build with participating students. They also noted that making and maintaining connections with faculty in other departments and an interest in the overall concept of the communities motivated their continued participation. They also indicated that continued participation had a positive impact on their teaching overall. Several faculty members expressed an ability to better relate to and understand their first-year students in other classes because of their participation in the communities. Along with this analysis of data, the researchers discussed opportunities for collaboration available in other programs that share the characteristics of residential learning communities and offered recommendations to improve educational practice.

KEY WORDS: faculty, learning communities, residential learning communities.

Henscheid, J. M. (Ed.). (2004). *Integrating the first-year experience: The role of learning communities in first-year seminars* (Monograph No. 39). Columbia, SC: University of South Carolina, National Resource Center for The First-Year Experience and Students in Transition.

This edited collection focuses on the theoretical and practical intersection of two of the most commonly used curricular interventions for first-year students: learning communities and first-year seminars. The monograph begins with an analysis of the learning outcomes associated with stand-alone, first-year seminars as compared to those linked with learning communities. This research, conducted through The First-Year Initiative Benchmarking Survey, indicates that linked courses are associated with greater perceived gains on numerous learning outcomes. The bulk of the monograph is devoted to case studies of 16 institutions that offer learning communities inclusive of first-year seminars. Each institution was selected for its excellence in these program offerings but also with an eye toward providing examples from a diverse set of institutions, as well as the generalizability of the approach, assessment, and outcomes associated with learning communities and first-year seminars. Each case study provides a brief history, description, and rationale for the program, details on administration of the programs, and a summary of processes and outcomes of learning assessments and program evaluations. With these examples, the monograph provides several models for institutions to consider when developing or improving their own first-year programs.

KEY WORDS: assessment, case studies, first-year seminars, learning communities.

Hoffman, M., Richmond, J., Morrow, J., & Salomone, K. (2002-3). Investigating "sense of belonging" in first-year college students. *Journal of College Student Retention: Research, Theory & Practice, 4*(3), 227-256.

The purpose of this study was to develop, test, and refine an instrument to measure students' sense of belonging in relation to persistence in college. The researchers first conducted focus groups with students enrolled in a university first-year seminar course to assess factors related to a sense of belonging, or perception of fit between the student and the institution. Some seminar students were part of a learning community cluster of courses linked by academic content; others were a heterogeneous population of students. The researchers found that the learning community students were more successful than the non-learning community students at forming new friendships. Specifically, the learning community students were able to establish relationships with peers around academic matters. Furthermore, though both learning community and non-learning community students found their faculty to be friendly and approachable, the learning community students responded with greater intensity. The researchers also administered a pretest to 205 first-year college students to further refine the main conceptual dimensions of a sense of belonging. They identified five underlying dimensions for the resulting Sense of Belonging (SB) instrument: (a) Perceived Peer Support, (b) Perceived Faculty Support/Comfort, (c) Perceived Classroom Comfort, (d) Perceived Isolation, and (e) Empathetic Faculty Understanding. Data analysis revealed that students in learning communities scored significantly better on all five factors of the SB instrument than students in stand-alone seminar courses. The authors assert that learning community students were better able to form helpful connections around a common agenda and similar challenges. The researchers suggest that sense of belonging stems from students' perceptions of "valued involvement" in the college setting, which is enhanced by establishing supportive peer relationships and by the belief that faculty are compassionate and see students as more than a number among many. They also conclude that their Sense of Belonging instrument is a useful tool for further understanding factors that contribute to student persistence.

KEY WORDS: assessment, first-year seminars, learning communities, peer support, sense of belonging.

Johnson, J. L. (2000-01). Learning communities and special efforts in retention of university students: What works, what doesn't, and is the return worth the investment? *Journal of College Student Retention: Research, Theory & Practice, 2*(3), 219-238.

Drawing on data collected from four programs intended to improve student retention at a four-year university, this study investigated the cost-effectiveness of these efforts. Grade point average, retention, and student survey data were collected for each of the following programs over a two-year period: (a) Conditional Contract Student Program, (b) Project 100: Early Alert/Early Intervention, (c) First-Year Alternative Experience (FYAE), and (d) Russell Scholars Program (RSP). Several of these, including the Conditional Contract Student Program, Project 100, and FYAE were created to serve students who were considered at-risk (less academically prepared) and/or were conditionally admitted to the university. In addition to programmatic data, cost data for each program were derived from a cost analysis conducted for the study. The results of the study indicated that several of the programs (RSP and FYAE, both learning community-based programs) boasted higher than average retention rates. Further, grade point average data indicated that students who persisted in each program performed at better-than-expected rates academically and were retained at better-than-expected rates, particularly those students who were academically most at risk. Findings from the study suggest that while the programs using the learning communities model were more expensive, these programs increased the likelihood that students involved would persist to graduation.

KEY WORDS: academic advising, at-risk students, early warning systems, learning communities, retention.

Kutnowski, M. (2005, March/April). This is why we teach: Igniting a passion for learning in linked courses. *About Campus 10,* 23-26.

This article explores the teaching and learning that takes place in two linked courses, music appreciation and an art and design course, at Queensborough Community College (NY). Course linkages described in the article were created to help establish a more learning-centered environment and better meet the needs of diverse students. The author describes several methods used to connect the courses, such as creating themes that transcend multiple courses and engaging in common and shared assignments. The author described a successful collaboration between his music appreciation course and the art and design course in which he used two versions of the film, *Metropolis*. Students in both courses were asked to compare the Japanese animated version to the original version released in the 1920s and were encouraged to connect ideas related to the films. The author discusses how personal connections made among students in the learning community increased the openness of classroom discussions and the sharing of diverse opinions. The author describes his enthusiasm for this type of teaching and the shared learning experience that results.

KEY WORDS: clustered/linked courses, learning communities.

Laufgraben, J. L. (2005). Learning communities. In M. L. Upcraft, J. N. Gardner, B. O. Barefoot (Eds.), *Challenging and supporting the first-year student: A handbook for improving the first year of college* **(pp. 371-387). San Francisco: Jossey-Bass.**

This chapter defines curricular learning communities, which national research indicates have become a cornerstone of first-year programming at many postsecondary institutions, particularly research universities, across the United States. The author offers a rationale for this curricular intervention and summarizes research findings on the academic benefits of student participation in learning communities, including higher first-year grades, greater intellectual and social development, appreciation of interdisciplinary education, and increased interactions with faculty. The chapter lists characteristics of learning communities and offers a typology of learning community models. The author describes a five-step plan for implementing learning communities, as well as specific strategies and practices for their maintenance, assessment, and improvement. The descriptions of theory and practice offered in this chapter are of value to researchers and educators working with first-year students.
KEY WORD: learning communities.

Logan, C. R., Salisbury-Glennon, J., & Spence, L. D. (2000). The learning edge academic program: Toward a community of learners. *Journal of The First-Year Experience & Students in Transition, 12*(1), 77-104.

This article examines the correlation between the Learning Edge Academic Program (LEAP) and the academic and social adjustment of participating first-year college students. LEAP is an optional six-week summer academic program open to all first-semester students enrolled at a large research institution. Students in the program are housed together, are mentored by upperclass undergraduates, and enroll in two courses required for graduation. Content and assignments of the two courses are linked and the courses, scheduled over a blocked time period, and encourage use of small "learning teams" composed of four to five students. Training for using technological and library resources is also embedded into the courses. To evaluate the program, 84 of the 100 LEAP students completed the University Experiences Scale (included as an appendix in the article); 48 students in a control group also completed the self-report. LEAP participants were significantly more likely to report positive classroom experiences, support inside and outside the classroom, and comfort using technology. The retention rate for LEAP students was 99% after two semesters, compared with a 94.2% retention rate for all students who entered the institution the same year. Suggestions for improving the effectiveness of the program are presented.
KEY WORDS: assessment, college adjustment, clustered/linked courses, retention, summer bridge programs, technology.

Longerbeam, S. D., & Sedlacek, W. E. (2006). Attitudes toward diversity and living-learning outcomes among first- and second-year college students. *NASPA Journal, 43*(1), 40-55.

This article offers findings from a study that compared diversity attitudes of first- and second-year students who participated in a civic-related living-learning program (CIVICUS) and a group of students who did not participate in the program. Data were collected from the two groups using the Miville-Guzman University Diversity Scale (M-GUDS-S) which was administered a total of three times (at orientation, at the end of the first semester of the first year, and during the sophomore year; two administrations of the survey took place in courses in the CIVICUS program or in introductory sociology courses). Analysis of data indicated no significant difference in attitudes about diversity between the two groups. However, the findings did indicate some change in behaviors related to issues of diversity; specifically, some improvement in behaviors was noted. The study also suggested that diversity awareness and appreciation might need to be cultivated over time. This, the authors suggest, is a limitation of a study that attempts to measure impacts of programs like CIVICUS during or shortly after the students' participation.

KEY WORDS: assessment measures, diversity, residential learning communities.

MacGregor, J., & Smith, B. L. (2005, May/June). Where are learning communities now? National leaders take stock. *About Campus, 10,* **2-8.**
An update on the status of learning communities nationwide is provided through the reflections of 56 leaders in the movement. The leaders present 15 lessons about learning communities, addressing the following: (a) acceptance and applicability of learning communities, (b) associated curricular and pedagogical transformations, (c) overall effects and measures of effectiveness, (d) connections between learning communities and institutional missions, and (e) continued opportunities for improvement. The authors acknowledge the accomplishments of the learning communities movement and offer suggestions for maintaining its vitality.

KEY WORDS: learning communities, national trends.

Maher, M. A. (2004, July/August). What really happens in cohorts. *About Campus, 9,* **18-23.**
This article offers a research-based definition of cohorts, identifies their primary characteristics, reviews their history, and summarizes their documented learning outcomes, including affective development, group cohesion, community development, leadership development, and rich dialogue among students. The author also shares findings from a yearlong qualitative study of a cohort of graduate students in an education program. Analysis of the data indicated that cohorts demand a sense of investment and community building among both faculty and students that is far greater than other course structures and that these structures typically require adjustment in modes of teaching and learning. The study also indicated that these structures tend to create a strong sense of cohort agency, which can result in the interests of the collective overriding those of the individual, particularly in times of duress. Other research on cohorts and observations of the education students involved in the study indicate that groupthink and collusion may emerge as a potentially negative outcome of the cohort format. Students in the cohort studied also appeared to adopt individual roles (e.g., organizer, tension breaker) that fulfilled interpersonal needs of the cohort. Findings of this study are important for faculty considering teaching in a cohort and for students exploring participation in a cohort. While students in the first year of college were not the focus of this study, the author suggests that lessons are applicable to other populations, including first-year students in learning communities.

KEY WORDS: cohorts, group development, learning communities.

Oates, K. K., & Leavitt, L. H. (2003). *Service-learning and learning communities: Tools for integration and assessment.* **Washington, DC: Association of American Colleges and Universities.**
This publication examines theories, programmatic assessment, and best practices associated with learning communities and service-learning, movements the authors describe as parallel. The first chapter provides a foundational description of learning communities and service-learning and discusses the connection between the two initiatives. Chapters 2, 3, and 4 address basic programmatic components of service-learning and assessment of this instructional approach. The authors also offer several models for integrating service-learning and learning communities including the Visible Credit Model, Add-On Model, Linked Model, and Comprehensive Integration Model. This chapter also lists several differences between traditional classroom instruction and approaches used in service-learning and learning communities. The chapter on assessment offers several examples of learning assessment used in service-learning and learning community practice, including student reflections and narrative

assessment. Chapters 5, 6, and 7 describe portfolios and portfolio evaluation and suggest use of case studies as an additional means for learning assessment. The remaining chapters (8-11) offer practical advice on involving community members in service-learning and learning community initiatives, address risk management, and describe best practices and lessons learned from educators involved in service-learning and learning communities. The final chapter also encourages institutions to make the changes necessary to foster development of service-learning and learning communities.

KEY WORDS: assessment, learning communities, service-learning.

Potts, G., Schultz, B., & Foust, J. (2003-4). The effect of freshman cohort groups on academic performance and retention. *Journal of College Student Retention: Research, Theory & Practice, 5*(4), 385-395.

This study examined the impact of placing students in first-year learning communities at the University of Wisconsin-River Falls (UWRF). The sample for the study included 308 first-year students who entered the university in fall 1998. The researchers performed *t*-tests and ANOVAs to compare grade point averages among business major cohorts, psychology major cohorts, a nonmajor cohort, and a control group, as well as one-semester and seven-semester retention rates for the four groups. While other elements of students' first-year experiences influence retention and grade point averages, participation in the learning community cohorts did not have an influence on grades or either measure of retention. The authors posit that more intensive institutional intervention may be necessary and note that the cohort structure of learning communities at UWRF has since been supplemented with a first-year seminar for students in the major.

KEY WORDS: academic performance, first-year seminars, learning communities, retention.

Stassen, M. L. A. (2003). Student outcomes: The impact of varying living-learning community models. *Research in Higher Education, 44*(5), 581-613.

The study explored the effect of three living-learning initiatives (Residential Academic Program, Talent Advancement Program, and the Honors College Learning Community) on the academic experience of students at a large university in the Northeast. Each of the communities incorporated linked courses, but executed the linkages in different ways. Student participants' entering characteristic data were collected from university records and a survey was administered at the end of the semester. The findings from the study suggested students who chose to participate in the program had somewhat greater levels of academic preparation, ultimately earned higher grade point averages in the first semester, and persisted at greater levels. Because the Residential Academic Program did not have admission criteria affiliated with it, there was a greater chance that less academically prepared students would participate in this community. The study revealed that the selectivity of a learning community did not appear to have an influence on the outcomes. In addition to influence on persistence and academic performance, the learning communities also appeared to have an impact on the social and academic integration of participants, although none of the communities yielded strong connections with faculty.

KEY WORDS: clustered/linked courses, residential learning communities.

Tinto, V. (2000). Linking learning and leaving: Exploring the role of the college classroom in student departure. In J. M. Braxton (Ed.), *Reworking the Student Departure Puzzle* **(pp. 81-94). Nashville, TN: Vanderbilt University Press.**

This chapter explored the relationship between students' experiences in the classroom and persistence. The aim was to expand current theories of student departure to include activities in the classroom as part of student departure from college, particularly during or just after the first year. One important vehicle for understanding the connection between the classroom and retention is the emergence of learning communities as a pedagogical technique. After defining learning communities, the author summarizes his recent body of research on the impact of first-year learning community programs on retention. His research found that learning communities help build supportive peer groups, bridge students' academic and social experiences during the first year, and increase involvement, effort, learning, and, ultimately, persistence. These impacts of learning communities are based on restructuring first-year classrooms to make them engaging, seamless educational environments that foster shared learning experiences. These findings provide support for the inclusion of learning communities in the first-year experience as well as provide insight into their design and development for maximum impact upon retention and other student outcomes.

KEY WORDS: learning communities, retention.

Walker, A. A. (2003). Learning communities and their effect on students' cognitive abilities. *Journal of The First-Year Experience & Students in Transition, 15*(2), 11-33.

The author investigated the effects of participation in learning communities at a large, public, highly selective research university on the development of students' cognitive abilities. Survey data were collected during orientation and at the end of the first year from 228 students who participated in the learning community program and 247 students who constituted a control group for the study. Four outcome measures—(a) critical thinking ability, (b) analytical thinking and problem solving ability, (c) reading speed and comprehension, and (d) writing skills—were regressed against a series of independent variables including pretests or proxy pretests for the outcome measures, personal and educational background measures, learning community themes, and college experiences potentially related to the outcome measure. Results of these analyses indicated that participation in learning communities was positively associated with all four cognitive outcomes at a statistically significant level. This study provides strong empirical support for the impact of learning communities on cognitive gains during the first year of college.

KEY WORDS: cognitive development, learning communities.

Zhao, C., & Kuh, G.D. (2004). Adding value: Learning communities and student engagement. *Research in Higher Education, 45*(2), 115-138.

Using a sample of 80,479 first-year and senior students at 365 four-year institutions across the country who completed the National Survey of Student Engagement (NSSE) in spring 2002, the authors examined the relationships between participation in learning communities and student engagement in educationally purposeful learning activities. Results of descriptive and multivariate analyses indicated that learning community participation is uniformly and positively linked with student academic outcomes. Specifically, participation in learning communities had a statistically significant impact on students' grades (even when controlling for previous academic achievement); various measures of student engagement with curricular opportunities, cocurricular activities, faculty, and other students; perceptions of the campus environment; and student gains in personal and social development, practical competence, and general education. Further, since many of these effects remain strong through the senior year, these results indicate that learning communities have a strong and lasting impact on undergraduate experiences and outcomes of college.

KEY WORDS: academic performance, engagement, learning communities, national data sets, student development.

Library and Information Literacy

Hardesty, L. (Ed.). (2007). *The role of the library in the first college year* (Monograph No. 45). Columbia, SC: University of South Carolina, National Resource Center for The First-Year Experience and Students in Transition.

This volume establishes the importance of library instruction and information literacy in the academic success and retention of first-year college students. The first section traces the history of information literacy instruction but also looks broadly at student engagement and the characteristics of entering college students with an eye toward describing how libraries and librarians contribute to student success. The second section outlines structures and initiatives used to deliver library and information literacy instruction in the first college year. Two chapters focus on national survey data—one outlining common models of library instruction and the other focusing on the delivery of library instruction within the first-year seminar. The remaining chapters in this section focus on the information competency initiative in the California State University system, the emergence of first-year experience librarian positions, strategies for designing effective information literacy assignments, and the development of cocurricular library activities that move beyond the scavenger hunt. A third section examines issues related to assessing information literacy initiatives, increasing librarian involvement in campus-wide retention efforts, and strengthening the connection between information literacy efforts and the first-year experience movement. A final section offers case studies from a dozen institutions describing successful informational literacy initiatives.

KEY WORDS: information literacy, library instruction.

Nugent, C., & Myers, R. (2000). Learning by doing: The freshman-year curriculum and library instruction. *Research Strategies, 17,* 147-155.

This article summarizes the planning, implementation, and evaluation of a library literacy project for first-year students at Maryville College (TN). Rather than creating a separate library literacy course, the project involved incorporating critical thinking and information retrieval and synthesis into existing first-year courses such as speech and composition. After identifying courses appropriate for inclusion of library content, librarians agreed on a conceptual framework for creating a three-part library literacy curricular component for these courses. The component called for a variety of instructional approaches, with an emphasis on active learning, and was comprised of a three-hour research introduction followed by opportunities for students to conduct independent research using an outline. Faculty and student impressions of the library literacy component were positive. While faculty feedback was anecdotal, student impressions were collected through completion of evaluations designed for the program and through answers to several questions on existing course evaluations. The authors conclude with recommendations for creating similar library literacy projects on other campuses that address the following: seeking opportunities to be involved in curricular decisions and committees, developing a conceptual framework that will encourage faculty buy-in, paying attention to details, keeping the students' interests in mind when developing programs, and soliciting and paying attention to programmatic feedback from students and faculty.

KEY WORDS: information literacy, library instruction.

Parang, E., Raine, M., & Stevenson, T. (2000). Redesigning freshman seminar library instruction based on information competencies. *Research Strategies, 17,* 269-280.

The purpose of this study was to examine the effectiveness of a redesigned library instruction session affiliated with a first-year seminar course at Pepperdine University in California. The goal of the library session is to foster information literacy and increase student familiarity with the tools used to seek information when conducting library research. The researchers noted that first-year seminar is mandatory at this institution and that all sections include a library component. Upon evaluation of existing technologies, educators involved in the first-year seminar course chose to replace the existing lecture-based library instruction session with a web-based library tour and hands-on research activities conducted during a class session. Following their participation in these activities, students completed an evaluation that measured their library literacy competencies. Analysis of these data indicated that the majority of students who participated in the instructional session and completed the online library tour were able to correctly answer questions about the library. Changes made to the library session in the first-year seminar program prompted discussions of revisions to other courses.

KEY WORDS: first-year seminars, information literacy, library instruction, technology and teaching.

Service-Learning

Oates, K. K., & Leavitt, L. H. (2003). *Service-learning and learning communities: Tools for integration and assessment.* Washington, DC: Association of American Colleges and Universities.
This publication examines theories, programmatic assessment, and best practices associated with learning communities and service-learning, movements the authors describe as parallel. The first chapter provides a foundational description of learning communities and service-learning and describes the connection between the two initiatives. Chapters 2, 3, and 4 address basic programmatic components of service-learning and assessment of this instructional approach. The authors also offer several models for integrating service-learning and learning communities including the Visible Credit Model, Add-On Model, Linked Model, and Comprehensive Integration Model. This chapter also lists several differences between traditional classroom instruction and approaches used in service-learning and learning communities. The chapter on assessment offers several examples of learning assessment used in service-learning and learning community practice, including student reflections and narrative assessment. Chapters 5, 6, and 7 describe portfolios and portfolio evaluation and suggest use of case studies as an additional means for learning assessment. The remaining chapters (8-11) offer practical advice on involving community members in service-learning and learning community initiatives, address risk management, and describe best practices and lessons learned from educators involved in service-learning and learning communities. The final chapter also encourages institutions to make the changes necessary to foster development of service-learning and learning communities.

KEY WORDS: assessment, learning communities, service-learning.

Zlotkowski, E. (Ed.) (2002). *Service-learning and the first-year experience: Preparing students for personal success and civic responsibility* (Monograph No. 34). Columbia, SC: University of South Carolina, National Resource Center for The First-Year Experience and Students in Transition.
This edited monograph offers the history, processes, and outcomes of service-learning in the first college year. The first section builds a case for service-learning in the first year by describing research findings, including new research on the relationship between service-learning and the experiences of high school and college students. Two essays follow characterizing the personal histories, previous experiences, and expectations of traditional and nontraditional first-year students with respect to prior and future service involvement. The bulk of the monograph is composed of six case studies illustrating various approaches to developing, implementing, and assessing outcomes of service-learning in the first year. A wide range of institutional types and service-learning programs are represented in the case studies

and provide useful models to guide development and delivery of service-learning programs in the first year of college.

KEY WORDS: case studies, service-learning, teaching strategies.

Zlotkowski, E. (2005), Service-learning and the first-year student. In M. L. Upcraft, J. N. Gardner, & B. O. Barefoot (Eds.), *Challenging and supporting the first-year student: A handbook for improving the first year of college* (pp. 356-370). San Francisco: Jossey-Bass.

This chapter begins with a definition of service-learning based in its academic intentionality. The author explores the dimensions of congruence between service-learning and the first-year experience of college students and makes the argument that service-learning represents a valuable curricular tool to enhance the meaning and relevance of coursework to first-year students. He notes that as a critical time in the development and receptivity of college students to new behaviors and activities, the first year can establish a foundation for service involvement during and after college. Two institutional models illustrate how service-learning and the first-year experience are complementary in theory and practice. The chapter concludes with recommendations for the development, implementation, and assessment of service-learning initiatives in the first year of college.

KEY WORDS: service-learning.

Supplemental Instruction and Other Forms of Academic Support

Hagedorn, L. S., Siadet, M. V., Fogel, S. F., Nora, A., & Pascarella, E. T. (1999). Success in college mathematics: Comparisons between remedial and nonremedial first-year college students. *Research in Higher Education, 40*(3), 261-284.

This study examined math achievement among first-year students from 23 postsecondary institutions in 16 states (852 students enrolled in remedial math courses and 928 in college-level math courses). Since the sample was derived from the National Center on Postsecondary Learning and Assessment (NCTLA), students in the sample had completed reading comprehension, math, and critical thinking units as part of a precollege experience. Second sets of data were collected when a follow-up test was administered (a modification of the first set of tests), along with the College Student Experiences Questionnaire (CSEQ), and an NCTLA questionnaire. Findings from the study suggested that students in remedial math courses were less likely to receive encouragement to attend college, and their families were more likely to be at a lower income and education level. Further, students in remedial courses had lower grade point averages and indicated they studied less (in high school) and not in groups. In addition to these findings, students in remedial courses reported less satisfaction with course instruction than their peers in nonremedial courses. Finally, the researchers indicate finding a disproportionate number of women and students of color in remedial courses.

KEY WORDS: academic achievement, assessment measures, developmental education, gender, STEM disciplines.

Hafer, G. R. (2001). Ideas in practice: Supplemental Instruction in freshman composition. *Journal of Developmental Education, 24*(3), 30-37.

This study explored student academic performance in an English composition course linked with Supplemental Instruction (SI) at a small northeastern liberal arts college. The researcher described this SI as similar to that associated with other courses, with an SI leader holding sessions each week. The SI sessions linked with the composition course focused on helping students plan and proofread their papers in preparation for the next week's class. The SI Leader attended regular meetings with the researcher to provide updates on the supplemental efforts, which included workshops and preparation sessions. Findings from this study indicated a lower number of students earned D/F/W grades in the composition course.

KEY WORDS: English composition, Supplemental Instruction.

Higbee, J. L. (2005). Developmental education. In M. L. Upcraft, J. N. Gardner, & B. O. Barefoot (Eds.), *Challenging & supporting the first-year student: A handbook for improving the first year of college* (pp. 292-307). San Francisco: Jossey-Bass.

This chapter begins with a definition of developmental education and offers a set of goals that promote academic success for students in developmental education. The author provides a typology of students with developmental needs who belong in college including students with disabilities, students with limited English proficiency, students who have made poor educational decisions, and students who fell through the cracks of the educational system. The chapter offers a review of theories that shape approaches to developmental education, program models, and best practices. Traditional developmental education programs are considered against newer, alternative methods for needs assessment, placement, and instruction of first-year students in developmental education. The author concludes with a discussion of assessment strategies and offers recommendations for design of research-based developmental programs and services.

KEY WORDS: developmental education, student development theory.

Hodges, R., Dochen, C. W., & Joy, D. (2001). Increasing students' success: When Supplemental Instruction becomes mandatory. *Journal of College Reading and Learning, 31*(2), 143-56.

This study measured the academic achievement of students in a history course linked to mandatory Supplemental Instruction (SI). The study was conducted at a southern university with an enrollment of approximately 21,000 with 432 students in the sample. Students were enrolled in a writing-intensive U. S. History course, referred to at this institution as a high-risk course. In three of the four sections of the course, one-hour SI sessions were offered several times per week for students enrolled in those sections. The other section of the history course mandated SI and incorporated it into the class meetings. Each of the two SI formats was presented by trained SI Leaders who were observed several times during the semester. Researchers collected data on the participants through two administrations of the Academic Motivation Scale (administered once before the students enrolled in the history course and SI and once after). Findings from this study indicated that students in the mandatory SI groups earned higher grades than students who participated in the voluntary SI groups and higher grades than a group of students who did not participate in SI. The mandatory SI groups also had the lowest number of D/F/W grades in the history course; however, the overall grade point average for the three categories indicated no difference between the mandatory and voluntary SI groups. While there was no difference between the grade point averages of either versions of SI, there was a grade point difference between those students who participated in SI and those who did not.

KEY WORDS: academic motivation, assessment, Supplemental Instruction.

Hodges, R., & White, W. G. (2001). Encouraging high-risk student participation in tutoring and Supplemental Instruction. *Journal of Developmental Education, 24*(3), 2-10.

Drawing on data collected on the use of tutoring and Supplemental Instruction (SI) by 103 conditionally admitted, academically at-risk students (i.e., those who had failed to meet the institution's admissions requirements), this study explored the influence of encouragement on participation in tutoring and SI. During the study, first-year seminar instructors used a variety of techniques to encourage students to participate in tutoring and SI. In addition to enrolling in first-year seminar (mandatory for all students at this institution), conditionally admitted students participated in a workshop introducing them to campus academic resources, basic study strategies, and other topics before classes began. These students also enrolled in at least one course linked to SI, and many were offered additional tutoring in that content area. Students in the sample were divided into three treatment groups: (a) the first received verbal reminders of tutoring and SI sessions and attendance was monitored by the students; (b) the second group did not receive verbal reminders and was also asked to monitor their own participation in the sessions; and (c) the third group received the reminders but were not required to monitor their participation in tutoring or SI. Findings indicated that the combination of treatments did not produce a greater level of attendance in tutoring or SI sessions. The researcher noted that time conflicts occurred between tutoring and SI and suggested that interventions stronger than verbal reminders and monitored attendance may have been necessary to impact participation rates. Data analysis indicated that students who took advantage of the tutoring sessions earned higher grade point averages than their counterparts who did not; the same was true of the students who participated in SI. The grade point averages of students who participated in SI were higher than those of students who participated in tutoring, and more students chose to participate in SI.

KEY WORDS: first-year seminars, Supplemental Instruction, tutoring.

Martin, D. C., & Hurley, M. (2005). Supplemental Instruction. In M. L. Upcraft, J. N. Gardner, & B. O. Barefoot (Eds.), *Challenging and supporting the first-year student: A handbook for improving the first year of college* **(pp. 308-319). San Francisco: Jossey-Bass.**

This chapter provides a definition and description of Supplemental Instruction, an initiative designed to improve success rates of academically underprepared first-year students. The authors provide six principles of Supplemental Instruction for first-year students: (a) develop a culture of learning, (b) provide access to academic advising, (c) provide underprepared students assistance with lectures, (d) increase the efficiency of study time, (e) support the acquisition of new learning skills, and (f) foster opportunities for students to become apprentice learners. This chapter also describes assessment of Supplemental Instruction programs at three institutions and offers results of a national SI study. The data indicate that SI is positively associated with first-year student grades, even when controlling for student motivation and self-selection.

KEY WORDS: assessment, Supplemental Instruction, underprepared students.

Murie, R., & Thomson, R. (2001). When ESL is developmental: A model program for the freshman year. In J. L. Higbee (Ed.), *2001: A developmental odyssey* **(p. 15-28). Warrensburg, MO: National Association for Developmental Education.**

This chapter provides details on the Commanding English (CE) program, an initiative designed to provide developmental support to students who do not have a strong command of the English language (e.g., immigrant and refugee students) at the University of Minnesota. The authors describe the program as one that incorporates learning communities, tutoring, and Supplemental Instruction to help students improve their English skills. Students participate in the CE program for a full academic year, taking courses with the same group of students and receiving advice from a professional advisor and additional intervention from peer tutors affiliated with the Writing Center. The students in the program enroll in a combination of courses offering CE sections (e.g., speech and writing) and choose from a number of general courses such as sociology and biology. Coursework affiliated with the program is offered for academic credit and courses have been purposefully selected to meet the goals of the program. The authors of the chapter view these program attributes as important because they provide students in CE with an opportunity for increased motivation and foster growth in literacy over time. The authors also provide insights into the rationale for selection of courses in the program and offer program results, including increased retention of students.

KEY WORDS: assessment, developmental education, ESL instruction, retention.

Perrine, R. M., & Wilkins, S. L. (2001). College students' reactions to tutoring: The role of prior attitudes and attachment. *Journal of The First-Year Experience & Students in Transition, 13*(2), 55-74.

This study examined the impact of first-year college students' attitudes and attachment styles on their cognitive and affective reactions toward tutoring. The 49 participants were first-year college students enrolled in Student Support Services orientation courses, through which they were required to receive tutoring. The assessment measured students' attachment styles (secure, dismissing, fearful, or preoccupied), attitudes toward tutoring, and resistance to tutoring. Resistance to tutoring was related to prior negative attitudes toward tutoring and to insecure attachment. Students with prior negative attitudes toward tutoring tended to feel more negatively after receiving tutoring. Tutoring centers might consider assessing the attachment style of incoming students in order to provide outreach to those students who might be resistant to using the services. In addition, marketing aimed at counteracting prior negative attitudes toward tutoring could help promote tutoring services and increase the likelihood that students are well served.

KEY WORDS: tutoring.

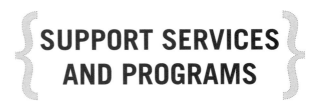

{ SUPPORT SERVICES AND PROGRAMS }

Academic and Career Advising

Gallagher, D. J., & Allen, N. (2000). First-year initiatives and results of a year-long advising pilot study: A proposed advising model. *Journal of The First-Year Experience & Students in Transition, 12*(2), 107-128.

Expectations and advising experiences of 140 first-year students at a college in Philadelphia with a full-time enrollment of 1,200 were measured over the course of one year. Through the administration of a pretest, periodic meetings with advisees, and administration of a posttest survey, the study explored the relationship between expectations of advising and the advising experience. Findings from the study indicated that expectations for advising were high and possibly not realistic. Analysis of the data also suggested the gap between expectation and experience resulted in dissatisfaction, particularly when students perceived advisors as being unavailable. Investigators suggested that students would be more satisfied knowing when advisors were available through posted office hours and e-mail. Finally, the study was used to offer suggestions for an advising model that involved emphasizing developmental rather than prescriptive advising, training advisors, recognizing and rewarding faculty for their work as advisors, and involving advisors in instruction of first-year seminars.

KEY WORDS: academic advising, student expectations, student satisfaction.

Gordon, V. N., Habley, W. R., & Associates. (2000). *Academic advising: A comprehensive handbook.* **San Francisco: Jossey-Bass.**

This book, a publication of the National Academic Advising Association (NACADA), provides a broad overview of the profession from more than 30 experts in the field. Part I describes the foundations of academic advising, including historical and philosophical foundations, use of theory, current practices, and ethical and legal issues. Part II presents issues and approaches to advising diverse students, such as those of different educational levels, multicultural students, those with special needs, and students in transition. Part III offers models of organizing and delivering advising services, including one-on-one and group advising, technological resources and assessment instruments, and the development of mission, goals, and objectives for advising programs. Part IV focuses on the training, evaluation, and recognition of advising professionals and services. The final chapters discuss how to manage change in the future of academic advising. NACADA's core values, Council for the Advancement of Standards, and NACADA resources are included in the appendices.

KEY WORDS: academic advising, assessment, CAS standards, diverse student groups, technology.

Gore, P. A., Jr. (Ed.), (2005). *Facilitating the career development of students in transition* **(Monograph No. 43). Columbia, SC: University of South Carolina, National Resource Center for The First-Year Experience and Students in Transition.**

This monograph, a collaborative effort of several authors with experience in various aspects of career development, provides a comprehensive overview of the essential components of career development and exploration for students in transition. The monograph is separated into two sections, the first focusing on foundational information about career development and the second emphasizing the application of that information. In the first section, the authors present theoretical and foundational information about career development, attending to specific career development theories, the incorporation of career development in first-year seminars, and the relationship between career centers and exploration and development in first-year students. The second half of the monograph provides a number of examples of career development efforts presented in a manner that highlights best practices at several institutions.

KEY WORDS: career development, first-year seminars.

Hunter, M. S., McCalla-Wriggins, B., & White, E. R. (Eds.). (2007). *Academic advising: New insights for teaching and learning in the first year* **(Monograph No. 46 [National Resource Center]; Monograph No. 14 [National Academic Advising Association]). Columbia, SC: University of South Carolina, National Resource Center for The First-Year Experience and Students in Transition.**

This volume posits a new way of understanding and delivering academic advising for first-year college students. In particular, the editors define advising as "a form of robust one-on-on teaching" (p. 1) and, thus, situate it as central to the educational mission of the institution. Section I explores the transition to college and characteristics of entering college students. In Section II, chapter authors describe a variety of approaches to academic advising including self-assessment, the use of technology,

and linking advising to other educational initiatives (e.g., first-year seminars and learning communities). The section concludes with a discussion of strategies for assessing the effectiveness of advising programs. Section III explores some of the unique needs and challenges presented by diverse student groups and offers strategies for serving these students more effectively. Chapters in this section focus on advising adult students, students of color, students with disabilities, honors students, undecided students, first-generation college students, and LGBT students. The volume concludes with a chapter outlining challenges facing first-year academic advisors and recommendations for effective practice. Three appendices included NACADA's statements on the concept of academic advising and the core values of academic advising and the CAS Standards for academic advising programs.
KEY WORDS: academic advising, diverse student groups.

Keeling, S. (2003). Advising the millennial generation. *The Journal of the National Academic Advising Association, 23*(1), 30-36.

The author provides information about the Millennial generation, compares this generation with others in recent history, and includes considerations for academic advisors as they work with Millennial students. Common characteristics of this generation include the desire to work in teams, increasing diversity, and awareness of diversity. This group may also be considered more protected than previous generations. The article includes additional considerations related to the generation with implications for academic advisors: increased expectations, pressure to exceed in all aspects of the college experience (academic and cocurricular), and a greater level of parental/familial involvement. Finally, the author provides suggestions for advisors working with this student population, specifically encouraging them to exercise creativity.
KEY WORDS: academic advising, Millennial students, student characteristics.

King, M. C., & Kerr, T. J. (2005). Academic advising. In M. L. Upcraft, J. N. Gardner, & B. O. Barefoot (Eds.), *Challenging & supporting the first-year student: A handbook for improving the first year of college* **(pp. 320-338). San Francisco: Jossey-Bass.**

The authors of this chapter provide an overview of academic advising, including examples of models of organization and delivery, key programmatic components, technology, diversity, challenges for the profession, and recommendations for future directions. Early in the chapter, the authors articulate the importance of advising in the undergraduate experience and offer several illustrations of the organization of advisement efforts on campuses. While they do not recommend one model over another, the authors do describe some preferred organizational models. The authors offer examples of programmatic elements they have identified as key to the success of advising programs (e.g., unified training efforts, coordination, recognition). The chapter also includes options for advising delivery methods and examples of uses for technology, including electronic appointment calendars, degree audit information, instant messaging, and use of electronic chats. The chapter concludes with a description of potential future challenges and recommendations. The authors encourage efforts aimed at assessing advising; relating advising efforts for first-year students to their needs and the institutional mission; and creating opportunities for training, support, and acknowledgement or reward for advisors.
KEY WORDS: academic advising, advisor training, assessment, diversity, institutional mission, technology.

Mastrodicasa, J. M. (2001, March). *But you teach chemistry, how can you advise me at orientation.* **Paper presented at the Annual Conference of the National Association of Student Personnel Administrators, Seattle, WA. (ERIC Document Reproduction Service No. ED 454485)**

This paper presents a model of using teaching faculty, rather than professional academic advisors, during orientation for first-year students at the University of Florida, a large public research university. Through this advising model, the university hoped to promote student-faculty interaction, create connected learning experiences, and personalize the large campus for students. Practically speaking, the model was a means of managing the large influx of students as a result of increased enrollments. The author provides information on the university's Universal Tracking system, which helps to improve advising and guarantees core classes for students. She also provides details about the orientation program, its organizational structure, and the hiring and training of the faculty advisors. Finally, the advantages and challenges of using such an advising model are presented. Assessment of the program revealed that students and families express high levels of satisfaction with the program.

KEY WORDS: academic advising, orientation, student-faculty interaction, student satisfaction.

Sams, W. P., Brown, L. S., Hussey, R. B., & Leonard, M. J. (2003). The development, implementation, and assessment of a systematic academic advising program for exploratory first-year students. *Journal of the National Academic Advising Association, 23*(1&2), 75-85.

This article describes the development, implementation, and assessment of a systematic academic advising program for exploratory (e.g., undecided) first-year students at The Pennsylvania State University. A core component of the program for exploratory first-year students is a series of paper and electronic guides that include time lines, worksheets, and supplemental information important for advancing the students' academic planning and success. These guides are distributed to students at key times during their first year. The assessment portion of the article focused on student and advisor perceptions of the effectiveness of four of these guides for six cohorts of exploratory first-year students participating in the program from 1996 through 2001. The four guides were (a) "How can I find out more about a major?" (b) "What courses should I take [each] semester?" (c) "Am I heading in the right direction?" and (d) "What should I schedule for [the next semester]?" Student survey data, telephone and individual interviews, and advisors' notes served as the data sources for the assessment of program effectiveness. The primary finding was that students in each cohort who completed the guides were more prepared to discuss majors and course selection than were students who only read the guides. Results suggest that this program was effective at encouraging students to thoughtfully engage in their academic planning process and at facilitating more productive interactions with academic advisors. Both are considered important elements to the success of all first-year students, particularly those who are undecided.

KEY WORDS: academic advising, academic planning, undecided students.

Smith, J. S., (2002). First-year student perceptions of academic advisement: A qualitative study and reality check. *The Journal of the National Academic Advising Association, 22*(2), 39-49.

The author of this article reports on a study that used qualitative data from 34 first-year students at the University of Albany to examine new students' perceptions of the role of an academic advisor, their preferences for type of academic advisement, and students' advisement experiences. Analyses of student feedback gathered from focus group discussions revealed that first-year students at this university expected and preferred prescriptive advising over developmental advising techniques. Students also likened the role of the academic advisor to their high school guidance counselor and thus expected that college advisors would merely hand them a course schedule or steer them toward classes that were considered easy. However, despite an overwhelmingly utilitarian view of the role of college advisors, the students indicated that, during their first year, some of their most meaningful and memorable experiences with academic advisors were more developmental in nature. Findings from this study highlight the complexity of first-year student preferences for and experiences with different types of academic advising. These results provide information to advisors working with new students and offer insights

into how to anticipate first-year student expectations for prescriptive advising and how to integrate developmental components into this advising.
KEY WORDS: academic advising, assessment.

Programs Designed to Support Social and Academic Adjustment

Beck, H. P., & Davidson, W. D. (2001). Establishing an early warning system: Predicting low grades in college students from survey of academic orientations scores. *Research in Higher Education, 42*(6), 709-723.

Using data collected from the Survey of Academic Orientations (SAO), this study explored whether scores on the SAO are useful as an early warning of academic trouble among college students. Survey data were collected from 536 first-year students at a university in the Southeast near the mid-point of the semester (between the third and seventh weeks) in introductory psychology classes. A comparison of scores from the SAO and first-semester grades revealed that survey data could serve as an early warning (to predict low grades). Particularly predictive items on the instrument were those that measured academic apathy and efficacy. The study highlighted a need to expand the type of data collected to predict student success beyond SAT scores, high school rank, and position in high school graduating class.
KEY WORDS: academic advising, early warning systems.

Colton, G. M., Connor, Jr., U. J., Schultz, E. L., & Easter, L. M. (1999-2000). Fighting attrition: One freshman year program that targets academic progress and retention for at-risk students. *Journal of College Student Retention: Research, Theory & Practice, 1*(2), 147-162.

This article describes Kutztown University's (PA) Student Support Services Freshman Year Program (SSFYP), a federally funded TRIO program designed to facilitate the college transition and promote the academic success of at-risk students. The authors provide relevant supporting literature and a detailed description of the program components. The program consists of the following elements: (a) academic advising/counseling, (b) freshman colloquium, (c) student mentor program, (d) academic skills training, and (e) social support activities. Program evaluation revealed that students expressed satisfaction with the availability of the SSFYP counselors, length of meeting times, and help from counselors on specific issues. An analysis of participants' grade point averages demonstrated that these students displayed satisfactory academic performance, especially given their at-risk status. Finally, SSFYP students were retained at higher rates than the general university population. The authors present the following components as keys to the success of the SSFYP program: (a) its intrusive nature, (b) the development of positive relationships between students and program faculty and staff, (c) the comprehensive nature of advisement, (d) the use of a targeted freshman colloquium, and (e) the use of extrinsic rewards.
KEY WORDS: academic advising, at-risk students, counseling, mentoring, retention, social support, student-faculty interaction, TRIO programs.

Cuseo, J. B. (2003). Comprehensive academic support for students during the first year of college. In G. Kramer and Associates (Eds.), *Student academic services: An integrated approach* (pp. 271-309). San Francisco: Jossey-Bass.

The author presents a case for providing comprehensive academic support during the first year of college and offers a description of several initiatives that build on collaboration to provide such support.

These include peer collaboration, such as peer tutoring, mentoring, study groups, and curricular models; early-alert systems that involve collaboration with faculty and academic support services; academic and student affairs partnerships such as living-learning centers, residential learning communities, and first-year seminars; and school-college collaborations that might include summer bridge programs, high school outreach programs, and academic alliances. The author concludes that first-year support programs are most effective when they are intrusive, proactive, and collaborative.

KEY WORDS: academic support, first-year seminars, mentoring, residential learning communities, summer bridge programs, tutoring.

Cutright, M. (2002, September/October). What are research universities doing for first-year students? *About Campus, 7,* **16-20.**
This study used qualitative data collected by the Policy Center on the First Year of College from more than 75 research universities as part of the project Strengthening First-Year Student Learning at Doctoral/Research-Extensive Universities. The project aimed to determine successful first-year initiatives at these types of institutions. The author identified seven themes common to first-year programs at research universities: (a) the proliferation of first-year programs, (b) first-year initiatives housed in a discipline or college, (c) integration of multiple strategies to support first-year programs, (d) learning communities as a cornerstone of first-year efforts, (e) a re-examination of teaching and learning, (f) strong academic and student affairs partnerships, and (g) intentional assessment and evaluation. These themes and the article's description of best practices provide the foundation for launching or examining first-year programs at research universities.

KEY WORDS: learning communities, research universities.

Engle, C. C., Reilly, N. P., & Levine, H. B. (2003-4). A case study of an academic retention program. *Journal of College Student Retention: Research, Theory & Practice, 5*(4), 365-383.
This research examined the impact of a voluntary 12-week retention program designed to promote the success of at-risk students through group and individual counseling and unmonitored study time. Students on academic probation at a mid-sized comprehensive university were invited to participate in the program, which focused on test taking, study skills, career options, motivation, and stress reduction. Among the 91 participants, 45 volunteered to participate in the program; the remaining 46 chose not to participate and were used as the control group. The researchers discovered that more students in the program remained after each semester compared to the control group. Furthermore, they learned that 69% of the program participants versus 43% of the control group were in good academic standing at the end of the spring semester; and 55% of the program participants versus 28% of the control group remained in good academic standing during the semester following the program. Program participants did not report an improvement in their study skills but did note enhanced self-esteem. The authors suggest that improving self-esteem, which is closely related to self-efficacy, can boost students' sense of academic competence and their subsequent academic performance.

KEY WORDS: at-risk students, counseling, retention, self-efficacy, self-esteem, student success.

Gold, J. M., Miller, M., & Rutholz, J. (2001). Grief experiences of first-year women students in the transition to college: Implications for individual and systematic interventions. *Journal of The First-Year Experience & Students in Transition, 13*(2), 37-54.
This study examined "disenfranchised grieving," or the normal grieving that often accompanies life transition, among women in their first semester of college. The researchers surveyed 289 first-year female students enrolled at a large southeastern university. At the sixth and seventh weeks of the fall

semester, participants completed an adapted Grief Experiences Questionnaire and a demographic survey. Their grade point average (GPA) and enrollment status were also collected at the conclusion of the spring semester. The researchers discovered that in-state students who had not visited home had a more severe grief reaction. High grievers had lower fall GPAs and persistence rates. Student ethnicity did not have a significant effect on grief experiences. The authors suggest residence hall programming and immediate individual or group counseling in order to help women cope with grief experiences and promote their persistence and success.

KEY WORDS: *female students, grief experiences, persistence, transition to college.*

Grant-Vallone, E., Reid, K., Umali, C., & Pohlert, E. (2003-4). An analysis of the effects of self-esteem, social support, and participation in student support services on students' adjustment and commitment to college. *Journal of College Student Retention: Research, Theory & Practice,* 5(3), 255-274.

The researchers surveyed 118 college students to assess the relationships among self-esteem, family support, peer support, and program use, academic and social support, and college commitment. The students were participants in one of the following support programs geared toward low-income and first-generation students: Educational Opportunity Program (EOP), Academic Support Program for Intellectual Rewards (A.S.P.I.R.E.), and Faculty Mentoring Program (FMP). The authors found that students with higher self-esteem and peer support reported better academic and social adjustment. Students who used the university support programs more frequently also tended to report higher levels of social adjustment. In addition, students who felt more involved in campus life and were better adjusted academically were more likely to report that they were committed to the university and the goal of a college degree. The researchers concluded that such support programs promote adjustment for economically disadvantaged and underrepresented students. They stressed the value of encouraging student involvement in campus life and university programs in facilitating student adjustment. The authors also suggested that since the support programs impacted social but not academic adjustment, more could be done to develop academic adjustment.

KEY WORDS: *college adjustment, first-generation students, student services.*

Hutto, C. P., & Fenwick, L. T. (2002). *Staying in college: Student services and freshman retention at historically black colleges and universities* (HBCUs). (ERIC Document Reproduction Service No. ED 468397)

This study focused on first-year student retention by measuring the perception of quality and accessibility of various student services at three private HBCUs (Historically Black Colleges and Universities). Data were collected from surveys completed by 1,014 first-year students who were surveyed at orientation and specifically measured perceptions about such areas as financial aid, residence life, and academic support. Findings from the study concluded that enrollment management, enrollment management/services, and financial aid were the focus of greatest concern among those in the sample. Specifically, students indicated a concern about the financial aid information received before attending the institution and the level of knowledge counselors had about financial aid and other forms of financial assistance. Other areas measured in the study indicated some level of satisfaction among the students in the sample. The article concludes that student retention, particularly that of students of color and/or those in lower socioeconomic groups, are impacted by financial aid and communication about financial resources and options for entering students.

KEY WORDS: *enrollment management, financial aid, HBCUs, student satisfaction, students of color, retention.*

Kuh, G. D., Kinzie, J., Schuh, J. H., Whitt, E. J., & Associates. (2005). Supportive campus environment. In *Student success in college: Creating conditions that matter* **(pp. 241-261). San Francisco: Jossey-Bass.**

This chapter presents a sampling of the policies, practices, and conditions of 20 institutions found to support their students at high levels, based on the findings of the National Survey of Student Engagement (NSSE). The institutions are diverse in terms of size, geographic region, Carnegie classification, and mission. Among the programs described are transition programs that welcome students and offer guideposts to their success; early warning systems and advising programs that respond efficiently and effectively to students, including those who may be at-risk; mentoring, learning, and peer support programs; residential living environments that provide academic and social support; and caring, accessible, and responsive faculty, staff, and administrators.

KEY WORDS: academic advising, assessment, early warning systems, engagement, mentoring, peer support, student support.

Mangold, W. D., Bean, L. G., Adams, D. J., Schwab, W. A., & Lynch, S. M. (2002-3). Who goes and who stays: An assessment of the effect of a freshman mentoring and unit registration program on college persistence. *Journal of College Student Retention: Research, Theory & Practice, 4*(2), 95-122.

This article presents a description and evaluation of a unit registration and mentoring program designed to improve student academic performance and persistence at a major state university. Through the program, students enroll in the same courses as a cohort, share six to nine hours of class time, meet once a week with a faculty mentor, and receive one hour of credit. Mentors receive training on student issues and are expected to engage students in a variety of academic and social events. To assess the program, data were analyzed from individual student records obtained from the Office of the Registrar over a four-year period. The researchers discovered that students who participated in the program were at a lower risk of leaving the university than those who did not participate. Furthermore, women and Black students were less likely to drop out than nonparticipants. The authors conclude that the program has a positive impact on graduation and persistence and note that the program was implemented at a total average cost of $73 per student. However, they note that the findings cannot be generalized to other populations given the self-selected nature of the program participants.

KEY WORDS: learning communities, mentoring, retention, students of color.

Martin Jr., W. E., Swartz-Kulstad, J. L., & Madson, M. (1999). Psychosocial factors that predict the college adjustment of first-year undergraduate students: Implications for college counselors. *Journal of College Counseling, 2,* 121-133.

This article reports on two studies designed to identify which psychosocial factors best predict the college adjustment of first-year undergraduates. The first study involved 60 first-semester students at a mid-size doctorate granting university in the southwest United States. Data were collected in the fall semester through the Student Adaptation to College Questionnaire and the Demographic Questionnaire. The second study replicated the first with 119 students at a smaller upper-midwest master's degree granting university. The results of both studies revealed that academic self-confidence, positive attitudes toward the university, and faculty and peer support significantly predicted a more successful adjustment to college. The authors recommended that college counseling centers implement outreach programming, consultation services, and research activities to promote student adjustment. Finally, they assert that these activities should be conducted collaboratively with colleagues from both student and academic affairs.

KEY WORDS: assessment, college adjustment, counseling services, faculty support, peer support.

Perrine, R. M. (2001). College stress and persistence as a function of attachment and support. *Journal of The First-Year Experience & Students in Transition, 13*(1), 7-22.

This research explored the relationship between attachment and perceived support on the stress levels and persistence rates of college students. First-year students ($N = 171$) were assessed for their attachment styles during the second week of classes. Level of stress and support data were collected during the sixth week of the semester. The researchers gathered persistence and grade point average data by checking student academic records at the end of the spring semester. They found that students with one type of insecure attachment style (fearful) persisted at lower rates, were least satisfied with their perceived support, and reported the most college-related stress. Women perceived more stress and had higher attrition rates than men. Dissatisfaction with perceived support and gender were the strongest predictors of stress. In addition, support mediated the relationship between attachment and stress, but not between gender and stress. Since a fearful attachment style is associated with social insecurity and lack of assertiveness, fearful students faced with stressors may be less likely to seek out help. The author recommends that automatic and intrusive interventions that provide services to students before they can become overly stressed may eliminate the need for students to seek out services on their own.
KEY WORDS: attachment, persistence, social support, stress.

Perrine, R. M., & Wilkins, S. L. (2001). College students' reactions to tutoring: The role of prior attitudes and attachment. *Journal of The First-Year Experience & Students in Transition, 13*(2), 55-74.

This study examined the impact of first-year college students' attitudes and attachment styles on their cognitive and affective reactions toward tutoring. The 49 participants were first-year college students enrolled in Student Support Services orientation courses, through which they were required to receive tutoring. The assessment measured students' attachment styles (secure, dismissing, fearful, or preoccupied), attitudes toward tutoring, and resistance to tutoring. Resistance to tutoring was related to prior negative attitudes toward tutoring and to insecure attachment. Students with prior negative attitudes toward tutoring tended to feel more negatively after receiving tutoring. Tutoring centers might consider assessing the attachment style of incoming students in order to provide outreach to those students who might be resistant to using the services. In addition, marketing aimed at counteracting prior negative attitudes toward tutoring could help promote tutoring services and increase the likelihood that students are well served.
KEY WORD: tutoring.

Perry, S. R., Cabrera, A. F., & Vogt, W. P. (1999). Career maturity and college student persistence. *Journal of College Student Retention: Research, Theory & Practice, 1*(1), 41-58.

This research examines the impact of career maturity on the persistence of first-year students at a public, four-year institution. The authors collected data from 307 college students during a precollege orientation session and again through a mail survey four weeks before the conclusion of the students' first year of college. The data provide support for the idea that goal commitment and career maturity are two independent constructs, despite the inclination of researchers to link the two. Though career maturity did not have a direct effect on persistence, it was significantly associated with various factors that could influence persistence, such as grade point average, academic integration, faculty contact, encouragement from family and friends, and goal and institutional commitment. The researchers assert that students with greater levels of career maturity are likely to engage in the learning process with a greater sense of purpose. They suggest that curricular offerings, faculty development programs, and career counseling should be evaluated for their ability to promote career maturity. Finally, the authors posit that financial resources should be allocated for services that facilitate career maturity, given its association with improved student integration and performance.

KEY WORDS: academic integration, career development, social support, goal commitment, institutional commitment, retention, student-faculty interaction.

Ting, S. R., Grant, S., & Pienert, S. L. (2000). The Excellence-Commitment-and-Effective-Learning (ExCEL) group: An integrated approach for first-year college students' success. *Journal of College Student Development, 41,* 355-362.

Drawing on student development theory and practice, the investigators in this study paired noncognitive variables and study skills to create an exploratory learning group, ExCEL. ExCEL groups were formed on two campuses, with 22 total participants, 17 of whom completed the program. Data were collected from the participants through administration of the Learning and Study Strategies Inventory (LASSI; this instrument served as a pre and posttest) and grade point average. Additionally, the ExCEL groups met weekly to explore study skills and learning strategies, as well as noncognitive subject matter (e.g., cocurricular involvement, issues relating to diversity.). The findings of the study indicated that ExCEL participants improved their study skills and grade point averages through participation in the program. Further, students involved in the program reported enjoying the experience and support extended by the group.

KEY WORDS: assessment, learning strategies, student development theory, student success, study skills.

{ INVOLVEMENT IN CAMPUS LIFE AND LIVING ENVIRONMENTS }

Blackhurst, A. E., Akey, L. D., & Bobilya, A. J. (2003). A qualitative investigation of student outcomes in a residential learning community. *Journal of The First-Year Experience & Students in Transition, 15*(2), 35-59.

The authors conducted a qualitative exploration of students' perceptions of learning community outcomes and the relationship between students' stated experiences in a learning community and the measurable outcomes associated with those experiences. The study complements findings from numerous quantitative studies on this subject. Analysis of data from interviews conducted with 20 first-year student members of a learning community yielded seven themes characterizing students' perceptions of their experience. Students perceived that participation in the learning community (a) eased the transition to college, (b) facilitated social integration, (c) helped develop personal relationships with faculty, (d) facilitated in-class learning, (e) created a positive living-learning environment, and (f) worked against peer norms of individualism and competitiveness. Students also perceived that the outcomes of their participation in the learning community could not be attributed solely to self-fulfilling expectations. These themes provide the foundation for marketing efforts to attract new students to the learning community program as well as for information to help faculty better understand the potential impact of the learning community experience.

KEY WORDS: assessment, college adjustment, learning communities, residential learning communities.

Dillon, J. (2003). Bringing counseling to the classroom and the residence hall: The university learning community. *Journal of Humanistic Counseling Education and Development, 42*(2), 194-208.

This article describes a first-year student learning community program at the State University of West Georgia involving partnerships among counselors, faculty, and residence life staff. The learning communities, organized around the theme "making decisions," include psychological, social, and academic components. During the first two years of the program, the author collected qualitative and quantitative data on 48 students to determine the relationship among learning communities, student development, and academic success. In assessing the psychological component, the author discovered a relationship between the following: (a) participation in the program and ease of transition to college, (b) students' feelings of acceptance and being valued, (c) increased alcohol awareness and improved eating habits. Assessment of the social elements revealed that students reported greater sensitivity to the role of race, learning styles, and the importance of serving the community; students also reported an improvement in ethical decision making. Learning community participants had higher grade point averages and persistence rates than those who did not participate. In addition, students reported increased academic excitement, increased faculty interaction, and competence in decision making. The author asserts that the learning communities appeared successful in promoting development and success among new students.
KEY WORDS: academic support, residential learning communities, retention, student-faculty interaction, student success.

Inkelas, K. K., & Weisman, J. L. (2003). Different by design: An examination of student outcomes among participants in three types of living-learning programs. *Journal of College Student Development, 44*(3), 335-368.

Drawing on data collected from 2,833 students living in university residence halls at a large, highly competitive, public research institution in the Midwest, the researchers sought to determine how the differences among students who participated in three types of living-learning programs—transitions, academic honors, or curriculum-based—compared with students who were not involved in any program. Using data collected from a 44-item survey developed for this study, the researchers found that students involved in any living-learning program tended to be more engaged in their activities and were more positive about their environments than were nonparticipants. They also found that students in the transitions and the academic honors programs were likely to use critical thinking skills, meet faculty in social settings outside of the classroom, and discuss sociocultural issues in nonclassroom settings. In addition, living-learning program participants were more likely to indicate that their residence hall environments were supportive than students not in such programs. The researchers provide separate analysis for each of the three types of programs, offer several implications for practice, and recommend areas for future research. The survey instrument's items, psychometric data, and demographic data on respondents are included in the appendices.
KEY WORDS: assessment, residential learning communities, residence life.

Kaya, N. (2004). Residence hall climate: Predicting first-year students' adjustments to college. *Journal of The First-Year Experience & Students in Transition, 16*(1), 101-118.

This study examined impacts of the physical and social climate of residence halls on college student adjustment. The sample included 245 first-year students at a large public university in the Southeast. Participants completed online versions of the Residence Hall Climate Scale and the Student Adaptation to College Questionnaire during the spring semester. Results revealed that group cohesiveness was significantly related to student adjustment. Disruption by noise and personalization of the residence hall environment had significant impacts on institutional attachment. The authors suggest that creating a sense of community, enforcing policies to limit noise, and providing opportunities for students to personalize their living space could promote student adjustment.

KEY WORDS: assessment, college adjustment, residence life.

Keup, J. R., & Stolzenberg, E. B. (2004). *The 2003 Your First College Year (YFCY) survey: Exploring the academic and personal experiences of first-year students* **(Monograph No. 40). Columbia, SC: University of South Carolina, National Resource Center for The First-Year Experience and Students in Transition.**

This monograph summarizes findings from the 2002-2003 administrations of two national instruments sponsored by the Cooperative Institutional Research Program (CIRP), the Freshman Survey and the Your First College Year (YFCY) survey. Drawing on data on nearly 30,000 students from 136 four-year institutions across the country, this monograph provides a general, empirical portrait of students' first-year experiences. Students reported low levels of engagement in academic activities, first-year pedagogical practices that relied heavily on lecturing and group discussion, a reliance upon peers rather than faculty and staff for information and support, and a high degree of overall satisfaction with college. Financial concerns topped the list of personal challenges for students. Further, the data reveal how students' behaviors, values, and self-image change during the first year of college. For example, drinking, socializing with friends, and self-understanding increase while attendance at religious services, participation in volunteer activities, and self-ratings of academic ability decline during the first year. Subgroup analyses of first-year experiences by gender and place of residence (i.e., on-campus vs. off-campus housing) help identify segments of the first-year student population that are particularly at risk. Overall, these data provide a national context for understanding first-year students.

KEY WORDS: national data, student characteristics.

Kuh, G., Palmer, M., & Kish, K. (2003). The value of educationally purposeful out-of-class experiences. In T. L. Skipper & R. Argo (Eds.), *Involvement in campus activities and the retention of first-year college students* **(Monograph No. 36, pp. 1-18). Columbia, SC: University of South Carolina, National Resource Center for The First-Year Experience and Students in Transition.**

This chapter reviews literature addressing the impact of out-of-class activities on desired college outcomes, including cognitive complexity, knowledge acquisition and application, humanitarianism, inter- and intrapersonal communication, and practical competence. The authors describe how the following cocurricular experiences influence students: fraternity and sorority membership, residence life, intercollegiate athletics, service-learning and volunteerism, tutoring, work, campus activities, student-faculty interaction, and diversity experiences. They conclude that life outside the classroom has great potential to enrich the undergraduate experience. Collaboration between academic and student affairs and positive peer influence can further enhance the positive effects of these activities. They assert that additional research and assessment is warranted in the following areas: the impact of these experiences on underrepresented students, service-learning and mentoring programs, and new academic initiatives such as the use of technology and cocurricular portfolios.

KEY WORDS: cocurricular activities, college outcomes, involvement.

Laar, C. V., Levin, S., Sinclair, S., & Sidanius, J. (2005). The effect of university roommate contact on ethnic attitudes and behavior. *Journal of Experimental Social Psychology, 41*(4), 329-345.

This study examined the influence of living with an African American, Asian American, Latino/a, or White roommate on the affective, cognitive, and behavioral indicators of prejudice among university students. Roommate contact for more than 2,000 students was examined in two ways: (a) prejudice as a function of living with randomly assigned roommates during the first year of colleges and (b) the impact of voluntary interaction with a roommate in the second and third years on the prejudicial views held by students during the fourth year of study. The findings reveal that overall, students randomly assigned to live with students from other races at the start of the first year of college displayed less prejudice by the end of the year. In addition, students who voluntarily continued to interact with roommates from different races during their second and third years of college also showed decreases in prejudice. One notable exception that emerged involved random assignment to an Asian American roommate during the first year of college and voluntary interaction with Asian American roommates in subsequent years of study. Both of these conditions resulted in the increase of prejudicial attitudes, particularly toward African American and Latino students. The study carries implications for residence life practitioners and other educators interested in decreasing prejudice and enhancing student success during and after the first year of college.

KEY WORDS: diversity education, prejudice, residence life.

Light, R. J. (2001). *Making the most of college: Students speak their minds.* **Cambridge, MA: Harvard University Press.**

This book offers a synthesis of findings from interviews conducted over the course of 10 years with college seniors at Harvard University focused on what students can do to get the most out of their college experience and how faculty, staff, and administrators can facilitate this process for students. Many of the findings summarized in the book are related to interactions with faculty, advisors, and fellow students; the importance of course selection, involvement in enriching educational opportunities both inside and outside the classroom, and time management skills; and social and intellectual interactions with diverse individuals. While implications for practice are highlighted throughout the book, the final chapter specifically identifies strategies for campus leaders to improve student life on campus, including adopting a policy of inclusion; building a strong campus culture; facilitating collaboration between institutional and student leadership; implementing innovative course schedules; and forging connections among students, faculty, staff, and administrators. The final chapter makes the critical point that these strategies are likely to be most successful and sustainable if they are instituted at the very beginning of the students' college careers. Student insights and institutional strategies lay an important foundation for first-year programs and student success throughout college.

KEY WORDS: diversity, involvement, research studies, student-faculty interaction.

Terenzini, P. T., Pascarella, E. T., & Blimling, G. S. (1999). Students' out-of-class experiences and their influence on learning and cognitive development: A literature review. *Journal of College Student Development, 40*(5), 610-623.

This article reviews literature that demonstrates the impact of cocurricular activities on the learning and cognitive development of college students. The authors examine research related to residence life, Greek life, intercollegiate athletics, employment, other cocurricular activities, and faculty and peer interactions. They conclude that while some out-of-class activities can have a positive effect on students (e.g., living in a residence hall, studying abroad, and socializing with others of different racial/ethnic groups), other activities are less effective (e.g., belonging to a Greek organization, working full time, participating in men's intercollegiate football or basketball). Out-of-class activities have the greatest impact on student learning when they actively engage students and involve interpersonal interactions with peers and faculty. The authors suggest that since no single policy or program is likely to have a complete impact on students, academic and student affairs educators must work collaboratively to provide students with experiences in multiple areas that promote learning and development. In order

for cocurricular activities to have the greatest impact on first-year students, educators should strive to engage them early in those opportunities that research indicates have the most positive effect.
KEY WORDS: cocurricular activities, cognitive development, engagement, involvement.

Zheng, J. L., Saunders, K. P., Shelley, II, M. C., & Whelan, D. F. (2002). Predictors of academic success for freshman residence hall students. *Journal of College Student Development, 43*(2), **267-283.**

This research examined the impact of background, psychological, and environmental variables on first-year student success. Participants included 1,167 residential students at a midwestern land-grant university enrolling more than 26,000 students. Data were obtained from the registrar's student information files, residence information files, and the Cooperative Institutional Research Program survey data. The researchers learned that grade point average is significantly related to precollege characteristics (i.e., high school rank, gender, ethnicity, parental education, divorced/separated parents, self-perception of abilities, expectation of honors and/or changing a major) and environmental variables (i.e., learning community membership, choice of academic college). Collecting such data can be used to identify potentially at-risk students and inform the establishment of necessary support mechanisms. The study described here also demonstrated the positive impact of learning communities when controlling for student motivation (i.e., self-selection).
KEY WORDS: national survey findings, residential learning communities.

TECHNOLOGY

Barone, C. A., & Hagner, P. R. (Eds.). (2001). *Technology-enhanced teaching and learning: Leading and supporting the transformation on your campus* **(Educause Leadership Strategies, Volume 5). San Francisco: Jossey-Bass.**

This multi-author book describes how technology is being integrated into college teaching and learning and transforming campuses. Several chapters address the role of faculty, focusing on how to engage faculty in technology use and examining the roles of faculty (i.e., traditional roles vs. those that prevail in the current technological environment). The book includes strategies for creating consensus among campus constituents about technology use, and suggestions for creating mechanisms and infrastructure to support the use of technologies to enhance teaching and learning. The book concludes with several observations about conditions needed to facilitate technologically driven campus transformations. Authors of this chapter offer 12 conditions they believe necessary for creating and sustaining campus transformation and offer examples of how each of those conditions can be applied at an institutional level.
KEY WORDS: technology, technology and teaching.

Flowers, L., Pascarella, E. T., & Pierson, C. T. (2000). **Information technology use and cognitive outcomes in the first year of college.** *The Journal of Higher Education, 71*(6), 637-667.

This study explored the relationship between computer use, including use of e-mail, and intellectual development of first-year students. The sample included 3,840 first-year students from several two- and four-year institutions. Data were collected by the National Study of Student Learning (NSSL) precollege survey and an instrument associated with the Collegiate Assessment of Academic Proficiency (CAAP). Follow-up data were collected using another CAAP instrument, the College Student Experiences Questionnaire (CSEQ), and an NSSL follow-up survey. Findings from the study indicated some difference in the level of technology use at two- and four-year institutions (there was greater use of technology on four-year campuses). When students on both types of campuses enrolled in technical or preprofessional courses, there was a greater likelihood that they would use computers. Students who were older (at either type of institution) tended to use e-mail, in particular, less than other students. Finally, the study found that use of technology had little impact on skill development, with the exception of word processing and reading comprehension.
KEY WORDS: assessment, technology and teaching.

Junco, R. (2005). **Technology and today's first-year students.** In M. L. Upcraft, J. N. Gardner, and B. O. Barefoot (Eds.), *Challenging and supporting the first-year student: A handbook for improving the first year of college* (pp. 221-238). San Francisco: Jossey-Bass.

The author of this chapter provides an overview of the relationship between networked technologies and first-year students. The following is discussed: (a) research associated with the use and impact of technology, (b) examples of technology in the classroom experience, (c) the gap between student and faculty experience with technology, and (d) recommendations for uses of technologies with first-year students. The chapter begins with examples of the types of technologies used most often by first-year students (e.g., instant messaging, cell phones, e-mail, Internet) and considers how and why students use these technologies. The author examines research that indicates differences in technology use among students by socioeconomic status and gender and suggests that appropriate uses of technologies can enhance the educational experience of first-year students. The chapter also offers negative and positive examples of technology use in and out of the classroom (with an emphasis on the impact on academic performance). The experience gap between students and faculty is also highlighted as a consideration as use of technologies becomes ubiquitous. For example, both students and faculty tend to use e-mail, but many faculty members do not have the same level of Internet experience as their students and, consequently, might not be as comfortable using the Internet in the classroom. The author recommends future uses of networked technologies with first-year students, suggests standardizing the types of technologies used on a campus, and recommends introducing these technologies early in the college experience.
KEY WORD: technology and teaching.

Kubey, R. W., Lavin, M. J., & Barrows, J. R. (2001). **Internet use and collegiate academic performance decrements: Early findings.** *Journal of Communication, 51,* 366-382.

This article details how students' Internet use affects academic performance and social integration. The authors discuss the concepts of Internet addiction and Internet dependence and apply these notions as a framework for analysis. The 43-item survey administered to participants ($N = 572$) directed students to respond only on their Internet usage during recreational times—not during course-mandated research or other uses. A small percentage of students (9.26%) agreed or strongly agreed that they may have a psychological dependence on the Internet. Of the entire sample population, 14% reported that their Internet usage had a negative impact on their academic performance. Students seemed more addicted to synchronous Internet applications (e.g., chat rooms, chat programs), where real-time discussions could occur, rather than asynchronous programs (e.g., e-mail, blogs) wherein a wait time existed before responses would be received. The authors suggest that academic administrators examine Internet usage among students and develop appropriate interventions to combat what the authors see as a "small but growing problem" (p. 380).

KEY WORDS: academic performance, Internet addiction, technology.

Shuell, T. J., & Farber, S. L. (2001). Students' perceptions of technology use in college courses. *Journal of Educational Computing Research, 24*(2), 119-138.

Drawing on data collected from 728 graduate and undergraduate students enrolled in courses in which the faculty reported using computer technologies, the researchers in this study used a survey to measure students' perceptions of technology use in 20 classes. The study's findings revealed that more than 85% of the sample perceived computer technology to be a helpful learning tool for them in their classes. Additionally, they reported improved interactions with their instructor and peers through the use of technology. Findings also suggested these perceptions might be influenced by the way in which technology was used in the course, by a student's learning style and background, and by the student's gender. In open-ended responses, some participants indicated that use of computer technologies in the course enabled them to self-pace.

KEY WORDS: technology and learning.

Thomson, J. S., & Stringer, S. B. (2000). First-year seminar: Using technology to explore professional issues and opportunities across locations. *Journal of General Education, 49*(1), 66-73.

The purpose of this study was to identify ways to enhance the first-year seminar at The Pennsylvania State University using a variety of means, including integration of computer technologies into the seminar. Students enrolled in the course in fall 1996 were surveyed about computer use and what they hoped to learn, with 142 students enrolled in the seminar completing the survey. The study's findings revealed a range of computer and other technological knowledge among the students and variations in accessibility to these technologies. Fifty-seven percent of students in the sample reported owning a computer, more than 50% reported daily computer use, either to access the Internet/World Wide Web or to complete class assignments. Results from the study informed creation of web-based resources for students and faculty to be used as enhancements to teaching and learning.

KEY WORDS: first-year seminars, technology and teaching.

{AGENTS OF SOCIALIZATION AND SUPPORT IN THE FIRST YEAR}

Faculty as First-Year Student Advocates

Boulter, L.T. (2002). Self-concept as a predictor of college freshman academic adjustment. *College Student Journal, 36*(2), 234-247.

This research examined the impact of 12 domains of self-concept and five sources of support (close friends, mother, father, instructors, and persons in campus organizations) on first-year college student adjustment (quantified as students' cumulative grade point average). Participants were 265 first-year students enrolled at a small southeastern private liberal arts college. Data were collected during orientation (two days before fall classes began) with the Self-Perception Profile for College Students, as well as a Student Questionnaire developed to obtain demographic information. Self-perception of intellectual ability and instructor support had positive influences on adjustment. Self-perception of creativity and the importance to men of close friendships negatively impacted adjustment. Boulter suggests that programs that encourage students to form challenging academic goals may bolster their academic self-concept, facilitating frequent contact with faculty members could help promote students' academic adjustment to college.

KEY WORDS: assessment, college adjustment, self-image, student-faculty interactions.

Braxton, J. M., Bray, N. J., & Berger, J. B. (2000). Faculty teaching skills and their influence on the college student departure process. *Journal of College Student Development, 41*(2), 215-227.

This study examined the impact of faculty teaching skills on college students' social integration, subsequent institutional commitment, and persistence. Tinto's interactionalist theory of student departure was used as the conceptual framework. Data from 696 first-year students at a highly selective, private Research I university were collected three times during the students' first year. Participants completed the Student Information Form of the Cooperative Institutional Research Program (CIRP) survey in August, the Early Collegiate Experiences Survey (ECES) in October, and the Freshman Year Survey (FYS) in March. Researchers discovered that teaching skills, including instructor organization, preparation, and clarity, positively impacted social integration, institutional commitment, and intent to reenroll. The authors assert that student classroom experience has a great impact on persistence in college and should be given more attention. This research provides support for the notion that first-year students should be taught by instructors with strong teaching skills. Institutions interested in improving student retention rates should also offer faculty development opportunities focused on teaching skills.

KEY WORDS: assessment, faculty, retention, social integration, teaching.

Donahue, L. (2004). Connections and reflections: Creating a positive learning environment for first-year students. *Journal of The First Year Experience & Students in Transition, 16*(1), 77-100.

This researcher used end-of-semester reflection essays from first-year seminars to analyze first-year students' perceptions of their learning environments and the aspects of their experiences that facilitated or impeded their learning process. Qualitative data analysis was conducted on 138 student essays randomly selected from 522 students who completed the first-year seminar at a small liberal arts institution. This analytical process focused on what students perceived they needed in order to feel connected with the campus community and to have effective curricular and cocurricular learning experiences. The data revealed that interpersonal relationships were the key to a positive learning environment and to

the students' feeling connected to the campus community. Students identified faculty as important, but interaction with peers both inside and outside the classroom also was considered necessary for academic growth. Small classroom size and interactive pedagogy were identified as strategies that effectively enhanced these interactions. Few students saw their growth and learning potential enhanced by cocurricular experiences, such as those available through residential life. While interconnectedness appeared to be the key element of a positive learning experience, students also recognized that college was a time for them to assume responsibility for their own learning and development. The results of this study identify and validate the role of campus community in the success of first-year students.
KEY WORDS: first-year seminars, learning, peer support, sense of belonging, student-faculty interaction.

Greiner, K., & Westbrook, T. S. (2002). Academic service quality and instructional quality. *Journal of The First-Year Experience & Students in Transition 14*(2), 7-30.
This study examined student perceptions of the relationship between academic service quality and instructional quality at a leading midwestern private university. The authors define academic service quality as nonclassroom services provided by faculty, such as availability, reliability, trustworthiness, and empathy. Instructional quality focuses on evaluations of learning, enthusiasm, organization, interaction, individual rapport, breadth, assignments, and workload. The researchers administered an adaptation of the Service Quality survey and the Students' Evaluation of Educational Quality survey to 360 undergraduates enrolled in an introductory biology class. Of these students, 82% were in their first semester of college. Students completed variants of these instruments at the start of the fall semester and again at the end of the semester, with 245 students completing both tests. Results revealed a high correlation between perceived academic service and instructional quality. Furthermore, perceptions of these concepts were similar across a variety of demographic characteristics.
KEY WORDS: assessment, faculty, teaching.

Hoffman, M., Richmond, J., Morrow, J., & Salomone, K. (2002-3). Investigating "sense of belonging" in first-year college students. *Journal of College Student Retention: Research, Theory & Practice, 4*(3), 227-256.
The purpose of this study was to develop, test, and refine an instrument to measure students' sense of belonging in relation to persistence in college. The researchers first conducted focus groups with students enrolled in a university first-year seminar course to assess factors related to a sense of belonging, or perception of fit between the student and the institution. Some seminar students were part of a learning community cluster of courses linked by academic content; others were a heterogeneous population of students. The researchers found that the learning community students were more successful than the non-learning community students at forming new friendships. Specifically, the learning community students were able to establish relationships with peers around academic matters. Furthermore, though both learning community and non-learning community students found their faculty to be friendly and approachable, the learning community students responded with greater intensity. The researchers also administered a pre-test to 205 first-year college students to further refine the main conceptual dimensions of a sense of belonging. They identified five underlying dimensions for the resulting Sense of Belonging (SB) instrument: (a) Perceived Peer Support, (b) Perceived Faculty Support/Comfort, (c) Perceived Classroom Comfort, (d) Perceived Isolation, and (e) Empathetic Faculty Understanding. Data analysis revealed that students in learning communities scored significantly better on all five factors of the SB instrument than students in stand-alone seminar courses. The authors assert that learning community students were better able to form helpful connections around a common agenda and similar challenges. The researchers suggest that sense of belonging stems from students' perceptions of "valued involvement" in the college setting, which is enhanced by establishing supportive peer

relationships and by the belief that faculty are compassionate and see students as more than a number among many. They also conclude that their Sense of Belonging instrument is a useful tool for further understanding factors that contribute to student persistence.

KEY WORDS: assessment, first-year seminars, learning communities, peer support, sense of belonging.

Kuh, G. D. & Hu, S. (2001). The effects of student-faculty interaction in the 1990s. *The Review of Higher Education, 24*(3), 309-332

This article examines student perceptions of the nature of student-faculty interactions, as well as the impact of these interactions on student learning, personal development, and student satisfaction. Using data collected through the College Student Experiences Questionnaire (CSEQ) from more than 5,000 full-time undergraduates (35% of whom were first-year students) at 126 colleges and universities nationwide, the authors found that the most frequent type of contact with faculty was informational and the least common type of interaction with faculty was working with a faculty member on a research project. Results of several multiple regressions yielded four main conclusions for the study. First, contact between faculty and students increases over time in college. Second, student-faculty interaction encourages students to devote greater effort to other educationally purposeful activities in college. Third, institutional type and selectivity have limited influence on the effect of student-faculty contact on student satisfaction and development. Finally, students' personal and academic characteristics need to be included in an analysis of the impact of student-faculty interaction. Overall, student-faculty contact is perceived by students to have a positive impact except for critique of written work, which has a slight negative impact on student satisfaction, and for informal socializing outside of class, which has no impact on student outcomes. The results of this study support the need to encourage students to forge academically meaningful connections with faculty as early in their college career as possible and to create structures that support the attention of faculty to building academic relationships with their students.

KEY WORDS: national survey findings, student development, student satisfaction, student-faculty interaction.

Kuh, G. D., Kinzie, J., Schuh, J. H., Whitt, E. J., & Associates. (2005). Student-faculty interaction. In *Student success in college: Creating conditions that matter* (pp. 207-218). San Francisco: Jossey-Bass.

This book presents the findings of the Documenting Effective Educational Practice (DEEP) project, a research initiative of the National Survey of Student Engagement (NSSE) and the American Association for Higher Education. The researchers conducted in-depth case studies of 20 institutions identified as having higher than predicted levels of student engagement (based on NSSE scores) and higher than predicted graduation rates after adjusting for institutional and student characteristics. The institutions were diverse in terms of size, geographic region, Carnegie classification, and mission. This chapter focuses on one of five effective practices used at DEEP campuses: effective student-faculty interaction both inside and outside the classroom. While the quantity of interaction with faculty is important, the authors posit that the quality of these interactions is even more significant. The authors also indicate that the accessibility and responsiveness of faculty at DEEP institutions is particularly noteworthy, as is the high quality of the academic advising relationship. The chapter also highlights specific strategies to encourage interaction between faculty and students, including undergraduate research opportunities, first-year seminars and senior capstone courses, effective use of electronic technologies, consideration of interaction with students in the faculty rewards structure, mentoring programs, and arrangement of the physical environment to facilitate these interactions.

KEY WORDS: engagement, student-faculty interaction, student success, technology.

Lundquist, C., Spalding, R. J., & Landrum, R. E. (2002-3). College students' thoughts about leaving the university: The impact of faculty attitudes and behaviors. *Journal of College Student Retention: Research, Theory & Practice, 4*(2), 123-133.

The researchers surveyed 729 undergraduates about 19 faculty attitudes and behaviors and how they would impact their general educational goals and plans to persist and graduate from the university. The participants were presented with several statements on faculty attitudes and behaviors then asked to respond on a Likert-type scale on the likelihood that observing such an attitude or behavior would encourage them to leave the university. The following three faculty attitudes and behaviors were most predictive of a student responding that he or she would consider leaving the institution: (a) lack of support from the faculty, (b) faculty members who do not return phone calls or e-mails in a timely fashion, and (c) professors who seem unapproachable. Women and upperclass students tended to be more sensitive to faculty attitudes and behaviors (i.e., more likely to leave because of them) than men and first-year students. The results affirmed that faculty attitudes and behaviors do have a significant impact on student retention. Despite the fact that first-year students reported being less impacted by these behaviors than their upperclass counterparts, professors who teach first-year students should make an effort to be supportive and approachable, and strive for timely communication with their students.
KEY WORDS: faculty, retention.

Nagda, B. A., Gregerman, S. R., Jonides, J., von Hippel, W., & Lerner, J. S. (1998). Undergraduate student-faculty research partnerships affect student retention. *The Review of Higher Education, 22*(1), 55-72.

This study reports on an Undergraduate Research Opportunity Program (UROP) at a large, public Research I institution. The goal of the program is to foster intellectual relationships between faculty and students through research partnerships. Though open to all first and second-year students, UROP specifically targets students of color and women with interest in the sciences. The researchers studied a random sampling of 1,280 African American, Hispanic, and White students. Of that number, 613 participated in UROP and 667 did not. The authors obtained data on the students' retention and academic performance from the Office of the Registrar. They learned that participation in UROP had the strongest impact on retention rates for African American students and for sophomores (rather than first-year students). For African American students, the program was particularly beneficial when their academic performance was below the median for their race/ethnic group. Furthermore, Hispanic and White students who participated in UROP during their sophomore year also experienced positive effects. The researchers concluded that different racial/ethnic groups face different challenges on college campuses, which can be positively impacted by faculty and peer interaction that promotes both the academic and social integration of students.
KEY WORDS: academic integration, retention, social integration, students of color, undergraduate research.

Pascarella, E. T., & Terenzini, P. T. (2001). Student-faculty and student-peer relationships as mediators of the structural effects of undergraduate residence arrangement. *Journal of Educational Research,* 344-353.

This study investigated the impact of a living-learning residential setting on academic achievement, institutional persistence, and intellectual and personal growth. The researchers used a longitudinal design with first-year students at a large, private, residential university. These students could choose to live in a conventional residence hall or an experimental living-learning residence (LLR), which included live-in academic staff, special courses, a faculty lecture series, and informal meetings with scholars and

administrators. In July, the researchers mailed a questionnaire to a random sample of 1,905 students to assess their expectations for college, background characteristics, and educational aspirations. In March, 1,457 students who had participated in the first data collection were sent a follow-up survey. Among the 733 respondents, 65 lived in the LLR and 708 lived in a conventional residence hall. The researchers found that, when student background characteristics were held constant, participation in the LLR had a significant positive impact on persistence, gains in intellectual and personal development, and perceptions of sense of community and intellectual curiosity. Furthermore, these positive outcomes were mediated by the quality of informal interaction with faculty and peers, as opposed to mere frequency of interaction. The study provides support for the importance of placing first-year students in settings (i.e., residential, classroom) that foster quality relationships among students and with faculty.
KEY WORDS: college outcomes, residence life, residential learning communities.

Santos, S. J., & Reigadas, E. T. (2004-5). Understanding the student-faculty mentoring process. Its effects on at-risk university students. *Journal of College Student Retention: Research, Theory & Practice, 6*(3) 337-357.
This study investigated the student-faculty mentoring process and how the nature and impact of mentoring relationships is affected when the student and mentor are from the same ethnic background. Framed by Tinto's Model of Student Departure and Social Network Theory, the study used survey data collected from 65 undergraduates at a comprehensive public institution in Los Angeles. Results of path analyses conducted through hierarchical regression analyses showed that students who had faculty mentors from the same ethnic background met with them more frequently than students who did not. Ethnic homogeneity and the greater frequency of interaction between students and faculty mentors that resulted had a positive influence on a number of outcomes, including attitudinal adjustment to college, academic performance, career and personal development, and satisfaction with the faculty mentoring program. The importance of ethnic homogeneity in the mentor-student relationship has important implications especially for the adjustment and retention of at-risk students from historically underrepresented ethnic groups and for structuring mentoring programs to assist these students.
KEY WORDS: at-risk students, mentoring, student-faculty interaction, students of color.

Academic Advisors and Other Professional Staff

Anttonen, R. G., & Chaskes, J. (2002). Advocating for first-year students: A study of the micropolitics of leadership and organizational change. *Journal of The First-Year Experience & Students in Transition, 14*(1), 81-98.
This article profiles the characteristics, strategies, and tactics employed by a group of award-winning campus leaders who were effective change agents on behalf of first-year students. The authors administered a survey to recipients of the "Outstanding First-Year Student Advocate Award," conferred annually by the National Resource Center for The First-Year Experience and Students in Transition. Responses to open-ended survey items indicated that presidential support, professional staff support, and the advocates' own persistence were critical to program success while faculty obstacles and, to a lesser extent, administrative staff obstacles were challenges to the success of first-year programs. Survey respondents also identified the ability to "play politics," work across boundaries, be persistent, and have a well-articulated game plan as the most critical elements of the advocacy process. The authors conclude that the decentralized nature of college campuses and their vague boundaries of responsibility require a postmodern leadership style for successful advocacy. Characteristics of postmodern leadership include

tolerating ambiguity, preferring process over prescription, having a sense of mission, creating a shared vision, learning from mistakes, and facilitating leadership in others. These findings lay the groundwork for more effective institutional advocacy for first-year programs as well as provide exploratory findings for future research on leadership and change in the first-year experience movement.

KEY WORDS: advocacy, leadership.

Kuh, G. D., Kinzie, J., Schuh, J. H., Whitt, E. J., & Associates. (2005). Shared responsibility for educational quality and student success. In *Student success in college: Creating conditions that matter* (pp. 157-172). San Francisco: Jossey-Bass.

This book presents the findings of the Documenting Effective Educational Practice (DEEP) project, a research initiative of the National Survey of Student Engagement (NSSE) and the American Association for Higher Education. The researchers conducted in-depth case studies of 20 institutions identified as having higher than predicted levels of student engagement (based on NSSE scores) and higher than predicted graduation rates, after adjusting for institutional and student characteristics. The institutions were diverse in terms of size, geographic region, Carnegie classification, and mission. This chapter focuses on one of six conditions common to educationally effective institutions: shared responsibility for educational quality and student success. The researchers assert that such an ethos must begin at the top with the senior leadership and permeate to faculty, student affairs professionals, staff, and students. They provide specific examples of how these various campus stakeholders work collaboratively to support students at these 20 institutions.

KEY WORDS: collaboration, engagement, student success.

Gallagher, D. J., & Allen, N. (2000). First-year initiatives and results of a year-long advising pilot study: A proposed advising model. *Journal of The First Year Experience & Students in Transition, 12*(2), 107-128.

Expectations and advising experiences of 140 first-year students at a college in Philadelphia with a full-time enrollment of 1,200 were measured over the course of one year. Through the administration of a pretest, periodic meetings with advisees, and administration of a posttest survey, the study explored the relationship between expectations of advising and the advising experience. Findings from the study indicated that expectations for advising were high and possibly not realistic. Analysis of the data also suggested the gap between expectation and experience resulted in dissatisfaction, particularly when students perceived advisors as being unavailable. Investigators suggested that students would be more satisfied knowing when advisors were available through posted office hours and e-mail. Finally, the study was used to offer suggestions for an advising model that involved emphasizing developmental rather than prescriptive advising, training advisors, recognizing and rewarding faculty for their work as advisors, and involving advisors in instruction of first-year seminars.

KEY WORDS: academic advising, student expectations, student satisfaction.

Smith, J. S., (2002). First-year student perceptions of academic advisement: A qualitative study and reality check. *The Journal of the National Academic Advising Association, 22*(2), 39-49.

The author of this article reports on a study that used qualitative data from 34 first-year students at the University of Albany to examine new students' perceptions of the role of an academic advisor, their preferences for type of academic advisement, and students' advisement experiences. Analyses of student feedback gathered from focus group discussions revealed that first-year students at this university expected and preferred prescriptive advising over developmental advising techniques. Students also likened the role of the academic advisor to their high school guidance counselor and thus expected

that college advisors would merely hand them a course schedule or steer them toward classes that were considered easy. However, despite an overwhelmingly utilitarian view of the role of college advisors, the students indicated that some of their most meaningful and memorable experiences with academic advisors during their first year were more developmental in nature. Findings from this study highlight the complexity of first-year student preferences for and experiences with different types of academic advising. These results provide information to advisors working with new students and offer insights into how to anticipate first-year student expectations for prescriptive advising and how to integrate developmental components into this advising.
KEY WORDS: academic advising, assessment.

Parents and Family Members

Daniel, B. V., & Scott, B. R. (Eds.). (2001). *Consumers, adversaries, and partners: Working with the families of undergraduates,* (New Directions for Student Services No. 94). San Francisco: Jossey Bass.

The purpose of this edited volume is to help college administrators develop a cohesive approach to creating and sustaining programs, services, and lines of communication between an institution and the families of that institution's students. Family expectations about this relationship are established at orientation and during the first year and last throughout the students' college careers. The first chapter explores how a new generation of families views higher education in a postmodern society and post-in loco parentis era. Other chapters establish ideals for working with families of college students in a number of areas including admissions, financial aid, orientation, residence life, legal issues, and institutional advancement. A presidential perspective on the relationship between institution and families is also offered. The final chapter summarizes the volume and provides a review of other resources on the topic. The ultimate aim of institutional work with families is to create productive learning experiences for the students during the first year and beyond.
KEY WORDS: orientation, parents, student services.

Elkins, S. A., Braxton, J. M., & James, G. W. (2000). **Tinto's separation stage and its influence on first-semester college student persistence.** *Research in Higher Education, 41*(2), 251-268.

This study examined the persistence of first-year students at a public, four-year institution. The researchers used Tinto's construct of separation from his interactionist theory of student departure as a framework. The Cooperative Institutional Research Program's Student Information Form was used to collect background information on the participants. The First Semester Collegiate Experiences Survey, which involves items derived from Tinto's notion of separation, was administered at the midpoint of the fall semester. Enrollment data were collected from the 411 respondents who completed both surveys. The researchers learned that support from family and friends in the students' previous communities was the most important factor in students' decisions to attend and remain in college. Members of racial/ethnic minority groups, students with lower levels of high school achievement, and those with parents in lower income brackets received less support. For students who did not receive this support, their ability to reject the attitudes and values of their past communities led to greater persistence. The researchers concluded that first-semester students who are able to successfully negotiate the separation stage are more likely to persist to their second semester. They also determined that Tinto's construct of separation is valid and recommend that higher education professionals work to involve family members in assisting students with negotiating the separation process. They suggest systematic communication with parents, as well as creation of programs that bring prospective students and their families to campus, especially for first-generation college students. Finally, they stress the importance of social and academic support to students, residence hall and student activities initiatives, and early warning systems that use absenteeism or low grades as a catalyst for outreach.

KEY WORDS: parental involvement, retention theory, social support.

Hickman, G. P., & Crossland, G. L. (2004-5). The predictive nature of humor, authoritative parenting style, and academic achievement on indices of initial adjustment and commitment to college among college freshmen. *Journal of College Student Retention: Research, Theory & Practice, 6*(2), 225-245.

This study examined the coping role of humor and familial factors in the academic achievement and adjustment of first-year college students at a large midwestern university. Self-report data were collected from 257 first-quarter students during their eighth week of college. These data included information on student demographics, family structure, birth order, college grade point average, student adjustment (via the Student Adaptation to College Questionnaire), use of humor (via the Coping Humor Scale), and parenting style (via the Parental Authority Questionnaire). The researchers learned that use of humor was an important factor in college adjustment for students of both genders, and for males in particular. Though birth order and family structure did not have a significant impact on adjustment, authoritative parenting styles of both mothers and fathers significantly predicted successful adjustment. The authors suggest that teaching faculty how to incorporate humor into instruction and encouraging students to use humor to cope with stress could help promote academic achievement and success. They also suggest that involving parents in the ongoing orientation of new students, both prior to and after they enroll, could ease student adjustment and increase persistence.

KEY WORDS: assessment, college adjustment, humor, parents, persistence, stress.

Hickman, G. P., Toews, M. L., & Andrews, D. W. (2001). The differential influence of authoritative parenting on the initial adjustment of male and female traditional college freshmen. *Journal of The First-Year Experience & Students in Transition, 13*(1), 23-46.

This study examined the relationship between gender, authoritative parenting style, aptitude, self-esteem, academic achievement, and adjustment for traditional-age first-year college students. Self-report data were collected from a sample of 101 first-year students at a large midwestern university. The researchers learned that an authoritative parenting style impacts the initial academic achievement (i.e., first-semester grade point average) of men, but not women. The data also revealed that aptitude was not correlated with self-reported initial academic achievement, self-esteem, or adjustment for students of either gender. The study also indicated that self-esteem was highly correlated with adjustment for both men and women and that male students' initial academic achievement was moderately correlated with overall initial college adjustment, regardless of parenting style, aptitude, and self-esteem. These same results were not found for female students. The authors recommend creation of programs and services to boost self-esteem of new students, since this factor appears closely related to adjustment. They also stress the importance of recognizing gender differences when designing services to promote student adjustment and success.

KEY WORDS: college adjustment, gender differences, parental involvement.

Hickman, G. P., Bartholomae, S., & McKenry, P. C. (2000). Influence of parenting styles on the adjustment and academic achievement of traditional college freshmen. *Journal of College Student Development, 41*(1), 41-54.

The purpose of this research was to examine the relationship between parenting style (authoritarian, authoritative, or permissive) and academic achievement, institutional commitment, and academic, social, and personal/emotional adjustment during the first year of college. The sample included 101 traditional-age first-year students at a large midwestern university who completed the Quick Word Test (a measure of general aptitude), the Rosenberg Self-Esteem Inventory, the Parental Authority Questionnaire, and the Student Adaptation to College Questionnaire. Descriptive and multivariate analyses using ordinary least square regression indicated that parenting had a statistically significant influence on only one of the outcome measures: a positive impact on academic adjustment. Further, contrary to the authors' hypotheses, results indicated that students from divorced families have higher levels of adjustment to college. Other results indicated that aptitude does not predict academic performance or institutional adjustment; parental education was a predictor of students' adjustment to college; and self-esteem was the most consistent predictor of all measures of adjustment to college. These findings provide important information for academic and student affairs educators linking student family environments and structures with academic adjustment as part of first-year programming.
KEY WORDS: academic achievement, assessment, college adjustment, parents.

Keppler, K., Mullendore, R. H., & Carey, A. (Eds.). (2005). *Partnering with the parents of today's college students.* Washington, DC: National Association of Student Personnel Administrators.
This volume contains seven articles focused on ways to promote student success through collaboration with parents. Topics include changing demographics and increasing diversity in higher education, parent orientation programs, legal issues, and managing parental expectations. The book includes an annotated bibliography for parents and educators. The appendices include practical information, such as model parent programs, activities, and related materials.
KEY WORDS: orientation, parents.

Nora, A. (2001). The depiction of significant others in Tinto's "Rites of Passage": A reconceptualization of the importance of family and community in the persistence process. *Journal of College Student Retention: Research, Theory & Practice, 3,* 41-56.
This article is a theoretical examination of the interrelation of the three rites of passage in Tinto's Student Integration Model: separation, transition, and incorporation. After a review of Tinto's model, the author summarizes previous research on the role of support systems in students' transition to college. The author draws five major conclusions from these studies. First, encouragement and support can ease the transition to college. Second, different sources of encouragement, including family, friends, faculty, and academic staff are critical in students' transition to college. Third, support and encouragement from various sources influences academic and social experiences and integration during the three stages of transition. Fourth, students' commitment to their institutions and the goal of attaining a degree at those colleges are both directly and indirectly influenced by their support systems. Finally, in addition to the components of Tinto's theoretical framework (e.g., precollege characteristics, integration, institutional commitment) students' persistence is influenced by their perceived support system from the moment they enter college. In sum, the author uses previous research to highlight the critical role of college faculty and staff as a complement to the role of family and friends in the support structure for students. This support structure is established during the student's first year and carries them through their entire college career.
KEY WORDS: faculty, retention, transition to college.

Schwartz, J. P., & Buboltz, Jr., W. C. (2004). The relationship between attachment to parents and psychological separation in college students. *Journal of College Student Development, 45*(5), 566-577.

This study investigates the relationship between attachment to parents and psychological separation in college students. The researchers used two surveys, the Inventory of Parent and Peer Attachment and the Psychological Separation Inventory, to collect data from 241 female undergraduates (30% were first-year students) and 127 male students (42% were first-year students) at a medium-sized public university in the South. These data were analyzed using two correlation analyses, one for men and one for women, which indicated that there is a connection between attachment and psychological separation from parents for both men and women. The association between attachment and psychological separation with fathers accounted for the most variance for both genders. Further, the results indicate that a successful balance between attachment and separation may include conflict with both parents as students forge an independent identity in college. The results of this study indicate the importance of counseling and programming for first-year students that assists them in separation from their parents and highlights the importance of efforts to work with parents during orientation and perhaps throughout the first year to assist their children in the transition to college.

KEY WORDS: college adjustment, parents, transition to college.

Sessa, F. M. (2005). The influence of perceived parenting on substance use during the transition to college: A comparison of male residential and commuter students. *Journal of College Student Development, 46*(1), 62-74.

This study offers a comparison of the experiences of commuter and residential students by focusing on the influence of the perceived parent-child relationship on the use of alcohol and marijuana. The researcher collected survey data from 50 residential and 57 commuter male college students who were an average of 18.5 years old and were attending two different baccalaureate-granting institutions in the same general region of a mid-Atlantic state. Demographic comparisons of the two student groups revealed no statistically significant differences. Results of descriptive analyses and MANOVAs yielded three main findings. First, residential and commuter first-year men had different patterns of substance use. Residential students used alcohol more frequently than commuter students, while commuter students reported more frequent use of marijuana than their residential peers. Second, residential and commuter first-year students in the sample have different relationships with their parents. Specifically, residential students in the study felt that their parents monitored their behavior more than commuter students did and that their parents were less encouraging of their independence. Finally, these results indicate that the effect of perceived parenting on substance use is significant for commuter college students but not for residential first-year male students in this study. This study highlights the importance of recognizing the diversity of first-year student experiences, particularly with respect to patterns of substance use and parental influence. These findings can be used to inform orientation and first-year intervention programs for both students and parents.

KEY WORDS: commuter students, parental involvement, substance abuse.

Torres, V. (2004). Familial influences on the identity development of Latino first-year students. *Journal of College Student Development 45*(4), 457-468.

This article expands upon previous work in the area of "situating identity" by exploring the impact of a construct called "Generation in the United States and Familial Influences" in the expression and development of ethnic identity of Latino first-year students. The study used theoretical sampling as part of a constructivist grounded theory methodology to select 83 self-identified Latino first-year students at seven institutions to participate in interviews. Analyses of data collected from these participants

identified three new issues to consider within the "Familial Influence and Generational Status in the U.S." construct. First, specific contexts (e.g., living near the Mexican-American border) may cause a student to choose a self-identifier that confounds their country of origin (i.e., the United States or Mexico) with their cultural heritage (e.g., Hispanic, Latino, Chicano), which make it challenging to understand fully a student's contextual experiences. Second, first-year students from Latino enclaves, particularly women, may appear acculturated to the United States but actually experience a variety of cultural conflicts with the college environment. Finally, students who come from mixed backgrounds or who are adopted by White parents are blending into the overall environment of their colleges but may have ethnic/racial identity issues that are not being fully addressed. This article provides information on the variety of cultural and familial influences for first-year Latino students so that college faculty, staff, and administrators may support these students and their families in their transition to college.
KEY WORDS: Latino students, racial/ethnic identity development.

Peer Influence, Interaction, and Training

Brissette, I., Scheier, M. F., & Carver, C. S. (2002). The role of optimism in social network development, coping, and psychological adjustment during life transition. *Journal of Personality and Social Psychology, 82*(1), 102-111.
The purpose of this research was to examine the relationship between optimism, social support, coping, and psychological adjustment during the transition to college. First-year students ($N = 89$) completed baseline and follow-up questionnaires at the beginning and end of the fall semester. The researchers found that optimism was related to greater increases in social support and more successful adjustment during the first college semester. Optimism was impacted by perceived support from on-campus, rather than off-campus, sources. The on-campus support tended to come from quality peer relationships as opposed to large friendship networks. Educators can use these findings to inform creation of opportunities for students to make quality, on-campus connections with peers as a means of promoting a more successful transition.
KEY WORDS: college adjustment, peer support, student optimism.

Coffman, D. L., & Gilligan, T. D. (2002). Social support, stress, and self-efficacy: Effects on students' satisfaction. *Journal of College Student Retention: Research, Theory & Practice, 4*(1), 53-6.
This research studied the impact of perceived stress, self-efficacy, and social support on life satisfaction among 94 first-year college students at a southeastern university. The Satisfaction With Life Scale, Support Evaluation List, the Perceived Stress Scale, and the College Self-Efficacy Inventory were used to measure the variables. The data revealed that higher levels of social support and self-efficacy and lower levels of perceived stress were related to higher levels of life satisfaction. Social support provided the largest contribution to life satisfaction. The researchers recommend that first-year student orientation programs, residence life programming, and classroom assignments be designed to promote social interaction, which can lead to increased peer support for students.
KEY WORDS: assessment, self-efficacy, social support, student satisfaction.

Crissman Ishler, J. L. (2002). First-year female students: Perceptions of friendsickness. *Journal of The First Year Experience & Students in Transition, 14,* 89-104.

This researcher examined the journal entries of first-year students to assess their level of friendsickness (the challenges students face letting go of precollege friendships) during their first year of college. The 96 participants (84 women, 12 men) wrote the entries as an assignment for a first-year seminar class. Key themes from the first semester included a reluctance to make new friends for fear of betraying old friendships, the amount of time spent keeping in touch with friends from home, feeling left out of activities with their old friends, and the use of the journal to explore friendsickness. Second semester themes included an acknowledgement of their overreaction to homesickness and friendsickness, an appreciation for their new college friends, and concerns over leaving their new college friends when they go home for the summer. The author concluded that students' precollege and college friendships impact their adjustment to college. She asserted that the use of journal writing in first-year seminars can be an effective way for students to work through feelings and experiences through self-reflection and metacognition. Group discussions on these topics can also help students to realize they are not alone and that other students have similar feelings of friendsickness. Such discussions might even foster social connections through shared experiences. Though there were fewer men than women in this sample, the male students were just as likely as the women to discuss feelings of friendsickness. The author stresses the importance of supporting both male and female students as they work to let go of precollege friendships and develop new social connections.
KEY WORDS: college adjustment, first-year seminars, friendship.

Donahue, L. (2004). Connections and reflections: Creating a positive learning environment for first-year students. *Journal of The First Year Experience & Students in Transition, 16*(1), 77-100.

This researcher used end-of-semester reflection essays from first-year seminars to analyze first-year students' perceptions of their learning environments and the aspects of their experiences that facilitated or impeded their learning process. Qualitative data analysis was conducted on 138 student essays randomly selected from all 522 students who completed the first-year seminar at a small liberal arts institution. This analytical process focused on what students perceived they needed in order to feel connected with the campus community and to have effective curricular and cocurricular learning experiences. The data revealed that interpersonal relationships were the key to a positive learning environment and to the students' feeling connected to the campus community. Students identified faculty as important, but interaction with peers both inside and outside the classroom also was considered necessary for academic growth. Small classroom size and interactive pedagogy were identified as strategies that effectively enhanced these interactions. Few students saw their growth and learning potential enhanced by cocurricular experiences, such as those available through residential life. While interconnectedness appeared to be the key element of a positive learning experience, students also recognized that college was a time for them to assume responsibility for their own learning and development. The results of this study identify and validate the role of campus community in the success of first-year students.
KEY WORDS: first-year seminars, learning, peer support, sense of belonging, student-faculty interaction.

Hoffman, M., Richmond, J., Morrow, J., & Salomone, K. (2002-3). Investigating "sense of belonging" in first-year college students. *Journal of College Student Retention: Research, Theory & Practice, 4*(3), 227-256.

The purpose of this study was to develop, test, and refine an instrument to measure students' sense of belonging in relation to persistence in college. The researchers first conducted focus groups with students enrolled in a university first-year seminar course to assess factors related to a sense of belonging, or perception of fit between the student and the institution. Some seminar students were part of a learning community cluster of courses linked by academic content; others were a heterogeneous population of students. The researchers found that the learning community students were more successful than the non-learning community students at forming new friendships. Specifically, the learning community students were able to establish relationships with peers around academic matters. Furthermore, though both learning community and non-learning community students found their faculty to be friendly and approachable, the learning community students responded with greater intensity. The researchers also administered a pre-test to 205 first-year college students to further refine the main conceptual dimensions of a sense of belonging. They identified five underlying dimensions for the resulting Sense of Belonging (SB) instrument: (a) Perceived Peer Support, (b) Perceived Faculty Support/Comfort, (c) Perceived Classroom Comfort, (d) Perceived Isolation, and (e) Empathetic Faculty Understanding. Data analysis revealed that students in learning communities scored significantly better on all five factors of the SB instrument than students in stand-alone seminar courses. The authors assert that learning community students were better able to form helpful connections around a common agenda and similar challenges. The researchers suggest that sense of belonging stems from students' perceptions of "valued involvement" in the college setting, which is enhanced by establishing supportive peer relationships and by the belief that faculty are compassionate and see students as more than a number. They also conclude that their Sense of Belonging instrument is a useful tool for further understanding factors that contribute to student persistence.

KEY WORDS: *assessment, first-year seminars, learning communities, peer support, sense of belonging.*

Maher, M. A. (2004, July/August). **What really happens in cohorts.** *About Campus, 9,* 18-23.

This article offers a research-based definition of cohorts, identifies their primary characteristics, reviews their history, and summarizes their documented learning outcomes, including affective development, group cohesion, community development, leadership development, and rich dialogue among students. The author also shares findings from a yearlong qualitative study of a cohort of graduate students in an education program. Analysis of the data indicated that cohorts demand a sense of investment and community building among both faculty and students that is far greater than other course structures and that these structures typically require adjustment in modes of teaching and learning. The study also indicated that these structures tend to create a strong sense of cohort agency, which can result in the interests of the collective overriding those of the individual, particularly in times of duress. Other research on cohorts and observations of the education students involved in the study indicate that groupthink and collusion may emerge as a potentially negative outcome of the cohort format. Students in the cohort studied also appeared to adopt individual roles (e.g., organizer, tension breaker) that fulfilled interpersonal needs of the cohort. Findings of this study are important for faculty considering teaching in a cohort and for students exploring participation in a cohort. While students in the first year of college were not the focus of this study, the author suggests that lessons are applicable to other populations, including first-year students in learning communities.

KEY WORDS: *cohorts, group development, learning communities.*

Paul, E. L., & Brier, S. (2001). **Friendsickness in the transition to college: Precollege predictors and college adjustment correlates.** *Journal of Counseling and Development, 79,* 77-89.

This study examined relationships among "friendsickness" (a preoccupation with a change in or loss of precollege friendships), precollege predictors, and dimensions of college adjustment. The participants, 70 first-year college students (52 women and 18 men), were mailed questionnaires in July and again 10 weeks into their first semester of college. The instruments assessed precollege concerns, discrepancies between precollege expectations and college experiences, and students' level of "friendsickness." The researchers found that more than half the participants (51%) experienced moderate to high levels of "friendsickness." Furthermore, students who were highly concerned about precollege friendships demonstrated poorer college adjustment along a number of dimensions. The researchers conclude that

"friendsickness" is a normal social challenge that students experience as they transition to college. However, students who are more focused on making new college friends than maintaining precollege friendships are less likely to experience "friendsickness" and more likely to have a successful adjustment process. The authors stress the importance of allaying students' precollege social concerns and helping them develop realistic social expectations for college. They recommend that institutions facilitate the development of student social networks before college begins through interventions such as precollege programs, discussion lists, or chat rooms. The researchers also suggest that programming just after Thanksgiving break (often the first prolonged visit home) can be a good time to decrease grief over diminished precollege friendships and foster building and strengthening of new relationships.
KEY WORDS: college adjustment, friends, social support.

Potts, G., Schultz, B., & Foust, J. (2003-4). The effect of freshman cohort groups on academic performance and retention. *Journal of College Student Retention: Research, Theory & Practice,* **5(4), 385-395.**

This study examined the impact of placing students in first-year learning communities at the University of Wisconsin-River Falls (UWRF). The sample for the study included 308 first-year students who entered the university in fall 1998. The researchers performed *t*-tests and ANOVAs to compare grade point averages among business major cohorts, psychology major cohorts, a nonmajor cohort, and a control group, as well as one-semester and seven-semester retention rates for the four groups. While other elements of students' first-year experiences influence retention and grade point averages, participation in the learning community cohorts did not have an influence on grades or either measure of retention. The authors posit that more intensive institutional intervention may be necessary and note that the cohort structure of learning communities at UWRF has since been supplemented with a first-year seminar for students in the major.
KEY WORDS: academic performance, first-year seminars, learning communities, retention.

Thomas, S. L. (2000). A social network approach to understanding student integration and persistence. *The Journal of Higher Education, 71*(5), 591-615.

This work studied the relationship between social integration (students' sense of connectedness with their peers) and persistence. One week prior to the beginning of the fall semester, 322 first-year students completed the Freshman Summer Survey, which assessed students' commitment to educational goals, confidence in their choice of college, and expectations for their first year. The same population completed the First-Year Experiences Survey (FYES) toward the end of their second semester. This survey was designed to assess students' social integration through their social networks and capture aspects of their college experiences to that point. The researchers concluded that students with a greater number of social connections outside their immediate peer groups tend to perform better academically and persist at higher rates. The same held true for students who developed relationships with those who had broad social ties. The implication is that students with greater social connectedness have broader access to academic and social resources that might promote their success in college. The author advocates creation of activities and residential situations that foster a sense of belonging and connectedness among students and "enhance cross-clique diversity." He also cautioned that there is an optimal size for social networks, and too much connectedness can detract from a student's academic performance.
KEY WORDS: peer support, retention, social integration.

Walker, S. C., & Taub, D. J. (2001). Mentoring relationship in first-year college students and their mentors. *Journal of The First-Year Experience & Students in Transition, 13*(1), 47-68.

The purpose of this research was to examine the impact of different mentoring relationship structures on the satisfaction of first-year college students. The 97 study participants were all part of a mentor program; 61 were first-year student mentees and 36 were upperclass mentors and network facilitators. The participants were randomly assigned to one of two mentoring conditions: one involved a dyadic mentor/mentee pairing; the other involved a small group of students (four to six) matched with one or two network facilitators. The mentoring program involved monthly programs and monthly contact between mentees and their mentors/network facilitators. Questionnaires collected in March from 62 participants assessed mentor/mentee satisfaction, frequency of contact, and degree of match. The researchers learned that there was no significant difference in satisfaction for those involved in a one-on-one mentoring relationship versus a network. Frequency of contact was related to satisfaction in both mentoring structures. There was no significant relationship between similarity of demographic variables and mentee satisfaction. Educators should consider using the network mentoring structure to support incoming students since they could serve greater numbers of students using fewer human resources. In addition, the authors contend that face-to-face contact is not the only means to connect with mentees in order to promote their satisfaction; frequent telephone and e-mail contact can also be effective.

KEY WORDS: mentoring, student satisfaction.

{ PART IV }

Other Aspects of the First-Year Experience

{ INTRODUCTORY OVERVIEW }

Part IV of this monograph consists of three subsections: (a) Access to College, (b) the First-Year Experience at Two-Year Institutions, and (c) The First-Year Experience at Specific Types of Four-Year Colleges & Universities. While the headings of these three subsections are relatively self-explanatory, we nevertheless provide some information to help readers place the content in the context of higher education in general and the previous edition of the publication.

Updates and Additions

We include Access to College subsection in this part of the monograph because access must be a concern for all institutions, regardless of type. This subsection serves as a replacement for the Financial Implications section found in the third edition of the monograph, with the current version focusing more on policy than the section it replaces.

The First-Year Experience at Two-Year Institutions includes annotations for sources that address the first-year experience at America's two-year colleges. This revised and updated subsection provides valuable insight into supporting first-year students at two-year institutions.

The First-Year Experience at Specific Types of Four-Year Colleges & Universities subsection is a new addition. It exists, at least in part, because of increasing attention being paid to the first-year experience by a variety of types of four-year colleges and universities such as, but not limited to, research institutions, tribal colleges, and historically Black colleges and universities. Sources included in this section reveal that despite obvious differences in these types of institutions, there are common elements in the approaches they use to the first-year experience. This should not be surprising, and on some level comforting, given the pluralistic context in which they all exist.

Ackerman, R., Young, M., & Young, R. (2005). A state-supported, merit-based scholarship program that works. *Journal of Student Financial Aid, 35*(3), 21-34.

This study examined five years of data collected on the merit-based Millennium Scholars Program in Nevada. The program, in existence since 2000, was created to increase the level of college attendance in the state. At the time the program was created, there was no limitation on the number of participants, and the criteria to continue to receive funding after the first year involved completing at least six college credit hours with a 2.0 or higher grade point average. The data collected indicated an increase in the number of Nevada high school students who decided to pursue higher education in the state following the implementation of the program. Further, the data suggested that the proportion of students attending college in- versus out-of-state shifted, with more students who may have previously chosen to leave the state staying to attend college. To measure the levels of academic preparedness of the students attending college in Nevada, the researchers examined the number of students receiving the Millennium scholarship who required remedial coursework. The number of students in this group who took remedial courses was lower than peers not in the scholarship group. In addition to the aforementioned data, the researchers also examined the impact the scholarship program had on high schools and student persistence.

KEY WORDS: financial aid, scholarship programs.

Cabrera, A. F., & La Nasa, S. M. (2001). On the path to college: Three critical tasks facing America's disadvantaged. *Research in Higher Education, 42*(2), 119-149.

Drawing on data collected through the National Education Longitudinal Study of 1988 (NELS, 1988), this study examined academic preparedness and overall college readiness of students who had lower socioeconomic status. The researchers in the study culled several variables they believed affected student preparedness, including socioeconomic status, at-risk factors (e.g., family dropouts, grades leading up to high school), parental involvement, high school support, and plans to attend college. The findings from the study identified several preparedness variables that the researchers categorized. The first of three categories, Parental Education and At-Risk Factors, suggested that level of parental education and other risk factors, such as academic performance leading up to high school, repeating a grade, being raised by a single-parent, and changing schools, contribute to the readiness of students to go to college. These characteristics were found to be more common among students of lower socioeconomic status. In addition to these risk factors, the study also suggested that fulfilling college qualifications and early planning for higher education (e.g., in middle school), as well as encouragement and parental and familial involvement with activities contribute to the likelihood of these students pursuing higher education. In the final category, Applying to College, the researchers found that students of lower socioeconomic status were less likely to complete college applications, although the students in this group did talk to counselors more about financial aid. Students who reported expectations about higher education and earning a degree were more likely to apply to college and those students who applied to college had greater parental and familial support than those who did not apply.

KEY WORDS: academic preparation, parental involvement, socioeconomic status.

Chenoweth, K. (1998). The College Board decries preparation gap. *Black Issues in Higher Education, 15*(15), 24.

This article examines differences of academic preparation among several first-year student populations. Drawing on data collected from the SAT, the findings indicated a gap between the SAT scores for students in suburban environments and those living in more rural or even urban areas. These data reflected the average test scores of 40-50% of the African American and Latino student population who had taken the SAT at the time the data were collected. In addition to the gap in SAT scores, the article also indicates some disparity between the number of AP offerings in the suburbs and in the more urban or rural areas and student populations enrolling in AP courses. The article suggests more effort be made to create additional opportunities for access to AP courses and exams through subsidization and allowing students to take these courses regardless of PSAT scores.

KEY WORDS: academic preparation, African American students, Latino students, standardized tests.

Heller, D. E. (Ed.). (2001). *The states and public higher education policy: Affordability, access and accountability.* **Baltimore: Johns Hopkins Press.**

This brief edited volume addresses affordability, access, and accountability as they relate to the current state of higher education. The book's three parts address (a) the increasing cost of education, reasons behind tuition growth, and a discussion of state and federal policies towards higher education funding; (b) strategies for refinancing higher education and the impact of court decisions (e.g., the Hopwood discrimination case in Texas) and state laws (e.g., California Proposition 209) on educational outcomes; and (c) strategies for reconciling the downward trends in access and affordability. Historical lessons presented in the first two thirds of the book and recommendations for change and outcomes in the latter third all have implications for the first year of college. Examples of programs in such states as Florida and New York demonstrate how different approaches have led to some preliminary increases in access to and affordability of college. Those with influence on institutional policy surrounding cost and access and those working to increase access and affordability of college education can use this text to better understand the impact their work can have on students and the academy.

KEY WORDS: access to higher education, college costs, policy.

Hu, S., & Hossler, D. (2000). Willingness to pay and preference for private institutions. *Research in Higher Education, 41*(6), 685-701.

This study examined student preference for private or public colleges and universities, with particular attention to the impact of tuition costs and availability of financial aid and ability (or willingness) to pay on those preferences. Researchers gathered survey data from 482 12th grade students in Indiana high schools who indicated an intention to pursue higher education. Findings from the study indicated that family characteristics (e.g., mother's education), as well as level of academic preparation, and financial situation influenced college choice. Further, the students were more likely to choose a private institution or indicate a preference for this when they had greater academic preparation in high school. The same was true for students whose mothers had attained a degree. To better understand how these factors are related to the cost of education, the authors suggest future research in the area of student response to tuition costs.

KEY WORDS: financial aid, private institutions.

Kim, D. (2004). The effect of financial aid on students' college choice: Differences by racial groups. *Research in Higher Education, 45*(1), 43-70.

Drawing from data collected through the administration of the 1994 Freshman Survey, the researcher examined the impact of financial aid on college choice. The sample included 5,136 students from four-year institutions; of that number, 3,391 were attending their first-choice institution and 1,183 were attending an institution other than their first-choice. From the sample, 1,300 students did not receive any form of financial aid. Findings from the study indicated differences in the effect financial aid has on the college choice of various student populations. For example, the researcher found that White students attended first-choice institutions when they received grants. Asian American students tended to attend first-choice institutions when they received monetary support from the institution; however, this was not the case with African American or Latino students. African American and Latino students' decision to attend a first-choice institution was more often influenced by background factors (e.g., high school achievement and family support and income) than by financial aid alone. The researcher posits that these students are less familiar with the benefits associated with attending a first-choice institution, and in this study some of those benefits included greater likelihood of earning a degree and greater levels of satisfaction with the overall college experience. Finally, the researcher suggests that consideration of the various effects financial aid has on college choice for different student populations is important.

KEY WORDS: access to higher education, college choice, financial aid, students of color.

Mortenson, T. G. (2005, September). *College affordability trends by parental income levels and institutional type 1990 to 2004* **(Postsecondary Education Opportunity Issue No. 159). Oskaloosa, IA: The Pell Institute for the Study of Opportunity in Higher Education.**

This report indicates that because the cost of education has outpaced parents' inflation-adjusted incomes, a growing number of undergraduates has been forced to shift their postsecondary enrollment to less costly institutions. An analysis of data from the National Center for Education Statistics' National Postsecondary Student Aid Studies from 1990 to 2004 findings show that students from high-income families have noticeably more financial aid resources at their disposal than students from low-income backgrounds. As a result, increasing numbers of low-income students are enrolling at cost-efficient community colleges. The implications of these findings are particularly important to educators at two-year institutions, who, by default, are more likely to work with low-income (and less-prepared) students who increasingly constitute the first-year class.

KEY WORDS: access to higher education, low-income students, two-year institutions.

Smith, J. S., & Wertlieb, E. C. (2005). Do first-year college students' expectations align with their first-year experiences? *NASPA Journal, 42*(2), 153-174.

Using expectancy-value theory and ecological theory as frameworks, this study investigates the alignment between academic and social expectations and first-year experiences of college students. The researchers also explore the potential relationships between expectations, experiences, and academic achievement. By administering a survey to 31 new prebusiness students at a four-year, public university at three points in time (two weeks after college entry, midway through the first year, and at the end of the spring semester), the researchers found that students' first-year experiences do not live up to their precollege expectations. While the findings show more significant decreases for social expectations than for academic ones, they did not indicate a statistically significant impact of unmet social or academic expectations on first-year grade point average. The authors share methodological and practical implications of this work and identify the disparity between expectations and experiences as symptomatic of an overall disconnect between high school and college that educators in both realms should work together to address.

KEY WORDS: academic achievement, Freshman Myth.

St. John, E. P., Chung, C., Musoba, G. D., Simmons, A. B., Wooden, O. S., & Mendez, J. P. (2004, February). *Expanding college access: The impact of state finance strategies.* **Indianapolis, IN: Lumina Foundation for Education.**

The authors of this report provide insight into state-level policies for funding access programs for students attending college. The report includes (a) a review of access studies conducted in the past, (b) a new model for assessing the impact of a state's funding strategy, (c) an analysis of strategies currently employed by states, and (d) program and funding examples. The authors conclude with recommendations for funding access programs for low-income students at the state level.

KEY WORDS: access to higher education, low-income students.

St. John, E. P., Gross, J. P. K., Musoba, G. D., & Chung A. S. (2005, August). *A step toward college success: Assessing attainment among Indiana's twenty-first century scholars.* **(Research Reports). Indianapolis, IN: Lumina Foundation for Education.**

A follow-up to the 2002 study, Meeting the Access Challenge: Indiana's Twenty-First Century Scholars Program, this report reveals that participation in Indiana's Twenty-First Century Scholars Program increases the odds that low-income students will enroll and succeed in college. The study indicates that Twenty-First Century Scholars are substantially more likely to enroll in college, are more likely to earn two-year degrees, are more likely to persist in college, and are no less likely to earn four-year degrees than their non-participating low-income peers. The findings suggest that precollege preparation combined with financial support enhances the likelihood that low-income students will enroll and succeed in both two- and four-year colleges.

KEY WORDS: access to higher education, low-income students, scholarship programs.

U. S. Census Bureau. (2005). *School enrollment: Social and economic characteristics of students: October, 2003.* **Washington, DC: U.S. Department of Commerce.**

Drawing from data obtained in the October 2003 Current Population Survey (CPS) conducted by the U.S. Census Bureau, this report highlights school enrollment trends of students from nursery school through graduate school as well as the social and economic characteristics of the diverse student population participating in the American education system. Findings with implications for higher education in general and the first year of college in particular include a greater representation of minority populations among high school students, which will increase the racial/ethnic diversity of the pool of college applicants. Greater high school dropout rates among African American and Latino students and students from lower-income families threaten the potential for gains in diversity at the college level. The report also summarizes changes in college enrollments, which increased by more than one million students in a decade. Numbers of traditional-aged students (i.e., 18-24 year olds) continue to grow while the college enrollment of students over the age of 25 has remained relatively constant since 1980. These data also indicate that women continue to outnumber men among college students, two thirds of all college students are enrolled full-time, two thirds of all undergraduates attend four-year institutions, and 60% of college students work at least part-time during college. These data provide a national context for understanding general college enrollment patterns and for identifying potential areas of need among first-year students.

KEY WORDS: enrollment data, national data sets, transition to college.

Young, J. W., & Johnson, P. M. (2004). The impact of an SES-based model on a college's undergraduate admissions outcomes. *Research in Higher Education, 45*(7), 777-797.

Drawing on admissions data from mostly in-state, first-year student applicants to a liberal arts college between 1994 and 1996, the researchers explored differences among three admissions models: original admissions decisions, purely academic, and socioeconomic status (SES), and the impact these models had on the college's admissions. Findings from the study revealed that the SES model, which considered variables such as level of parents' education, family income, and background, yielded more diverse and academically prepared students, who persisted at greater levels than other traditionally admitted students of color.

KEY WORDS: admissions, socioeconomic status.

THE FIRST-YEAR EXPERIENCE AT TWO-YEAR INSTITUTIONS

Bailey, T. R., & Alfonso, M. (2005, January). *Paths to persistence: An analysis of research on program effectiveness at community colleges* (New Agenda Series, Vol. 6, No. 1). Indianapolis, IN: Lumina Foundation for Education.

The authors of this report completed a critical analysis on the effectiveness of community colleges' practices in four areas: (a) advising, counseling, mentoring and orientation programs; (b) learning communities; (c) developmental education and other services for academically underprepared students; and (d) collegewide reform. Key findings suggest that learning communities generally have a strong positive correlation with student retention and graduation. The researchers note that no one form of developmental education, counseling, or advising programs is best at increasing students' ability to succeed in college. All are important to student success. The authors present several suggestions for improving research on community colleges and offer six strategies for fostering a research culture on these campuses.

KEY WORDS: research studies, retention, two-year institutions.

Fabich, M. (Ed.). (2004). *Orientation planning manual.* Flint, MI: National Orientation Directors Association.

This manual includes 10 articles that address the design and implementation of first-year college student orientation programs. Topics included are (a) the connection of orientation and student retention; (b) staff selection and training; (c) developing programs for special populations, transfer students, and families; (d) orientation for two-year institutions; (e) use of technology; and (f) assessment. Half of the volume is composed of appendices, which provide practical resources for orientation planning and implementation. For example, the manual offers an orientation leader job description, application, training syllabus, training schedule, and contract; sample orientation schedules for use at two-year colleges and for working with special populations, transfer students, and families; sample assessment questions; as well as Council for the Advancement of Standards and National Orientation Directors Association standards for orientation programs.

KEY WORDS: CAS standards, diversity, orientation, technology, two-year institutions.

Freer-Weiss, D. (2004-5). Community college freshmen: Last in, first out? *Journal of College Student Retention: Research, Theory & Practice, 6*(2), 137-154.

This study sought to discover the characteristics of late-admission first-time, first-year students who enrolled at an open-access institution. The author examined the relationship between students' date of admission and their subsequent academic success and persistence. Guided by Tinto's (1987) theoretical framework, the researcher examined students' pre-entry attributes, academic abilities, and goals from closed admission files at a two-year metropolitan regional campus. The investigator discovered that students who apply late have different characteristics from those who apply early. For example, students who apply late are less academically successful and are less likely to re-enroll for the next term. The author concluded that a strong relationship exists between a high-risk student profile, late application, and attrition. She suggests that admissions policies be reconsidered to ensure that the needs of all students are met. Earlier admissions dates might provide more time to offer services, such as orientation and advising, that would optimize student success and promote their persistence.

KEY WORDS: academic success, admissions standards, at-risk students, two-year institutions.

Kutnowski, M. (2005, March/April). This is why we teach: Igniting a passion for learning in linked courses. *About Campus 10,* 23-26.

This article explores the teaching and learning that takes place in two linked courses, music appreciation and an art and design course, at Queensborough Community College (NY). Course linkages described in the article were created to help establish a more learning-centered environment and better meet the needs of diverse students. The author describes several methods used to connect the courses, such as creating themes that transcend multiple courses and engaging in common and shared assignments. The author described a successful collaboration between his music appreciation course and the art and design course in which he used two versions of the film, *Metropolis.* Students in both courses were asked to compare the Japanese animated version to the original version released in the 1920s and were encouraged to connect ideas related to the films. The author discusses how personal connections made among students in the learning community increased the openness of classroom discussions and the sharing of diverse opinions. The author describes his enthusiasm for this type of teaching and the shared learning experience that results.

KEY WORDS: clustered/linked courses, learning communities.

Tsao, T. M. (2005). Open admissions, controversies, and CUNY: Digging into social history through a first-year composition course. *The History Teacher, 38*(4), 469-482.

This article traces the development and delivery of a first-year composition course taught at LaGuardia Community College (NY) that used the topic of open admissions as a vehicle for teaching the course content. Using both primary and secondary documents, students analyzed the history of open admissions in the CUNY system in their class assignments and discussions. Based on what they had learned, students expressed deep concern about the relationship between race and educational opportunity—particularly their own opportunities. They also reported a deeper value for the educational opportunities that were available to them.

KEY WORDS: access to higher education, English composition, race/ethnicity.

Weissman, J., Bulakowski, C., & Jumisko, M. (1998). A study of White, Black, and Hispanic students' transition to a community college. *Community College Review, 26*(2), 19-42.

This study draws on data collected from 71 first-year students at the College of Lake County (IL) who participated in focus group sessions, organized by race, with the intent of better understanding their college transition. Academic information about the students who participated in the focus group was obtained from survey data collected in the fall, as well as institutional records. These data were considered in the study, in addition to the focus group data collected in the fall and spring. Findings from the study indicated marked differences among racial groups (White, Black, and Hispanic). Some of the most significant differences between the groups included perceived goals and expectations of the college; Black and Hispanic students indicated college attendance helped fulfill their desire to be a role model for family members and others in their community. The focus group data also suggested that White students had higher academic aspirations, often articulating a desire to earn more advanced degrees, a desire not as commonly reported among the Black and Hispanic students. Additionally, expectations of what the college experience would be like varied from group to group, with the White and Hispanic students indicating that college was more like high school—easier than they had anticipated. Conversely, most of the Black students commented on the difficulty of college overall. Finally, perceptions of the institution differed by racial groups, with Black and Hispanic students indicating that they felt uncomfortable, to some extent, with classroom conversations about racism. They also reported experiencing a level of isolation and loneliness on campus. To combat this, the researchers suggested that more diverse faculty and staff be recruited, in addition to creating mechanisms to help students of color feel greater support on campus.

KEY WORDS: academic aspirations, African American students, focus groups, Latino students, students of color, transition to college.

THE FIRST-YEAR EXPERIENCE AT SPECIFIC TYPES OF FOUR-YEAR COLLEGES AND UNIVERSITIES

Cutright, M. (2002, September/October). What are research universities doing for first-year students? *About Campus, 7,* 16-20.

This study used qualitative data collected by the Policy Center on the First Year of College from more than 75 research universities as part of the project Strengthening First-Year Student Learning at Doctoral/Research-Extensive Universities. The project aimed to determine successful first-year initiatives at these types of institutions. The author identified seven themes common to first-year programs at research universities: (a) the proliferation of first-year programs, (b) first-year initiatives housed in a discipline or college, (c) integration of multiple strategies to support first-year programs, (d) learning communities as a cornerstone of first-year efforts, (e) a re-examination of teaching and learning, (f) strong academic and student affairs partnerships, and (g) intentional assessment and evaluation. These themes and the article's description of best practices provide the foundation for launching or examining first-year programs at research universities.

KEY WORDS: learning communities, research universities.

First-year experience to help students succeed. (2005). *Tribal College, 16*(3), 41-44.

This article offers an overview of the First-Year Experience (FYE) program at the Lummi campus of Northwest Indian College (NWIC). The program is described as a cohort experience (one of the first at a tribal college), focusing on building community through experiential projects and incorporating opportunities to learn more about the perspectives of Native American peoples. Additionally, the FYE course also contains content specific to the seasons. For example, during the winter, students are encouraged to reflect and consider Native American history and communication. Finally, the course also encourages connection to the campus and local community through service-oriented activities and the incorporation of guest speakers from the Native American community.

KEY WORDS: first-year seminars, Native American students, tribal colleges.

Hutto, C. P., & Fenwick, L. T. (2002). *Staying in college: Student services and freshman retention at historically black colleges and universities* (HBCUs). (ERIC Document Reproduction Service No. 468 397)

This study focused on first-year student retention by measuring the perception of quality and accessibility of various student services at three private HBCUs (Historically Black Colleges and Universities). Data were collected from surveys completed by 1,014 first-year students who were surveyed at orientation and specifically measured perceptions about such areas as financial aid, residence life, and academic support. Findings from the study concluded that enrollment management/services and financial aid were the focus of greatest concern among those in the sample. Specifically, students indicated a concern about the financial aid information received before attending the institution, and the level of knowledge counselors had about financial aid and other forms of financial assistance. Other areas measured in the study all indicated some level of satisfaction among the students in the sample. The article concludes that student retention, particularly that of students of color and/or those in lower socioeconomic statuses, are impacted by financial aid and communication about financial resources and options for entering students.

KEY WORDS: enrollment management, financial aid, HBCUs, student satisfaction, students of color, retention.

Mastrodicasa, J. M. (2001, March). *But you teach chemistry, how can you advise me at orientation?* Paper presented at the Annual Conference of the National Association of Student Personnel Administrators, Seattle, WA.

This paper presents a model of using teaching faculty, rather than professional academic advisors, as advisors during the orientation of first-year students at the University of Florida, a large public research university. Through this advising model, the university hoped to promote student-faculty interaction, create connected learning experiences, and personalize the large campus for students. Practically speaking, the model was a means of managing the large influx of students as a result of increased enrollments. The author provides information on the university's Universal Tracking system, which helps to improve advising and guarantees core classes for students. She also provides details about the orientation program, its organizational structure, and the hiring and training of the faculty advisors. Finally, the advantages and challenges of using such an advising model are presented. Assessment of the program revealed that students and families express high levels of satisfaction with the program.

KEY WORDS: academic advising, orientation, student-faculty interaction, student satisfaction.

Ness, J. E. (2002). Crossing the finish line: American Indian completers and non-completers in a tribal college. *Tribal College, 13*(4), 36-40.

This qualitative study examined the reasons why Native American students either completed or did not complete their collegiate programs of study. Thirteen interview participants suggested various societal, programmatic, organizational, and/or personal factors that influenced their decision to finish or abandon their higher education efforts. In addition to providing lists of retention risk factors and characteristics of degree completers germane to Native Americans, the article provides suggestions on policies and directions for future research that merit consideration for faculty and staff seeking ways to enhance the success of Native American students both during and after the first year of college.
KEY WORDS: Native American students, research studies, retention, tribal colleges.

Schwartz, R. A., & Washington, C. M. (2002). Predicting academic performance and retention among African American freshmen men. *NASPA Journal, 39,* 355-370.

This study described in this article sought to identify patterns of academic performance and retention among 229 African American first-year students at Bethel College (a small, private historically Black college located in the South). In the study, several variables (e.g., high school grades, class rank, and SAT scores) were observed for predictive value when coupled with the results of two measures: the Noncognitive Questionnaire Revised (NCQ-R) and the Student Adjustment to College Questionnaire (SACQ). The two questionnaires were used to measure noncognitive variables such as college expectations, self-esteem, and social and institutional adjustment. In addition, researchers also considered the academic performance of the students in the sample during their first year of college using the following dependent variables: grade point average earned in the first semester, academic status (probation), and persistence to the second semester. Findings from the study indicated that high school class rank and grades were most predictive of academic success in the first year of college. Further, when considering retention, the data collected indicated a correlation between high school class rank and social adjustment in college. Finally, the findings also suggested that academic achievement could be predicted by measuring institutional attachment.
KEY WORDS: academic performance, African American students, assessment measures, college adjustment, self-esteem, student expectations.

Walker, A. A. (2003). Learning communities and their effect on students' cognitive abilities. *Journal of The First-Year Experience & Students in Transition, 15*(2), 11-33.

The author investigated the effects of participation in learning communities at a large, public, highly selective research university on the development of students' cognitive abilities. Survey data were collected during orientation and at the end of the first year from 228 students who participated in the learning community program and 247 students who constituted a control group for the study. Four outcome measures—(a) critical thinking ability, (b) analytical thinking and problem solving ability, (c) reading speed and comprehension, and (d) writing skills—were regressed against a series of independent variables including pretests or proxy pretests for the outcome measures, personal and educational background measures, learning community themes, and college experiences potentially related to the outcome measure. Results of these analyses indicated that participation in learning communities was positively associated with all four cognitive outcomes at a statistically significant level. This study provides strong empirical support for the impact of learning communities on cognitive gains during the first year of college.
KEY WORDS: cognitive development, learning communities.

PART V

Transforming the First-Year Experience

{ INTRODUCTORY OVERVIEW }

In this final section, we offer content that either addresses or impacts the transformation of the first-year experience. By transformation, we mean the positive growth and development of students, institutions, and the cultures and communities in which they are situated. This part of the monograph includes five subsections, each examining an aspect of institutional or student transformation through the first-year experience. These subsections include (a) Critical Competencies and Attitudes in the First Year of College (b) Promising Institutional Practices in the First-Year Experience (c) Retention and Success of First-Year Students (d) Reports with Implications for the First-Year Experience, and (e) Assessment and Evaluation.

Updates and Additions

The first two subsections did not exist in the prior version of this monograph. The Critical Competencies and Attitudes in the First Year of College subsection includes sources that examine ways in which changes in student emotional intelligence, motivation, integration, self-efficacy, skills, civic engagement, humanitarianism, and leadership can be measured and/or impacted by first-year programs. The Promising Institutional Practices in the First-Year Experience subsection includes annotations on sources that help answer the question, "What are we presently doing that is measurably improving the first year of college?"

The third, fourth, and fifth subsections provide readers with updated information associated with headings identical to those from the previous edition. These updates are important for understanding how the first-year experience is seen through nationally circulated reports, assessment and evaluation practices, and measurements of retention and success.

CRITICAL COMPETENCIES AND ATTITUDES IN THE FIRST YEAR OF COLLEGE

Bean, J. P., & Eaton, S. B. (2000). A psychological model of student retention. In J. M. Braxton (Ed.), *Reworking the student departure puzzle* (pp. 48-61). Nashville: Vanderbilt University Press.

This chapter presents a psychological model of college student retention, which is different from the more common sociological theories of student departure. The authors first present several existing theories used to help explain student departure decisions, including attitude-behavior theory, coping behavioral theory, self-efficacy theory, and attribution theory. The authors' own theory assumes that students enter college with personal characteristics that are affected by the institutional environment. Students will respond to future situations using psychological assessments of environmental conditions. The successful student will experience positive self-efficacy, reduced stress, and internal locus of control, which can lead to increased academic motivation, social and academic integration, institutional loyalty, and persistence. The authors suggest creation of campus initiatives that promote desired psychological outcomes that result in new student success and persistence.

KEY WORDS: locus of control, motivation, retention, self-efficacy, student success.

Boyd, V. S., Hunt, P. F., Kandell, J. J., & Lucas, M. S. (2003). Relationship between identity processing style and academic success in undergraduate students. *Journal of College Student Development, 44*(2), 155-167.

This study explored the relationship between self-efficacy and identity processing among first-year students through administrations of the Identity Styles Inventory (ISI) and the University New Student Census (UNSC) to 2,818 first-year students during orientation. The researchers posed three questions that guided design of the study: (a) Does identity processing vary by gender or race in first-year students? (b) Is there a relationship between identify processing and self-reported skills and goals? and, (c) What is the connection between identity processing and retention and academic achievement? The findings suggested that students with an identity processing style (32% of the sample) had stronger levels of college preparedness than other students, had a level of self-efficacy that indicated a readiness for college, and had a willingness to receive new information. Students who were normative (lacking interest in exploring or exploration) indicated preparedness for college and tended not to change their advising college or academic major. In the study, 32% of students were normative and 36% of the students were diffused (perceived a lack of college preparedness and parent/family support). The researchers indicated that the latter group included a higher number of Asian American women than some other groups, and although they were included in the diffused group, these students performed well academically. Male students in the diffused group did not perform as well. The study revealed that fewer males in this group were in good academic standing after several semesters and did not persist at the same level as their peers in other categories.

KEY WORDS: assessment measures, identity development, retention, self-efficacy, student success.

Chemers, M. M., Hu, L., & Garcia, B. F. (2001). Academic self-efficacy and first-year college student performance and adjustment. *Journal of Educational Psychology, 93*(1), 55-64.

This longitudinal study examined the impact of academic self-efficacy and optimism on first-year college students' academic performance, stress, health, and commitment to remain in school. Questionnaire data were obtained from 256 first-year students at the University of California, Santa Cruz during the first week of winter quarter and the last week of the spring quarter. The researchers found that self-efficacy and optimism had strong relationships with academic performance and personal adjustment. Further, academic self-efficacy was significantly related to academic expectations, which was, in turn, related to academic performance. That is, students with higher expectations for their academic performance and with greater levels of confidence in themselves performed better academically. In addition, confident and optimistic students were more likely to view college as a challenge rather than a threat; students with a challenge outlook experienced less stress, better health, and greater personal adjustment and satisfaction with college life. Programs and services that increase new students' sense of efficacy and optimism would help to promote a challenge versus threat perspective that could promote their success in college.

KEY WORDS: academic performance, college adjustment, optimism, self-efficacy, stress.

Coffman, D. L., & Gilligan, T. D. (2002). Social support, stress, and self-efficacy: Effects on students' satisfaction. *Journal of College Student Retention: Research, Theory, & Practice, 4*(1), 53-6.

This research studied the impact of perceived stress, self-efficacy, and social support on life satisfaction among 94 first-year college students at a southeastern university. The Satisfaction With Life Scale, Support Evaluation List, the Perceived Stress Scale, and the College Self-Efficacy Inventory were used to measure the variables. The data revealed that higher levels of social support and self-efficacy and lower levels of perceived stress were related to higher levels of life satisfaction. Social support provided the largest contribution to life satisfaction. The researchers recommend that first-year student orientation programs, residence life programming, and classroom assignments be designed to promote social interaction, which can lead to increased peer support for students.

KEY WORDS: assessment, self-efficacy, social support, student satisfaction.

Hoover, K. G. (2003). The relationship of locus of control and self-efficacy to academic achievement of first-year students. *Journal of The First-Year Experience & Students in Transition, 15*(2), 103-123.

In this study, the researcher examined whether factors such as locus of control and self-efficacy can predict college student achievement beyond measures such as standardized tests, high school rank, and grade point average. Several measures were administered to 1,218 first-year students at a private midwestern university, including the Nowicki-Strickland Internal-External Control Scale for Adults, the Academic Locus of Control Scale for College Students, Self-Efficacy Scale, and the College Academic Self-Efficacy Scale. Results indicate that there is a positive correlation between self-efficacy and locus of control and academic achievement. Based on the findings of this study, educators may wish to consider measuring self-efficacy and locus of control along with reviewing high school grade point average and standardized test scores to strengthen prediction of academic success.

KEY WORDS: academic achievement, academic success, assessment measures, locus of control, self-efficacy.

Parker, J. D. A., Duffy, J. M., Wood, L. M., Bond, B. J., & Hogan, M. J. (2005). Academic achievement and emotional intelligence: Predicting the successful transition from high school to university. *Journal of The First-Year Experience & Students in Transition, 17*(1), 67-78.

The influence of emotional intelligence on the transition from high school to higher education was measured in this study. The sample—1,426 first-year students at four institutions in three states—was provided a short version of the Emotional Quotient Inventory (EQ-i: Short) at the beginning and end of the semester. This inventory provided an opportunity to self-assess levels of emotional intelligence. From the data collected, coupled with grade point average information, the sample was divided into two groups: "successful" (students with a 3.0 or greater grade point average), and "unsuccessful" (students with a grade point average of less than a 2.0, or those who withdrew from the institution). When the EQ-i: Short data from both groups were compared, there was an association between academic achievement and some levels of emotional intelligence. Several components of emotional intelligence were cited in the study including abilities to manage stress, adapt, and relate on an interpersonal level. These are factors the researchers suggest are important to consider when working with students in transition. *KEY WORDS: academic achievement, emotional intelligence, stress management, student success.*

Pritchard, M. E., & Wilson, G. S. (2003). Using emotional and social factors to predict student success. *Journal of College Student Development, 44*(1), 18-28.

While demographic and retention variables have been the primary focus of previous studies on college students' academic success and persistence, the current study sought to identify potential relationships between student emotional and social health and grade point average and retention. While the sample included undergraduates at all levels of study at a private, midwestern university, 50% of the sample were first-year students. Data from first-year students were not included in the analyses that predicted GPA, but results showed that aspects of students' emotional health, such as self-esteem, fatigue, and coping tactics, had a significant impact on the intent to drop out of school. However, the combined influence of social health measures (e.g., introversion/extroversion, alcohol behaviors, involvement in campus organizations) did not have a significant effect on the intent to leave college. Based on these findings, it appears that providing students with the skills to "deal successfully with the multitude of emotional stresses encountered in college life" (p. 25) is perhaps more important for persistence than attention to social health issues and should be a priority of student support programs in the first year and beyond. *KEY WORDS: mental health, persistence, social support, student success.*

Schlosser, L. Z., & Sedlacek, W. E. (2001). The relationship between undergraduate students' perceived past academic success and perceived academic self-concept. *Journal of The First-Year Experience & Students in Transition, 13*(2), 95-105.

This research studied the relationship between perceived past academic success and current academic self-concept (e.g., career aspirations, self-confidence related to academics). The participants were 3,271 entering first-year students at a large, eastern, four-year public university. Ninety percent of these students completed the University New Student Census, which assesses background, attitudes, goals, interests, campus service needs, expectations, and academic self-concept. The results showed that students who experienced past academic successes were more likely to have positive academic self-concepts. Academic advisors and admissions professionals can use this research to identify potentially at-risk students and design interventions to bolster their academic self-concept. *KEY WORDS: assessment measures, self-image/concept, student success.*

Stage, F. K., & Hossler, D. (2000). Linking student behaviors, college choice, and college persistence. In J. M. Braxton (Ed.), *Reworking the student departure puzzle* (pp. 170-195). Nashville: Vanderbilt University Press.

This chapter examines students' college choice and departure decisions, with a specific focus on student behaviors and agency. As agents of their own experience, students are viewed as active, as opposed to passive, participants in the process. The researchers' student-centered theory of persistence links students' background characteristics, college behaviors and experiences, student intentions and engagement, college entry, and student persistence. The authors assert that student motivation and self-efficacy are

central to their model. They recommend that educators promote self-efficacy in precollege students by providing them with opportunities to succeed in college-like courses; allowing them to view the successes of siblings and friends; helping them experience persuasion from counselors, teachers, and family; and helping them develop positive, not fearful, feelings about the college experience.
KEY WORDS: *college choice, motivation, retention, self-efficacy.*

Swing, R. L. (Ed.). (2004a). *Proving and improving, volume II: Tools and techniques for assessing the first college year* **(Monograph No. 37). Columbia, SC: University of South Carolina, National Resource Center for The First-Year Experience and Students in Transition.**

This six-part monograph compiles information about instruments related to first-year assessment and culminates with a comprehensive typology. The volume begins with an introduction to assessment of the first year including definitions of various forms of assessment and suggestions for organizing and preparing for assessment efforts. Authors of the first part describe assessment efforts that rely on data available through institutional records. In addition to highlighting specific tools (e.g., Data Audit and Analysis Toolkit and Enrollment Search), the authors provide suggestions on working with campus offices of institutional research and course records to assess aspects of the first year. Part 1 also includes a description of the Freshman Absence-Based Intervention program at the University of Mississippi. The second part of the monograph describes methods for collecting qualitative data including focus groups, and "think aloud" protocols. This part also includes an overview of a "promise audit" used to examine student perspectives on services and other campus features and a case study on involving faculty in assessment planning and implementation. The third part of the monograph offers examples of course evaluations and the fourth and largest part of the monograph describes numerous first-year survey instruments. Surveys featured in this section include the Cooperative Institutional Research Project (CIRP) Freshman Survey and the Your First College Year (YFCY) follow-up survey, the College Student Experiences Questionnaire (CSEQ), the Study Behavior Inventory, and the National Survey of Student Engagement (NSSE). Part five of the monograph offers several examples of cognitive tests including those to measure critical thinking, general education outcomes and assessment, and writing assessment. The final part of the monograph brings the discussion about first-year assessment from specific examples back to a broad discussion about purpose and future directions. This part includes a description of the Hope Scale and assessment of learning styles.
KEY WORDS: *assessment, assessment measures, cognitive measures.*

Terenzini, P. T., Pascarella, E. T., & Blimling, G. S. (1999). Students' out-of-class experiences and their influence on learning and cognitive development: A literature review. *Journal of College Student Development, 40*(5), 610-623.

This article reviews literature that demonstrates the impact of cocurricular activities on the learning and cognitive development of college students. The authors examine research related to residence life, Greek life, intercollegiate athletics, employment, other cocurricular activities, and faculty and peer interactions. They conclude that while some out-of-class activities can have a positive effect on students (e.g., living in a residence hall, studying abroad, and socializing with others of different racial/ethnic groups) other activities are less effective (e.g., belonging to a Greek organization, working full time, participating in men's intercollegiate football or basketball). Out-of-class activities have the greatest impact on student learning when they actively engage students and involve interpersonal interactions with peers and faculty. The authors suggest that since no single policy or program is likely to have a complete impact on students, academic and student affairs educators must work collaboratively to provide students with experiences in multiple areas that promote learning and development. In order for cocurricular activities to have the greatest impact on first-year students, educators should strive to engage them early in those opportunities that research indicates have the most positive effect.

KEY WORDS: cocurricular activities, cognitive development, engagement, involvement.

Tuckman, B. W. (2003). The effect of learning and motivation strategies training on college students' achievement. *Journal of College Student Development, 44*(3), 430-437.

Drawing on data collected from 397 students enrolled in "Individual Learning and Motivation: Strategies for Success in College," a five-credit elective course, this study explored the effect of learning and motivation strategies taught in the course on the students' academic achievement (measured by grade point average). The course content included several modules related to motivation and was taught through the use of what the author defined as "Active Discovery and Participation Through Technology" (ADAPT). The ADAPT approach makes use of both classroom-based and computer-based instruction. Findings from the study indicated that students who took the strategies course earned higher grade point averages than comparable level students who did not take the course. The researcher removed the class grade from consideration in the comparisons between grade point averages.

KEY WORDS: academic achievement, learning, motivation, student success.

Zajacova, A., Lynch, S. M., & Espenshade, T. J. (2005). Self-efficacy, stress, and academic success in college. *Research in Higher Education, 46*(6), 677-706.

Using data from a sample of 107 students in their first semester of college, this study explored the relationship between academic self-efficacy, stress, and academic performance. All students in the sample had entered the institution in the spring semester with an average age of 20.7. This age was consistent with the average age of all students who entered the institution in the spring of the year the study was conducted. The study was conducted using a survey administered during the second-to-last week of an orientation seminar that included measures of stress and self-efficacy. The measures of self-efficacy were drawn from multiple existing instruments. Information on grades, number of credits, and other registration data were obtained for the sample one year after initial enrollment. Findings from the study indicated a negative correlation between self-efficacy and stress and suggested that students' sense of academic self-efficacy is the strongest predictor of academic performance (measured by grade point average). In this study, stress was found to have little impact on grade point average but did have a marginal impact on persistence.

KEY WORDS: academic success, effects of stress, self-efficacy.

{ PROMISING INSTITUTIONAL PRACTICES IN THE FIRST-YEAR EXPERIENCE }

Barefoot, B. O. (2000, January/February). The first-year experience: Are we making it any better? *About Campus, 4,* 12-18.

This article begins with a brief summary of the history of the first-year experience and provides a broad overview of the first college year at American institutions. The author highlights successful first-year initiatives and identifies institutions that have used these practices to boost first-year retention, increase student involvement and satisfaction, enhance student intellectualism, and reduce behavior problems. The article identifies objectives that typically guide the development and delivery of many first-year programs, including increasing interaction between students and faculty, increasing student involvement on campus, linking the curriculum and the cocurriculum, and increasing the academic engagement and success of all students, particularly for those who do not have sufficient academic preparation for college. The article ends with suggestions for continuing to improve the first year of college and identifies previously unsuccessful initiatives and new challenges that will impact future work with first-year students.
KEY WORDS: engagement, student success.

Barefoot, B. O., Gardner, J. N., Cutright, M., Morris, L. V., Schroeder, C. C. Schwartz, S.W., et al. (2005). *Achieving and sustaining institutional excellence for the first year of college.* San Francisco: Jossey-Bass.

The authors share case studies of 13 institutions selected as Institutions of Excellence in the First College Year through a project administered by the Policy Center on the First Year of College. These colleges and universities represent a wide range of institutional sizes, including two-year, four-year, public, and private institutions and were identified through the project as exemplars for achieving excellence in the first year of college. Each chapter highlights one institution, summarizes findings from investigations into institutional history, culture, and leadership, and describes programmatic and student-level assessments related to the first-year experience. The final chapter summarizes findings from all 13 case studies and identifies 12 common features of the Institutions of Excellence in the First College Year. The five criteria for selecting the Institutions of Excellence and the descriptions of these institutions offer valuable guidance for evaluating and improving institutional practices and first-year student outcomes.
KEY WORDS: case studies, first-year comprehensive initiatives, student success.

Braxton, J. M., & McClendon, S. A. (2001-2). The fostering of social integration and retention through institutional practice. *Journal of College Student Retention: Research, Theory & Practice, 3*(1), 57-71.

The authors describe policies, programs, and practices that influence social integration and retention. They present 20 recommendations across eight domains of practice: academic advising, administrative policies and practices, enrollment management, faculty development, faculty reward system, student orientation programs, residential life, and student affairs programming. The authors conclude that there are multiple ways to impact student integration and persistence, and practices should be adapted to institutional type and culture. The article reinforces the notion that the success and retention of first-year students is a campuswide responsibility that should not be relegated to one campus division or office.
KEY WORDS: retention, social integration.

Cutright, M. (2002, September/October). What are research universities doing for first-year students? *About Campus, 7,* 16-20.

This study used qualitative data collected by the Policy Center on the First Year of College from more than 75 research universities as part of the project Strengthening First-Year Student Learning at Doctoral/Research-Extensive Universities. The project aimed to determine successful first-year initiatives at these types of institutions. The author identified seven themes common to first-year programs at research universities: (a) the proliferation of first-year programs, (b) first-year initiatives housed in a discipline or college, (c) integration of multiple strategies to support first-year programs, (d) learning communities as a cornerstone of first-year efforts, (e) a re-examination of teaching and learning, (f) strong academic and student affairs partnerships, and (g) intentional assessment and evaluation. These themes and the article's description of best practices provide the foundation for launching or examining first-year programs at research universities.

KEY WORDS: learning communities, research universities.

Hossler, D., Kuh, G. D., & Olsen, D. (2001). Finding (more) fruit on the vines: Using higher education research and institutional research to guide institutional policies and strategies (Part II). *Research in Higher Education, 42*(2), 223-235.

The authors demonstrate how research can be used to shape practices and policies designed to promote the success of first-year college students. Based on a review of literature on effective colleges, teaching and learning, and student development processes and outcomes, the authors present four clusters of activities they consider critical to fostering first-year student success. These clusters include (a) anticipatory socialization experiences, (b) strengthening academic foundations, (c) the integration of academic and social experiences, and (d) campus-wide collaboration. The authors provide examples of how practices at Indiana University Bloomington were designed to influence these key areas. They conclude that educators can act confidently and swiftly when they know their strategies are grounded in literature on best practices.

KEY WORDS: anticipatory socialization, collaboration, student services, student success.

Kuh, G. D., Kinzie, J., Schuh, J. H., Whitt, E. J., & Associates. (2005). *Student success in college: Creating conditions that matter.* **San Francisco: Jossey-Bass.**

This book presents the findings of the Documenting Effective Educational Practice (DEEP) project, a research initiative of the National Survey of Student Engagement (NSSE) and the American Association for Higher Education. The researchers conducted in-depth case studies of 20 institutions identified as having higher than predicted levels of student engagement (based on NSSE scores) and higher than predicted graduation rates, after adjusting for institutional and student characteristics. The institutions were diverse in terms of size, geographic region, Carnegie classification, and mission. The first part of the book introduces the research project and its rationale, as well as the concept of student engagement and its relationship with student success. Part two presents six properties and conditions common to educationally effective institutions: (a) a "living" mission and "lived" educational philosophy, (b) a strong focus on student learning, (c) environments adapted for educational advantage, (d) clear pathways to student success, (e) an improvement-oriented ethos, and (f) shared responsibility for educational quality. The third part of the book presents effective practices used at the DEEP institutions, organized around the five NSSE clusters of effective educational practice: (a) academic challenge, (b) active and collaborative learning, (c) student-faculty interaction, (d) enriching educational experiences, and (e) supportive campus environment. Part four offers principles and recommendations for promoting student success.

KEY WORDS: case studies, engagement, student success.

Light, R. J. (2001). *Making the most of college: Students speak their minds.* **Cambridge, MA: Harvard University Press.**

This book offers a synthesis of findings from interviews conducted over the course of 10 years with college seniors at Harvard University focused on what students can do to get the most out of their college experience and how faculty, staff, and administrators can facilitate this process for students. Many of the findings summarized in the book are related to interactions with faculty, advisors, and fellow students; the importance of course selection, involvement in enriching educational opportunities both inside and outside the classroom, and time management skills; and social and intellectual interactions with diverse individuals. While implications for practice are highlighted throughout the book, the final chapter specifically identifies strategies for campus leaders to improve student life on campus, including adopting a policy of inclusion; building a strong campus culture; facilitating collaboration between institutional and student leadership; implementing innovative course scheduling; and forging connections between students, faculty, staff, and administrators. The final chapter makes the critical point that these strategies are likely to be most successful and sustainable if they are instituted at the very beginning of the students' college careers. Student insights and institutional strategies highlighted in the book lay an important foundation for first-year programs and student success throughout college.

KEY WORDS: diversity, involvement, research studies, student-faculty interaction.

Mandel, R. G., & Evans, K. (2003, March/April). First choice: Creating innovative academic options for first-year students. *About Campus, 8,* **23-26.**

This article chronicles the nearly 20-year process of institutionalizing a comprehensive and successful first-year experience at SUNY Oswego and offers a valuable example of an institutional effort to develop a comprehensive and integrated first-year experience. Early efforts for a first-year seminar were challenged by suspicions regarding its academic rigor, its relegation to student affairs with little support from faculty, and difficulty marketing the opportunity to students. Several institutional transitions led to increased receptivity to this and other first-year programming efforts. Specifically, the key issues that primed the campus for a renewed focus on first-year student success were (a) concerns about retention, (b) momentum established by a few successful collaborative projects for first-year students, (c) an assessment of student advising, and (d) enhanced interest in self-evaluation. As a result, the campus established a First-Year Advisory Council, which developed an institutional philosophy on the importance of first-year programs, established criteria for programs to be included in a comprehensive first-year experience, integrated the existing first-year programs, and developed new courses and services that prepared the institution to offer a first-year academic experience to 85% of new students. The article ends with reflections on lessons learned in this process, such as the value of collaboration between academic and student affairs, the significance of academic support, and the importance of assessment in the evolution of first-year programming.

KEY WORDS: academic and student affairs collaboration, assessment, first-year comprehensive initiatives.

Pascarella, E. T., & Terenzini, P. T. (2005). *How college affects students: A third decade of research.* **San Francisco: Jossey-Bass**

This book provides an examination of the myriad factors that contribute to the effect higher education has on student development and change, and updates the first edition of the book published in 1991. In the first chapter, the authors present six key questions and identify and define important terms used throughout. Most of the chapter describes how the literature about students has changed in the years since the first edition, prompting the need for the new edition. The second chapter summarizes several student development theories, identifies commonalities among the theories, and provides several models of college impact on students (e.g., Astin's I-E-O model). The third chapter focuses on changes related to learning. Specifically, this chapter explores how the college experience impacts the development of academic skills and knowledge of subject matter and includes examples of instructional techniques and learning opportunities (e.g., Supplemental Instruction, learning communities). Chapter 4 examines the development of general skills and cognitive abilities such as critical thinking and decision making. Chapter 5 explores the psychosocial changes and development students often experience, including personal changes in identity and academic and social concepts and changes in the ways students view others. Chapters 6 and 7 provide discussion of changes in attitudes, values, and moral development among college students. Chapter 8 examines the relationship education can have on socioeconomic status, as well as the accessibility of higher education to various groups of students, and chapters 9 and 10 provide insight into the career/economic and personal (e.g., health and wellness, connection to community) gains associated with earning a college degree. Drawing on information presented in chapters 1 through 10, chapter 11 summarizes how students are affected by the college experience and leads the reader to the final chapter detailing implications for practice and research.

KEY WORDS: college outcomes, student characteristics, student development theory.

Schroeder, C. (2003, September/October). The first year and beyond: Charles Schroeder talks to John Gardner. *About Campus, 8,* 9-17.

In this interview, John Gardner reflects on the history, current state, and future directions of the first-year experience movement. The successes and challenges of several first-year best practices are discussed, including partnerships between faculty and student affairs in the delivery of first-year programs, a holistic approach to student learning, the role of Supplemental Instruction, and the integration of curricular initiatives such as first-year seminars, service-learning, and learning communities. The article focuses on best practices, new tools, and assessment approaches useful in work with first-year students.

KEY WORDS: assessment, collaboration, learning.

Smith, R. (2003, March/April). Changing institutional culture for first-year students and those who teach them. *About Campus, 8,* 3-8.

This article summarizes an institutional initiative to increase student retention launched in the 1990s by Indiana University Bloomington (IUB) and funded by the Lilly Foundation. The initiative's focus was on assisting students in the transitions they experience during the first year of college. Institutional efforts on 4 of 12 initiatives are highlighted. Orientation was moved closer to the beginning of classes, more academically focused programming was created for the residence halls, and technological resources were used more effectively. A video for students and parents was produced and a web guide to college success was designed. Instructional approaches in introductory mathematics courses, often a problem point for first-year students, were enhanced, the availability of math tutoring was increased, a companion to the math course was offered, and televised supplemental instruction was made available. Faculty from other key introductory courses elected to participate in a two-week seminar on reshaping gateway courses to improve student success while maintaining high intellectual and academic standards. These efforts to reshape the first-year experience at IUB required working across administrative silos, a collaboration aided by the formation of "Frosh-Up," a cross-campus committee to coordinate campus retention efforts. At the time of the article, the authors were still awaiting calculation of retention rates for students who had experienced the changes. However, institutional results of the National Survey of Student Engagement (NSSE) suggest that the efforts had yielded promising early outcomes.

KEY WORDS: gateway courses, orientation, retention.

Upcraft, M. L., Gardner, J. N., Barefoot, B. O. & Associates. (2004). *Challenging and supporting the first-year student: A handbook for improving the first year of college.* San Francisco: Jossey-Bass.

This comprehensive guide to promoting first-year student success serves as an update to the 1989 book, *The Freshman Year Experience: Helping Students Survive and Succeed in College,* written by M. Lee Upcraft, John Gardner, and Associates. The first part of the update provides an overview of today's first-year students and keys to their persistence and success. Part 2 presents issues related to recruiting and challenging new students, including student expectations and engagement, and the enrollment management process. The third part offers methods for creating a culture of success for first-year students. The chapters examine issues for underrepresented students, different institutional types, uses of technology, and campus collaboration. Part 4 provides suggestions for challenging and supporting first-year students in the classroom and part 5 looks at out-of-class offerings that accomplish these goals. The final chapters provide methods for assessing the impact of campus initiatives on first-year student success.

KEY WORDS: first-year experience, retention, academic success.

{ RETENTION AND SUCCESS OF FIRST-YEAR STUDENTS }

Arredondo, M., & Knight, S. (2005), Estimating degree attainment rates of freshmen: A campus perspective. *Journal of College Student Retention: Research, Theory, and Practice, 7*(1-2), 91-115.

The authors use assessment models developed by the Higher Education Research Institute (HERI) to estimate four- and six-year degree completion rates of students who enrolled as first-year students at Chapman University (CA) in 1996. Degree attainment estimates obtained by applying these models, which included measures of high school grades, SAT scores, gender, and race/ethnicity, were compared to actual enrollment and degree attainment rates obtained through student records in 2002. Findings suggested that the models were better able to predict four-year retention rates than six-year rates but yielded generally accurate degree completion rates by gender, the majority of racial/ethnic groups, and admit status (e.g., regular, honors, or provisional admission). These models were a less accurate predictor of degree attainment rates for out-of-state students and when the data were analyzed by high school grades. These statistical estimates helped the institution identify first-year students who were more likely to depart college prior to degree completion and to develop and deliver appropriate interventions to enhance student success at the institution.

KEY WORDS: degree attainment, gender, retention, students of color.

Bauer, K. W., & Liang, Q. (2003). The effect of personality and precollege characteristics on first-year activities and academic performance. *Journal of College Student Development, 44*(3), 227-290.

This study draws on data from a sample of 265 first-year science and engineering majors to examine the effect personality, gender, and predicted grade point average have on academic performance. Data were collected from three instruments: (a) the NEO Five-Factor Inventory (NEO FFI), measuring personality; (b) the Watson-Glaser Critical Thinking Appraisal (WGCTA), which measures inquiry; (c) and the College Student Experiences Questionnaire (CSEQ), measuring perceptions of campus, perceived gains in academic and personal areas and other factors. Additional demographic and high school grade point average and SAT data were collected from university records. Findings from the study indicated that academic performance is impacted by personality and the precollege factors considered in predicted grade point average (e.g., SAT/ACT scores and high school grade point average). Further, the study suggested a relationship between effort exerted toward academic activities and grade point average.

KEY WORDS: academic success, assessment measures, involvement, STEM disciplines, student characteristics.

Braunstein, A., McGrath, M., & Pescatrice, D. (2000-01). Measuring the impact of financial factors on college persistence. *Journal of College Student Retention: Research, Theory & Practice, 2*(3), 191-203.

In an extension of another study on how financial factors impact college enrollment, the authors analyze the impact of financial aid and family income on college persistence. Institutional data from the 1991-92 ($N = 636$) and 1993-94 ($N = 615$) cohorts of first-year students from the same college were examined. The authors found that the receipt of financial aid did not have a bearing on students' decision to persist, but that first-year students from families with higher incomes tended to be retained to the second year at higher rates than students from lower-income families. Overall, though, students' academic performance was the greatest predictor of persistence into the sophomore year.

KEY WORDS: academic performance, financial aid, persistence, socioeconomic status.

Braxton, J. M. (Ed.). (2000). *Reworking the student departure puzzle.* **Nashville: Vanderbilt University Press.**

This two-part book is a compilation of writings about student departure from college. The first part is focused on revising Tinto's theory of college student departure and the second suggests new theoretical directions for understanding student departure. Academic integration, a key concept in Tinto's theory, is closely examined, with the authors suggesting that economic and financial influences, including the ability to pay and the effects of financial aid and tuition, should also be considered in predicting student departure. The authors also describe student departure as a psychological process and present psychological theories that may be useful in revising the current theory of departure. The book describes other factors that influence the college student experience, including campus climate and classroom learning, and offers a sociological perspective on student departure. New theoretical directions offered in the second half begin with a description of issues related to retention of students of color. The authors explore the concept of persistence as a process, an alternative to some traditional retention research between student behaviors, college choice and persistence. The book also offers models of student success and persistence based on issues of power and identity and ends with a call for reinvigoration of scholarship on student departure. The book concludes with a summary of suggested revisions to Tinto's theory and with recommendations for future research.

KEY WORDS: retention theory.

Braxton, J. M., Milem, J. F., & Sullivan, A. S. (2000). The influence of active learning on the college student departure process. *The Journal of Higher Education, 71*(5), 569-590.

Drawing on data collected from 718 first-year students through the administration of the Student Information Form (SIF), the Early Collegiate Experience Survey (ECES), and the Freshman Year Survey (FYE), this study sought to measure student persistence and retention and to identify common factors impacting both. The instruments were administered throughout the first year, beginning at orientation and continuing through the first and second semesters. Six measures emerged from data analysis including institutional commitment, aspects of active learning, and departure decisions, as well as all characteristics described in Tinto's *Leaving College: Rethinking the Causes and Cures of Student Attrition*. Additional composite measures were identified to gauge levels of active learning. Findings from this study indicated a connection between active learning and persistence. Additionally, the researchers found an influence of social integration on persistence, with interaction with faculty and active learning playing a strong role on social integration. The influence of teaching and the effects of various teaching pedagogies (e.g., lecture) and relationship to student learning are additional areas that researchers in this study suggested for further examination.

KEY WORDS: active learning, assessment, persistence, retention.

Braxton, J. M., & McClendon, S. A. (2001-2). **The fostering of social integration and retention through institutional practice.** *Journal of College Student Retention: Research, Theory & Practice, 3*(1), 57-71.

The authors describe policies, programs, and practices that influence social integration and retention. They present 20 recommendations across eight domains of practice: academic advising, administrative policies and practices, enrollment management, faculty development, faculty reward system, student orientation programs, residential life, and student affairs programming. The authors conclude that there are multiple ways to impact student integration and persistence, and practices should be adapted to institutional type and culture. The article reinforces the notion that the success and retention of first-year students is a campuswide responsibility that should not be relegated to one campus division or office.

KEY WORDS: retention, social integration.

Clark, M. R. (2005). **Negotiating the freshman year: Challenges and strategies among first-year students.** *Journal of College Student Development, 46*(3), 296-316.

This study was explored and expanded upon the concept of student strategies to understand how new students transition to college. The researcher conducted a series of 10 individual interviews with eight traditional-aged first-year students during the second semester of their first year at a public, four-year, commuter college located in a major eastern city. Analyses of these data suggest that students' transition to college includes "an active process of strategizing" (p. 302). Further analyses revealed that challenges to the process of transition for first-year students and the related strategies that the students devised to cope with these challenges could be categorized into four broad themes: (a) overcoming an obstacle, (b) seizing an opportunity, (c) adapting to a change, or (d) pursuing a goal. However, the researcher noted that similar challenges did not necessarily yield similar strategies among the students in this study, but instead reflected other, often interconnected, influences such as the students' perceptions of their own personal responsibility, available resources, and available options as well as personal characteristics such as persistence and confidence. By acknowledging these strategies and recognizing their influences, it is possible for campus personnel and programs that serve first-year students to help them recognize these challenges during their transition to college, help students clarify appropriate college role responsibilities, and enhance students' strategies for success.

KEY WORDS: college adjustment, locus of control, student success.

Daempfle, P. A. (2003-04). An analysis of the high attrition rates among first-year college science, math, and engineering majors. *Journal of College Student Retention: Research, Theory & Practice, 5*(1), 37-52.

In a study of science, math, and engineering (SME) students who were not retained into their second year of college, the author found two factors contributing to attrition among these students. The first involved perceived differences between expectations of students by college instructors and the expectations of the students' high school teachers. The researcher notes that this seems to indicate a desire by college faculty for changes in secondary education with regard to SME classes. The second factor was students' epistemological beliefs, which involves the degree to which students believe that knowledge about a subject is certain. These two factors (high levels of difference and strong epistemological beliefs) led to a higher percentage of SME students leaving college than their non-SME peers. Academic performance, ability to do college-level work, and the size of classes did not have a statistically significant impact on student retention.

KEY WORDS: persistence, retention, STEM disciplines, student expectations.

Elkins, S. A., Braxton, J. M., & James, G. W. (2000). Tinto's separation stage and its influence on first-semester college student persistence. *Research in Higher Education, 41*(2), 251-268.

This study examined the persistence of first-year students at a public, four-year institution. The researchers used Tinto's construct of separation from his interactionalist theory of student departure as a framework. The Cooperative Institutional Research Program's Student Information Form was used to collect background information on the participants. The First Semester Collegiate Experiences Survey, which involves items derived from Tinto's notion of separation, was administered at the midpoint of the fall semester. Enrollment data were collected from the 411 respondents who completed both surveys. The researchers learned that support from family and friends in the students' previous communities was the most important factor in students' decisions to attend and remain in college. Members of racial/ethnic minority groups, students with lower levels of high school achievement, and those with parents in lower income brackets received less support. For students who did not receive this support, their ability to reject the attitudes and values of their past communities led to greater persistence. The researchers concluded that first-semester students who are able to successfully negotiate the separation stage are more likely to persist to their second semester. They also determined that Tinto's construct of separation is valid and recommend that higher education professionals work to involve family members in assisting students with negotiating the separation process. They suggest systematic communication with parents, as well as creation of programs that bring prospective students and their families to campus, especially for first-generation college students. Finally, they stress the importance of social and academic support to students, residence hall and student activities initiatives, and early warning systems that use absenteeism or low grades as a catalyst for outreach.

KEY WORDS: parental involvement, retention theory, social support.

Hagedorn, L. S., Siadet, M. V., Fogel, S. F., Nora, A., & Pascarella, E. T. (1999). Success in college mathematics: Comparisons between remedial and nonremedial first-year college students. *Research in Higher Education, 40*(3), 261-284.

This study examined math achievement among first-year students from 23 postsecondary institutions in 16 states (852 students enrolled in remedial math courses and 928 in college-level math courses). Since the sample was derived from the National Center on Postsecondary Learning and Assessment (NCTLA), students in the sample had completed reading comprehension, math, and critical thinking units as part of a precollege experience. Second sets of data were collected when a follow-up test was administered (a modification of the first set of tests), along with the College Student Experiences

Questionnaire (CSEQ), and an NCTLA questionnaire. Findings from the study suggested that students in remedial math courses were less likely to receive encouragement to attend college, and their families were more likely to be at a lower income and education level. Further, students in remedial courses had lower grade point averages and indicated they studied less (in high school) and not in groups. In addition to these findings, students in remedial courses reported less satisfaction with course instruction than their peers in nonremedial courses. Finally, the researchers indicate finding a disproportionate number of women and students of color in remedial courses.

KEY WORDS: academic achievement, assessment measures, developmental education, gender, STEM disciplines.

Hoover, K. G. (2003). The relationship of locus of control and self-efficacy to academic achievement of first-year students. *Journal of The First-Year Experience & Students in Transition, 15*(2), 103-123.

In this study, the researcher examined whether factors such as locus of control and self-efficacy can predict college student achievement beyond measures such as standardized tests, high school rank, and grade point average. Several measures were administered, including: the Nowicki-Strickland Internal-External Control Scale for Adults, the Academic Locus of Control Scale for College Students, Self-Efficacy Scale, and the College Academic Self-Efficacy Scale to 1,218 first-year students at a private midwestern university. Results indicate that there is a positive correlation between self-efficacy and locus of control and academic achievement. Based on the findings of this study, educators may wish to consider measuring self-efficacy and locus of control along with reviewing high school grade point average and standardized test scores to strengthen prediction of academic success.

KEY WORDS: academic achievement, academic success, assessment measures, locus of control, self-efficacy.

Johnson, J. L. (2000-2001). Learning communities and special efforts in retention of university students: What works, what doesn't, and is the return worth the investment? *Journal of College Student Retention: Research, Theory & Practice, 2*(3), 219-238.

Drawing on data collected from four programs intended to improve student retention at a four-year university, this study investigated the cost-effectiveness of these efforts. Grade point average, retention, and student survey data were collected for each of the following programs over a two-year period: (a) Conditional Contract Student Program, (b) Project 100, (c) Early Alert/Early Intervention, (d) First-Year Alternative Experience (FYAE), and (d) Russell Scholars Program (RSP). Several of these, including the Conditional Contract Student Program, Project 100, and FYAE were created to serve students who were considered at-risk (less academically prepared) and/or conditionally admitted to the university. In addition to programmatic data, cost data for each program were derived from a cost analysis conducted for the study. The results of the study indicated that several of the programs (RSP and FYAE, both learning-community based programs) boasted higher than average retention rates. Further, grade point average data indicated that students who persisted in each program performed at better-than-expected rates academically and were retained at better-than-expected rates, particularly those students who were academically most at risk. Findings from the study suggest that while the programs using the learning communities model were more expensive, these programs increased the likelihood that students involved would persist to graduation.

KEY WORDS: academic advising, at-risk students, early warning systems, learning communities, retention.

Kahn, J. H., & Nauta, M. M. (2001). Social-cognitive predictors of first-year college persistence: The importance of proximal assessment. *Research in Higher Education, 42*(6), 633-652.

The persistence of 400 first-year students at a public midwestern university was predicted before college entrance and measured in the second semester. Data were collected using The Social Cognitive Career Theory (SCCT), which relates measurements of self-efficacy, performance goals, and expectations to persistence to the second year. To measure academic ability and performance, the researchers collected data about high school class rank, ACT scores, and first- and second-semester grade point averages. Self-efficacy was measured using a modified version of the Self-Efficacy for Broad Academic Milestones Scale (SE-Broad). Outcomes expectations, performance goals, and first-to-second-year persistence were also measured. The researchers concluded that social-cognitive factors influence persistence of first-year students when students have completed at least one semester. The most significant predictors of persistence were ability and past performance (e.g., ACT scores, high school class rank). The researchers also concluded that while persistence can partially be predicted by ability and past performance, factors such as self-efficacy must also be considered.
KEY WORDS: assessment measures, persistence, self-efficacy.

Lounsbury, J. W., Saudargas, R. A., & Gibson, L. W. (2004). An investigation of personality traits in relation to intention to withdraw from college. *Journal of College Student Development, 45*(5), 517-534.

The researchers in this article drew on models of retention to relate personality traits to first-year student withdrawals. With a sample of 233 first-year students enrolled in an introductory psychology course, the researchers administered an online personality survey. Personality was measured through the Resource Associates' Adolescent Personal Style Inventory (APSI) for College Students. Findings indicated that personality traits are related to first-year students' intention to withdraw. Several traits, agreeableness, conscientiousness, emotional stability, and extroversion, were negatively correlated with the intention to withdraw. The study also measured Sense of Identity and Work Drive; both accounted for some variance in the intent to withdraw. The researchers suggest that this information be used to help identify students at risk of withdrawing and to inform the practices used to help those students.
KEY WORDS: persistence, student characteristics.

Murtaugh, P. A., Burns, L. D., & Schuster, J. (1999). Predicting the retention of university students. *Research in Higher Education, 40*(3), 355-371.

This study identified common factors associated with student retention among 8,867 first-year students at one university. Data were collected from the university's data warehouse and included demographic and academic information, including precollege data such as SAT scores and high school grade point averages. A survival or failure-time analysis of the data was used beginning at the students' point of entry to the university. Univariate and multiple-variable analyses indicated an attrition rate of approximately 40% over four years and suggested that high school grade point average may be the greatest predictor of academic success. The researchers also found that attrition tended to increase with increased age at the point of enrollment.
KEY WORDS: retention, student characteristics.

Parker, J. D. A., Duffy, J. M., Wood, L. M., Bond, B. J., & Hogan, M. J. (2005). Academic achievement and emotional intelligence: Predicting the successful transition from high school to university. *Journal of The First-Year Experience & Students in Transition, 17*(1), 67-78.

The influence of emotional intelligence on the transition from high school to higher education was measured in this study. The sample—1,426 first-year students at four institutions in three states—was provided a short version of the Emotional Quotient Inventory (EQ-i: Short) at the beginning and end of the semester. This inventory provided an opportunity to self-assess levels of emotional intelligence. From the data collected, coupled with grade point average information, the sample was divided into two groups: "successful" (students with a 3.0 or greater grade point average), and "unsuccessful" (students with a grade point average of less than a 2.0, or those who withdrew from the institution). When the EQ-i: Short data from both groups were compared, there was an association between academic achievement and some levels of emotional intelligence. Several components of emotional intelligence were cited in the study including abilities to manage stress, adapt, and relate on an interpersonal level. These are factors the researchers suggest are important to consider when working with students in transition.
KEY WORDS: academic achievement, emotional intelligence, stress management, student success.

Pike, G. R., & Staupe, J. L. (2002). Does high school matter? An analysis of three methods of predicting first-year grades. *Research in Higher Education, 43*(2), 187-207.

To better identify students who will benefit from first-year academic intervention programs, this study examined multiple ways of predicting grade point averages of 8,764 first-year students at a major research university. The authors compared typically used (a) regression models that included a students' standardized test scores, high school grades, and high school coursework; (b) high school effects models, which also included four characteristics of the sending high school (i.e., size, control, average ability of students, and percent attending college); and (c) hierarchical linear models that included both the individual and high school variables in a nested structure. When the estimates gained from these three models were compared with students' actual first-year grades, the researchers found that the high school effects model produced the most accurate prediction and hierarchical linear modeling produced the least accurate prediction for the data overall. However, both the high school effects model and hierarchical linear model were slightly more accurate than the typically used model for classifying at-risk students. While the ability to generalize is somewhat limited by the institutional sample, these results suggest the most accurate methods of using existing data to identify new students who may be most in need of academic interventions during the first year.
KEY WORDS: academic performance, assessment, intervention strategies.

Schwartz, R. A., & Washington, C. M. (2002). Predicting academic performance and retention among African American freshmen men. *NASPA Journal, 39*, 355-370.

This study described in this article sought to identify patterns of academic performance and retention among 229 African American first-year students at Bethel College (a small, private historically Black college located in the South). In the study, several variables (e.g., high school grades, class rank, and SAT scores) were observed for predictive value when coupled with the results of two instruments: the Noncognitive Questionnaire Revised (NCQ-R) and the Student Adjustment to College Questionnaire (SACQ). The two questionnaires were used to measure noncognitive variables such as college expectations, self-esteem, and social and institutional adjustment. In addition, researchers also considered the academic performance of the students in the sample during their first year of college using the following dependent variables: grade point average earned in the first semester, academic status (probation), and persistence to the second semester. Findings from the study indicated that high school class rank and grades were most predictive of academic success in the first year of college. Further, when considering retention, the data collected indicated a correlation between high school class rank and social adjustment in college. Finally, the findings also suggested that academic achievement could be predicted by measuring institutional attachment.

KEY WORDS: academic performance, African American students, assessment measures, college adjustment, self-esteem, student expectations.

{ REPORTS WITH IMPLICATIONS FOR THE FIRST-YEAR EXPERIENCE }

Black, S. E., & Amir, S. (2002). *Who goes to college? Differential enrollment by race and family background.* Cambridge, MA: National Bureau of Economic Research.

This study attempted to ascertain the factors driving the differences between Black and White college student enrollment. Based on an analysis of data collected from the Current Population Survey (CPS) between 1968 and 1998, the authors discovered that African American students at the lower end of the financial spectrum were more likely to attend college than higher income African Americans and their low-income White counterparts; however, as tuition increased over the period examined, the differences between college enrollment among the groups dissipated. The findings suggest that low-income African American students are more sensitive to changes in tuition and that policies aimed at increasing college attendance rates for underrepresented groups must take into account different behavioral responses associated with family socioeconomic status. These are important considerations for institutions interested in enrolling, educating and, graduating a diverse group of first-year students.

KEY WORDS: access to higher education, low-income students, race/ethnicity, students of color.

Chen, X., & Carroll, C. D. (2005, July). *First-generation students in postsecondary education: A look at their college transcripts* (Postsecondary Education Descriptive Analysis Report). Washington, DC: National Center for Education Statistics.

This report explores the college course-taking experiences of first-generation students using data from the Postsecondary Education Transcript Study of the National Education Longitudinal Study of 1988 (NELS, 1988). Researchers examined majors and course enrollment patterns of students who were the first members of their families to attend college and compare this information to outcomes for students whose parents went to college. The study demonstrates that first-generation status had a significant correlation with lower bachelor's degree completion rates, even after controlling for an array of factors such as demographics, prior academic preparation, course taking, and academic performance. Of particular note, taking more credits and earning higher grades in the first year of college were strongly correlated with higher persistence and baccalaureate degree completion rates. The outcomes suggest that first-generation college students can benefit from support, particularly during the first year.

KEY WORDS: demographics, enrollment data, first-generation students, graduation rates, retention.

Harvey, W. B., & Anderson, E. L. (2005). *Minorities in higher education: Twenty-first annual status report 2003-04.* Washington, DC: American Council on Education.

This 21st edition report uses data from the U.S. Census Bureau and the U.S. Department of Education National Center for Education Statistics to track the movement of students of color into and through postsecondary institutions in the United States between 1991 and 2001. Findings indicate that during this period, overall enrollment in American higher education increased by 1.6 million students—reaching nearly 16 million students by 2001. A large increase in enrollments of students of color countered declines in the number of Whites attending college—although the decline in Whites was largely due to a decrease in college-aged White students, not a decrease in overall college participation rates for Whites. While the college participation rate for African Americans increased over this period, the rate for Hispanics showed little improvement when compared to the college attendance rate of the overall population. The college participation rate for men increased slightly, while the participation rate of women went up by more than five percentage points. The findings indicate that today's first-year students are increasingly non-White and female and that African Americans and Hispanics, in particular, comprise a disproportionately large part of the enrollment at two-year institutions. The report also includes information on faculty diversity, persistence rates, and graduation rates. The report serves as an important source of national demographic and achievement data.

KEY WORDS: demographics, enrollment data, graduation rates, race/ethnicity, retention, students of color.

Horn, L., & Carroll, C. D. (2004, November). *College persistence on the rise? Changes in 5-year degree completion and postsecondary persistence rates between 1994 and 2000.* Postsecondary Education Descriptive Analysis Report). Washington, DC: National Center for Education Statistics.

This study uses two longitudinal data sets—the 1990-94 and 1996-2001 Beginning Postsecondary Students Longitudinal Studies—to determine whether students who enrolled in college in the beginning of the 1990s were more or less likely to complete a college degree than those who enrolled later. Data analysis indicated that the five-year persistence rate increased over this period. However, baccalaureate degree completion rates remained relatively stable, indicating that students are taking longer to complete their degrees. The authors suggest that a greater reliance on loans seems to have motivated students to keep studying rather than leave college in debt. In addition, the job market and increases in the number of students who had parents who earned college degrees also seemed to have a positive impact on keeping students enrolled in college. However, not all students fared as well as the general student population in the study. In particular, historically at-risk students, who represented a large portion of the beginning student cohorts included in the study, showed losses in degree completion rates over the time period. This finding suggests that faculty and staff working with students who are historically at-risk should make a concerted effort to help these students, particularly during the first year of college.

KEY WORDS: at-risk students, graduation rates, research studies, retention.

Lumina Foundation for Education. (2004, Spring). *Refuse to lose: Today's colleges and universities must work to foster student success* (Lumina Foundation Focus). Indianapolis, IN: Author.

This report uses real-life stories of students at a variety of colleges and universities throughout the United States and the perspectives of higher education researchers, campus officials, and retention experts to explore what institutions can do to enhance student success. The report offers a description of persistence issues associated with different types of student subpopulations (e.g., low-income, students of color) and reviews initiatives such as mentoring, orientation programs, first-year seminars, and other approaches for enhancing success in the first year of college and beyond.

KEY WORDS: retention, student success.

Lumina Foundation for Education. (2005, Fall). *Dreams detoured: Rising college costs alter plans and threaten futures* (Lumina Foundation Focus). **Indianapolis, IN: Author.**

This report explores the plight of students who are denied an opportunity to attend college because of spiraling costs. The report draws on research from the Institute for Higher Education Policy, the College Board, and the Center for Higher Education Policy Analysis to make the case that many students are left out of higher education because they cannot afford it—they either never go or they become college cost casualties. The report offers the insights of postsecondary institutional leaders, higher education policy makers, and heads of college-level associations and organizations on strategies for making college more affordable. The report includes real-life stories of students whose paths to, or away from, college degrees have been determined by the high cost of attendance.
KEY WORDS: access to higher education, college costs.

Mortenson, T. G. (2004, December). *College participation rates for students from low income families by state 1992 to 2002* (Postsecondary Education Opportunity Issue No. 150). **Oskaloosa, IA: The Pell Institute for the Study of Opportunity in Higher Education.**

This report uses data from the National School Lunch Program to demonstrate that students from low-income families constitute an increasing proportion of America's future citizenry. Yet, during the 1990s, the higher education funding policies employed by states across the country seem to have had a negative impact on the proportion of low-income students who participate in postsecondary education. These findings have implications for the first year of college and beyond. The manner in which these students are educated will factor heavily into the health of the American economy and sustainability of a democratic society. The findings suggest that educators and policy makers must step up efforts to provide access to all students, regardless of class background.
KEY WORDS: access to higher education, low-income students.

Mortenson, T. G. (2005, August). *Minority undergraduate enrollments at leading public and private colleges and universities* (Postsecondary Education Opportunity Issue No. 158). **Oskaloosa, IA: The Pell Institute for the Study of Opportunity in Higher Education.**

This report presents information on the overall growth in the proportion of high school graduates of color in the United States since 1960 and contrasts that with the proportion of students of color enrolled in college. The analysis calculates the share of undergraduates from three major underrepresented groups—African Americans, Hispanics and Native Americans—enrolled at public flagship and land-grant institutions, and the *U.S. News and World Report's* top-ranked national universities and national liberal arts colleges. Using a "minority equity index"—calculated by comparing the institutional share of undergraduate students from the three groups to the share of undergraduates in the state where the institutions are located—the report assigns grades to the institutions examined. All four-institution classifications earned F grades for their enrollments of students of color, enrollments that actually shrank between 1992 and 2002. The findings suggest that the colleges and universities in the analysis—considered America's best and most prestigious postsecondary institutions—are grossly underserving some students of color. As the share of high school graduates of color grows, it is a paramount priority for the nation's leading public and private institutions to find ways to expand the proportion of students of color enrolling in their first-year classes and earning degrees. Findings from this report suggest that failure to increase enrollments of students of color will weaken the overall educational experience these institutions offer and have a deleterious impact on the development of tomorrow's workers, taxpayers, parents and voters.
KEY WORDS: access to higher education, students of color.

Mortenson, T. G. (2005, September). *College affordability trends by parental income levels and institutional type 1990 to 2004* (Postsecondary Education Opportunity Issue No. 159). Oskaloosa, IA: The Pell Institute for the Study of Opportunity in Higher Education.

This report indicates that because the cost of education has outpaced parents' inflation-adjusted incomes a growing number of undergraduates have been forced to shift their postsecondary enrollment to less costly institutions. An analysis of data from the National Center for Education Statistics' National Postsecondary Student Aid Studies from 1990 to 2004 revealed that students from high-income families have noticeably more financial aid resources at their disposal than students from low-income backgrounds. As a result, increasing numbers of low-income students are enrolling at cost-efficient community colleges. The implications of these findings are particularly important to educators at two-year institutions, who, by default, are more likely to work with the low-income (and less prepared) students who increasingly constitute the first-year class.

KEY WORDS: access to higher education, low-income students, two-year institutions.

National Center for Education Statistics. *The condition of education, 2005* (NCES 2005-094). Washington, DC: Department of Education.

This congressionally mandated report provides current information on 40 indicators of success in the American education system from elementary school through higher education, including enrollment trends, student achievement, school environment, dropout rates, degree attainment, financial support, and outcomes of education. Findings from the report with implications for the first year of college include stable high school completion rates overall but a decline in dropout rates among White, African American, and Hispanic high school students, which diversifies the pool of applicants for American colleges and universities. Similarly, the report identifies that the rate of enrollment in postsecondary education after graduation from high school has remained constant but also reveals a variation in enrollment among specific sub-populations of high school graduates. Specifically, an increasing number of students are enrolling in college immediately after completing high school. However, African Americans and Hispanics are enrolling at a much lower rate than White high school graduates and more often enroll in two-year colleges than baccalaureate institutions. Further, women outpace men in higher education enrollment, a trend that is expected to continue well into the future.

KEY WORDS: enrollment data, national data sets, transition to college, two-year institutions.

St. John, E. P., Musoba, G. D., Simmons, A. B., & Choong-Geun, C. (2002, August). *Meeting the access challenge: Indiana's twenty-first century scholars program* (New Agenda Series Vol. 4 No. 4). Indianapolis, IN: Lumina Foundation for Education.

Authors of this article report outcomes of a study that examined the impact of Indiana's Twenty-first Century Scholars Program—an initiative that provides academic support for low-income middle and high school students and financial support once these students enter college. Hierarchical regression analyses revealed that eighth grade students who participated in the program were more likely to apply for college than comparable nonparticipating peers—suggesting that the program had an influence on precollege preparation. In addition, aid-receiving program participants were more likely to enroll in college than their peers—suggesting that the initiative also has a positive impact on higher education enrollment. Implications of the report should be considered by educators interested in enhancing access to and success in the first year of college.

KEY WORDS: access to higher education, low-income students.

St. John, E. P., Gross, J. P. K., Musoba, G. D., & Chung A. S. (2005, August). *A step toward college success: Assessing attainment among Indiana's twenty-first century scholars.* (Research Reports). Indianapolis, IN: Lumina Foundation for Education.

A follow-up to the 2002 study, Meeting the Access Challenge: Indiana's Twenty-First Century Scholars Program, this report reveals that participation in Indiana's Twenty-First Century Scholars Program increases the odds that low-income students will enroll and succeed in college. The study indicates that Twenty-First Century Scholars are substantially more likely to enroll in college, are more likely to earn two-year degrees, are more likely to persist in college, and are no less likely to earn four-year degrees than their nonparticipating low-income peers. The findings suggest that precollege preparation combined with financial support enhances the likelihood that low-income students will enroll and succeed in both two- and four-year colleges.

KEY WORDS: access to higher education, low-income students, scholarship programs.

{ ASSESSMENT AND EVALUATION }

Andrade, S. J. (2001). Assessing the impact of curricular and instructional reform—A model for examining gateway courses. *AIR Professional File* **(79).**

This article is based on the premise that many faculty want to improve the introductory courses that often defeat first-year students and discourage them from pursuing particular majors or career paths, most notably in the sciences. However, efforts to introduce instructional reform to transition these "gatekeeper" courses to "gateway" courses are challenged by a lack of assessment results that could help determine if innovations improve student learning. The author introduces an evaluation process, Indices of Course Efficiency and Effectiveness (ICE2) as a model for assessing curricular innovation for gateway courses. Rather than relying on students' grades or satisfaction ratings, ICE2 identifies students' grades in the next course in the curricular sequence (i.e., the majority of students who successfully complete the initial course should be able to pass the next course in the sequence on the first try) as the success measure for a new curricular approach. The author provides detailed steps for implementation of the ICE2 assessment strategy and a case study of an ICE2 assessment on instructional reform of the calculus curriculum at the University of Texas, El Paso.

KEY WORDS: academic achievement, curriculum reform, STEM disciplines.

Arredondo, M., & Knight, S. (2005), Estimating degree attainment rates of freshmen: A campus perspective. *Journal of College Student Retention: Research, Theory, and Practice, 7*(1-2), 91-115.

The authors use assessment models developed by the Higher Education Research Institute (HERI) to estimate four- and six-year degree completion rates of students who enrolled as first-year students at Chapman University (CA) in 1996. Degree attainment estimates obtained by applying these models, which included measures of high school grades, SAT scores, gender, and race/ethnicity, were compared to actual enrollment and degree attainment rates obtained through student records in 2002. Findings suggested that the models were better able to predict four-year retention rates than six-year rates but yielded generally accurate degree completion rates by gender, the majority of racial/ethnic groups, and admit status (e.g., regular, honors, or provisional admission). These models were a less accurate predictor of degree attainment rates for out-of-state students and when the data were analyzed by high school grades. These statistical estimates helped the institution identify first-year students who were more likely to depart college prior to degree completion and to develop and deliver appropriate interventions to enhance student success at the institution.

KEY WORDS: degree attainment, gender, retention, students of color.

Barefoot, B. O. (2004). Foundations of excellence: A new model for first-year assessment. *Assessment Update: Progress Trends, and Practices in Higher Education, 16*(2).

The author introduces the "Foundations of Excellence in the First College Year," sponsored by the Policy Center on the First Year of College. The goals of the "Foundations" project are to establish a definition of, and standards for, first-year excellence that goes beyond a single initiative or program and to characterize an institution's overall approach to the first year in an effort to produce higher levels of student learning and retention. With the input of hundreds of colleges and universities, staff at the Policy Center established a set of common standards—Foundational Dimensions—for the first year. Survey data collected from students, faculty, and administrators quantifies an institution's achievement of the "Dimensions." The signature innovation of the "Foundations" project is the creation of institutional task forces to conduct qualitative analyses of institutional performance around the "Dimensions." Staff members of the Policy Center encourage institutions to include faculty, student affairs professionals, academic administrators, institutional research and assessment staff, and students in these task forces. In their analyses of the institutions' performances in relation to the Dimensions, these task forces have engaged in thorough examinations of their institutional environments and campus cultures as they relate to the first-year experience. The author of this report suggests that allowing key campus leaders to engage in a close examination of the institutional environment is valuable and should serve as a model for assessment of the first-year at other institutions.

KEY WORDS: assessment, first-year program standards.

Belcher, A. R. (2005). Assessment of the first-year experience at the University of Charleston: Using portfolio completion rates as an indicator. *Assessment Update: Progress Trends, and Practices in Higher Education, 17*(2), 1-2,10.

This article summarizes the transition to an outcomes-based learning environment at the University of Charleston (SC). In this environment, students earn academic credit for introductory courses based on competencies mastered rather than on credits completed. A continuous assessment process involving a review of data, identification of areas for improvement, and establishing a corrective course of action served as the foundation for this competency-based practice. As part of the process, students are required to create a portfolio of work from their first-year learning communities and other introductory courses. If the work meets established standards for writing, speaking, and computer skills, the student earns credit toward graduation. Faced with problems with the program, a task force of faculty, administrators, and student affairs professionals met to identify opportunities across the first-year curriculum and cocurriculum for students to create portfolios. A more integrated approach to assignments across the first year provided more opportunities for students to complete their requirements and resulted in a higher overall portfolio completion rate.

KEY WORDS: outcomes-based learning, performance indicators, transition to college.

Braunstein, A., McGrath, M., & Pescatrice, D. (2000-2001). Measuring the impact of financial factors on college persistence. *Journal of College Student Retention: Research, Theory & Practice, 2*(3), 191-203.

In an extension of another study on how financial factors impact college enrollment, the authors analyze the impact of financial aid and family income on college persistence. Institutional data from the 1991-92 ($N = 636$) and 1993-94 ($N = 615$) cohorts of first-year students from the same college were examined. The authors found that the receipt of financial aid did not have a bearing on students' decision to persist, but that first-year students from families with higher incomes tended to be retained into the second year at higher rates than students from lower income families. Overall, though, students' academic performance was the greatest predictor of persistence into the sophomore year.

KEY WORDS: academic performance, financial aid, persistence, socioeconomic status.

Carini, R. M., Hayek, J. C., Kuh, G. D., Kennedy, J. M., & Ouimet, J. A. (2003). College student responses to web and paper surveys: Does mode matter? *Research in Higher Education, 44*(1), 1-19.

This article examines the potential difference between administering a survey in paper format and via the web. The authors used more than 58,000 cases from the 2000 academic year administration of the National Study on Student Engagement (NSSE) to determine if there were differences in responses between students taking the NSSE online or in a paper format. The researchers looked for differences on three levels: (a) general differences between responses based on mode, (b) differences specific to the college experience based on mode, and (c) differences by sex and age based on mode. Eight scales involving 53 survey items were examined using a multivariate logistic regression and ordinary least squares. The researchers found that students taking the NSSE online had statistically significant ($p < .001$) more positive and favorable responses than those responses provided on a paper survey, but that the effect sizes for each of the eight scales were very small. Similar results were identified when the sample was stratified based on specific questions and by sex and age. Thus, even though the differences in responses were statistically significant based on mode of survey, the small effect sizes mitigate this finding, and, as the researchers conclude, indicate that there is not a substantial difference in overall responses gathered on a web-based versus paper survey. The researchers also indicate a need for further research on this topic, specifically with noncognitive mechanisms that may explain responses and differences within the larger population beyond sex and age.

KEY WORDS: assessment measures, web-based surveys.

Crissman Ishler, J. L., & Upcraft, M. L. (2001). Assessing first-year programs. In J. H. Schuh, M. L. Upcraft, & Associates (Eds.), *Assessment practice in student affairs: An applications manual* (pp. 261-274). San Francisco: Jossey-Bass.

This chapter offers a comprehensive model for assessing first-year programs. The tenets of the model include the assessment of first-year students' background, needs, satisfaction with the first-year program under consideration, and gains resulting from program participation. The model also identifies the importance of considering the scope and cost-effectiveness of any first-year assessment effort. The authors use the model to work through 11 steps of an assessment example, new student orientation attendance, and student satisfaction.

KEY WORDS: assessment, orientation, student affairs practice.

Dooris, M. J., & Blood, I. M. (2001). Implementing and assessing first-year seminars. *Assessment Update, 13*(4), 1-2, 12-13.

The authors review the implementation and assessment of an institution-wide first-year seminar at The Pennsylvania State University that is considered the hallmark of a new general education curriculum. The design of the new first-year seminar and general education curriculum reflected input from alumni, students, and analysis of student registration data as well as a review of the literature and existing best practices. The new first-year seminar became a campuswide requirement, although individual colleges, departments, and campuses were given considerable autonomy with regard to course content and structure. Although this variation created some challenges to assessing the new first-year seminar program, the faculty senate and central administration were committed to understanding the program's effects. A General Education Assessment Interest group was formed to assess use, impact, and outcomes of the first-year seminars during their inaugural year. Information on course offerings and enrollment patterns comprised the bulk of the utilization study, while faculty and student focus groups and student surveys gauged the impact and outcomes of the courses. Overall, the assessments yielded data in favor of the program and identified specific areas of positive impact (e.g., small class sizes and longer duration of the course). This case study provides an example of how assessment can be used in planning, implementing, and evaluating a new first-year program.
KEY WORDS: assessment, first-year seminars, general education.

Evenbeck, S. E., & Borden, V. M. H. (2001). Assessing the impact of learning communities: Research in progress. *Assessment Update: Progress Trends, and Practices in Higher Education, 13*(4), 4-5, 9.

This brief article describes the development of a model for evaluating learning communities at Indiana University–Purdue University Indianapolis (IUPUI), a large, public urban commuter campus. The authors offer a history of the institution's learning community program, beginning with first-year seminars in the 1980s and building to include seminars and learning communities. The authors note that program evaluation was initially focused on examining differences between participants and nonparticipants. They discuss the merits of evolving the program evaluation to look at within-group differences (e.g., gender, age, ethnicity) and note that publicizing program outcomes revealed through these evaluation processes prompted funding for additional personnel to assess outcomes of these and other programs at the institution.
KEY WORDS: assessment, program evaluation.

Fenske, R. H., Porter, J. D., & DuBrock, C. P. (2000). Tracking financial aid and persistence of women, minority, and needy students in science, engineering, and mathematics. *Research in Higher Education, 41*(1), 67-94.

In this article, the authors outline a descriptive and inferential longitudinal study in which the impact of financial aid on persistence among women and students of color in Science, Engineering, or Mathematics (SEM) was assessed. Four consecutive cohorts beginning with the fall 1989 class were examined, using data obtained by the Financial Aid and Academic Progress (FAAP) data clearinghouse. The study found that students without financial need had the highest level of persistence. The researchers also noted that students in SEM majors tended to have lower rates of departure from college than students in other fields, but they also took longer to graduate, and women in general, as well as Whites and Asians, tended to persist and graduate at rates greater than all men and all other minority groups in the SEM fields. The authors also found that students of color at this institution tended to finance their education with several different kinds of aid (e.g., gifts, loans, grants) confirming an earlier study. When comparing financial aid packages and persistence rates, those receiving gift aid only (e.g., merit scholarships, other non-loan aid) persisted at higher rates than those financing their education through a combination of aid or through self-help aid (loans). The authors suggest that financial aid administrators, as well as faculty and staff in SEM fields, should recognize that SEM majors tend to take longer to graduate from college than students in other fields, which could impact their aid levels in later years. They also suggest that the amount of gift aid received by underrepresented populations should be evaluated and that additional research should be conducted to determine why discrepancies in who receives this aid exist.

KEY WORDS: financial aid, graduation rates, persistence, research studies, retention, STEM disciplines.

Hayek, J., & Kuh, G. (2004). Principles for assessing student engagement in the first year of college. *Assessment Update: Progress Trends, and Practices in Higher Education, 16*(2), 11-13.

The authors of this article offer five principles to guide assessment efforts that use the National Survey of Student Engagement (NSSE) and posit that effective incorporation of these principles into first-year assessment efforts will yield a deeper understanding of student experiences and institutional practices that contribute to a high quality college first year. The authors suggest that those involved in the assessment should first become familiar with the conceptual and empirical foundation of student engagement. Second, they should be sure to employ sampling strategies that maximize the utility and validity of the data (e.g., population sampling, efforts to increase response rates). Third, they should merge student survey data with other relevant sources of information on the first-year experience such as admissions data, transcripts, faculty data, or student data collected using other instruments. Fourth, they should be sure to share assessment results in multiple modes and settings as well as organize discussions about implications for and application to practice. Fifth, they should consider using multiple approaches (e.g., both normative and criterion-referenced) to estimating student performance. While the article elaborates on these assessment principles as they relate to use of NSSE data, the authors encourage using them as a guide to take maximum advantage of any first-year data.

KEY WORDS: assessment measures, engagement.

Ishitani, T. T. (2003). A longitudinal approach to assessing attrition behavior among first-generation students: Time-varying effects of pre-college characteristics. *Research in Higher Education, 44*(4), 433-449.

This article describes a longitudinal study on first-generation college students and their persistence through college. The author examined nine consecutive semesters of data from a cohort of 1,747 students that began college in the fall of 1995 at a four-year comprehensive public university in the Midwest. Using an event history model of analysis combined with product-limit estimation, the author found that first-generation college students persisted into their second year of college at a rate much lower than that of their peers, and that this trend of lower persistence continued throughout the duration of the study. Female first-generation students and students from families with yearly incomes less than $25,000 dropped out of college at rates significantly higher than their peers. The author notes that first-generation college students had a much higher risk of departure from college after their first year than their peers, but the timing of departure for these students varied from that point. Women in the study were at greatest risk of leaving in the third year. The author suggests that administrators and researchers could use this information and the event history model to determine when students fitting a specific description would be most likely to leave college. Educators could also use findings from this study to help explain risk factors associated with student attrition on their campuses.

KEY WORDS: assessment, first-generation students, persistence.

Kahn, J. H., & Nauta, M. M. (2001). Social-cognitive predictors of first-year college persistence: The importance of proximal assessment. *Research in Higher Education, 42*(6), 633-652.

The persistence of 400 first-year students at a public midwestern university was predicted before college entrance and measured in the second semester. Data were collected using The Social Cognitive Career Theory (SCCT), which relates measurements of self-efficacy, performance goals, and expectations to the first- to second-year persistence of first-year students. To measure academic ability and performance, the researchers collected data about high school class rank, ACT scores, and first- and second-semester grade point averages. Self-efficacy was measured using a modified version of the Self-Efficacy for Broad Academic Milestones Scale (SE-Broad). Outcomes expectations, performance goals, and first-to-second-year persistence were also measured. The researchers concluded that social-cognitive factors influence persistence of first-year students when students have completed at least one semester. The most significant predictors of persistence were ability and past performance (e.g., ACT scores, high school class rank). The researchers also concluded that while persistence can partially be predicted by ability and past performance, factors such as self-efficacy must also be considered.
KEY WORDS: assessment measures, persistence, self-efficacy.

Keup, J. R. (2004). The Cooperative Institutional Research Program Freshman Survey and Your First College Year: Using longitudinal data to assess the first year of college. *Assessment Update: Progress Trends, and Practices in Higher Education, 16*(2), 8-10.

This article introduces the two instruments that comprise the Cooperative Institutional Research Program (CIRP) at the University of California Los Angeles' Higher Education Research Institute (HERI): (a) the Freshman Survey, administered at college entry, and (b) the Your First College Year (YFCY) Survey, which serves as a one-year follow-up to the Freshman Survey. The author also discusses the types of analyses to consider when working with the Freshman Survey, YFCY, or other first-year assessment data. For example, comparative analyses offer the ability to evaluate elements of the first-year experience among institutions and peer groups as well as across segments of one college's first-year student population. Measures of association provide valuable information about the direction and the strength of the relationship between various aspects of the first-year experience, while factor analyses provide a means of distilling the vast data supplied by these instruments, simplifying the data analysis process, and streamlining presentation of results. Multivariate analyses provide the maximum amount of information about the relationships between variables such as students' individual characteristics and backgrounds, institutional characteristics, and first-year student involvement in the curriculum and cocurriculum. The particular value of the CIRP instruments is their longitudinal nature. This allows institutions to track students' change and development during the first year as well as more precisely estimate the effects of certain first-year experiences on student outcomes.
KEY WORDS: assessment measures, research design.

Pike, G. R., & Staupe, J. L. (2002). Does high school matter? An analysis of three methods of predicting first-year grades. *Research in Higher Education, 43*(2), 187-207.

To better identify students who will benefit from first-year academic intervention programs, this study examined multiple ways of predicting grade point averages of 8,764 first-year students at a major research university. The authors compared typically used regression models that included (a) standardized test scores, high school grades, and high school coursework; (b) high school effects models, which also included four characteristics of the sending high school (size, control, average ability of students, and percent attending college); and (c) hierarchical linear models that included both the individual and high school variables in a nested structure. When the estimates gained from these three models were compared with students' actual first-year grades, the researchers found that the high school effects model produced the most accurate prediction and hierarchical linear modeling produced the least accurate prediction for the data overall. However, both the high school effects model and hierarchical linear model were slightly more accurate than the model typically used for classifying at-risk students. While generalizability is somewhat limited by the institutional sample, these results suggest the most accurate methods of using existing data to identify new students who may be most in need of academic interventions during the first year.

KEY WORDS: academic performance, assessment, intervention strategies.

Sax, L. J., Gilmartin, S. K., & Bryant, A. N. (2003). Assessing response rates and nonresponse bias in web and paper surveys. *Research in Higher Education, 44*(4), 409-432.

The authors used 2000-2001 data from two Cooperative Institutional Research Program (CIRP) surveys administered nationally to first-year college students, the Freshman Survey and the Your First College Year (YFCY) survey, to examine response rates and nonresponse bias across various modes of YFCY survey administration: paper, paper with a web option, web-only with an incentive, and web-only without an incentive. Responses for each mode of administration indicated that the paper with a web option mode yielded the highest response rate while web-only administration (both with and without the incentive) resulted in the lowest response rates. Further analyses of response rates indicate that women, Asian American students, students categorized as social activists, and students with higher high school grade point averages and SAT scores were more likely to respond to the YFCY than their peers. African-American and Native American students and students characterized as status strivers, hedonists, or leaders were least likely to respond to the YFCY. An analysis of data from students who were given the choice of completing the survey via paper or web indicated that web response was more likely from men, students who attend college farther from home, students who report higher levels of emotional health, and students who more strongly value the learning opportunities provided by college attendance. The results of this study may be used to inform selection of institutional strategies for survey administration.

KEY WORDS: assessment, response rates, web-based surveys.

Schuh, J. H. (2005). Assessing programs and other student experiences designed to enrich the first-year experience. In R. S. Feldman (Ed.), *Improving the first-year of college: research and practice* (pp. 141-157). Mahwah, NJ: Lawrence Erlbaum Associates.

This chapter offers an overview of assessment strategies for programs, services, and experiences of first-year students. It begins with a discussion of how theory shapes effective first-year assessment. The author also defines assessment, offers three reasons to conduct assessment (measure effectiveness, accountability, and program improvement), and presents a typology of assessment activities. Twelve questions that can be used to guide every stage of assessment are identified, from questions about problem identification to questions about reporting results. Two case studies of assessment projects at fictitious institutions are used to illustrate implementation of the principles outlined in the chapter.

KEY WORD: assessment.

Swing, R. L. (Ed.). (2004a). *Proving and improving, volume II: Tools and techniques for assessing the first college year* (Monograph No. 37). Columbia, SC: University of South Carolina, National Resource Center for The First-Year Experience and Students in Transition.

This six-part monograph compiles information about instruments related to first-year assessment and culminates with a comprehensive typology. The volume begins with an introduction to assessment of the first year including definitions of various forms of assessment and suggestions for organizing and

preparing for assessment efforts. Authors of the first part describe assessment efforts that rely on data available through institutional records. In addition to highlighting specific tools (e.g., Data Audit and Analysis Toolkit and Enrollment Search), the authors provide suggestions on working with campus offices of institutional research and course records to assess aspects of the first year. Part 1 also includes a description of the Freshman Absence-Based Intervention program at the University of Mississippi. The second part of the monograph describes methods for collecting qualitative data including focus groups, and "think aloud" protocols. This part also includes an overview of a "promise audit" used to examine student perspectives on services and other campus features and a case study on involving faculty in assessment planning and implementation. The third part of the monograph offers examples of course evaluations and the fourth and largest part of the monograph describes numerous first-year survey instruments. Surveys featured in this section include the Cooperative Institutional Research Project (CIRP) Freshman Survey and the Your First College Year (YFCY) follow-up survey, the College Student Experiences Questionnaire (CSEQ), the Study Behavior Inventory, and the National Survey of Student Engagement (NSSE). Part five of the monograph offers several examples of cognitive tests including those to measure critical thinking, general education outcomes and assessment, and writing assessment. The final part of the monograph brings the discussion about first-year assessment from specific examples back to a broad discussion about purpose and future directions. This part includes a description of the Hope Scale and assessment of learning styles.
KEY WORDS: assessment, assessment measures, cognitive measures.

Swing, R. L. (2004b). What's so special about assessment in the first year of college? *Assessment Update: Progress, Trends, and Practices in Higher Education, 16*(2), 1-4.

In this introductory article in a special issue of *Assessment Update* on first-year assessment issues, the author introduces the evolution of the first-year assessment movement. The author also offers five conditions unique to assessment of the first year of college, and recommends strategies for managing under these conditions. Finding space in the list of institutional priorities and in a typically packed orientation schedule to collect baseline data on incoming students is one such condition. Another condition impacting assessment in the first year is the demographic profile (i.e., age and maturity level) of traditional-age new college students and the issues inherent in applying commonly used assessment theories, approaches, and instruments to nontraditional-age students. The power differential between first-year students and those who collect data from them is a third condition that can threaten data integrity and follow-up assessments. The fourth condition, student unfamiliarity with educational jargon and institutional vernacular, can also threaten data integrity. Ethical, practical, and other issues surrounding selection or creation of comparison or control groups comprise the fifth condition with implications for assessment approaches and data interpretation.
KEY WORD: assessment.

Swing, R. L., & Upcraft, M. L. (2005). Choosing and using assessment instruments. In M. L. Upcraft, J. N. Gardner, & B. O. Barefoot (Eds.), *Challenging & supporting the first-year student: A handbook for improving the first year of college* **(pp. 501-514). San Francisco: Jossey-Bass.**

This chapter identifies issues to consider when choosing approaches and instruments to assess the first college year. The authors discuss key issues in choosing an assessment instrument, including design of the study, purposes of the study, and the soundness and credibility of the instruments. The chapter also identifies quantitative instruments readily available for first-year assessment initiatives, outlines a typology for understanding the general classes of survey instruments and describes national instruments commonly used in first-year assessments. The chapter offers nine strategies to aid in selecting a quantitative instrument, discusses five qualitative approaches to assessment of the first college year (e.g., focus groups, portfolios, field observations), and outlines approaches for using existing data to better understand the first-year experience.

KEY WORDS: assessment, assessment measures, research design, research studies.

Upcraft, M. L. (2005). Assessing the first year of college. In M. L. Upcraft, J. N. Gardner, & B. O. Barefoot (Eds.), *Challenging & supporting the first-year student: A handbook for improving the first year of college* (pp. 469-485). San Francisco: Jossey-Bass.

This chapter offers basic definitions of terms used in assessment practice and identifies seven reasons to conduct assessment. An eight-step comprehensive model for assessing the first year of college is recommended, and the author identifies major barriers to successful first-year assessment efforts (e.g., lack of support from institutional leadership, limited fiscal and human resources, lack of expertise, and fear of the results). Ethical standards for conducting assessment in the first year are described and the author closes with recommendations to guide assessment activities.

KEY WORDS: assessment, ethics.

Stephanie M. Foote is the director of the Academic Success Center and First-Year Experience at the University of South Carolina Aiken. Stephanie has served as chairwoman of the ACPA Commission for Admissions, Orientation, and the First Year Experience. She has presented and written about the transition from high school to college, the first-year and sophomore-year experience, and the use of peers in the first-year seminar classroom. Her current research interests include examining the relationship between first-year student self-efficacy and academic achievement. Stephanie also coordinates and teaches the First-Year Seminar at USC Aiken and is a doctoral student in the Educational Administration – Higher Education program at the University of South Carolina.

Sara E. Hinkle has been professionally promoting first-year college student success for 11 years through research and practice, including work in residence life, orientation, student activities, precollege programming, and academic advising. She currently serves Hofstra University as associate dean of student affairs and community development. Sara earned a B.A. in psychology from Gettysburg College, a M.S. in counseling from Georgia State University, and a Ph.D. in higher education from Indiana University Bloomington. Her dissertation research focused on the adjustment issues of students who attended a precollege academic program. In addition, she served as a research associate on Project DEEP (Documenting Effective Educational Practice), a collaboration of the National Survey of Student Engagement (NSSE) and the American Association of Higher Education (AAHE), which conducted case studies of high-performing colleges and universities. The project resulted in the publication *Student Success in College: Creating Conditions That Matter* (Kuh, Kinzie, Schuh, Whitt, & Associates, 2005).

Andrew (Drew) K. Koch presently serves as the director of Purdue University's Student Access, Transition, and Success Programs department. He has been professionally involved with student access and success efforts for nearly 15 years. During that time, he has worked with learning communities, summer bridge programs, first-year seminars, precollege outreach programs, orientation programming, efforts for first-year honors students, Supplemental Instruction, diversity initiatives, and a host of other initiatives designed to enhance the first college year. He holds a B.A. in history and German from the University of Richmond, a M.A. in history from the University of Richmond, and a M.A. in Higher Education Administration from the University of South Carolina. In addition to his professional responsibilities, he is completing the requirements for a Ph.D. in American Studies at Purdue University where he is writing a dissertation titled *Rage Against the Machine: The University Military Industrial Complex and Contemporary American Culture.*

Jennifer R. Keup earned her doctorate in higher education and organizational change from the UCLA Graduate School of Education and Information Studies and served as a research analyst and project director at the Higher Education Research Institute (HERI) for seven years. Keup is currently the director of the UCLA Student Affairs Information and Research Office. Her professional roles, personal research agenda, and publications focus on issues of student learning and development, particularly at points of transition; the impact of college on student outcomes; and the practice of assessment in higher education.

Matthew (Matt) D. Pistilli is the assistant director and coordinator for Databases & Statistics for Student Access, Transition, and Success Programs at Purdue University. Pistilli has worked with learning communities at Purdue since February 2004 as the coordinator of Entrepreneurial and Multicultural Learning Communities. In his role, he created and implemented the Entrepreneurial Learning Communities and enhanced curriculum development pieces associated with new learning communities. During his tenure in higher education, Matt has also worked in residence life and on retention and summer bridge programs. His research interests include the impact of diversity perceptions on learning and retention, understanding the impact of orientation and academic success initiatives on student retention and graduation rates, and the transition process for graduating college seniors. Matt holds a B.A. in Psychology and Spanish, a M.S.Ed. in Counseling and College Student Affairs, and is in the final year of coursework for his Ph.D. in Higher Education Administration at Purdue University.

INDEX

Academic
Achievement
Andrade (2001) 139
Hagedorn, Siadet, Fogel, Nora, & Pascarella (1999) 70, 131
Hickman, Bartholomae, & McKenry (2000) 97
Hoover (2003) 120, 132
Parker, Duffy, Wood, Bond, & Hogan (2005) 120, 134
Smith & Wertlieb (2005) 42, 109
Tuckman (2003) 123
Advising
Beck & Davidson (2001) 77
Colton, Connor, Schultz, & Easter (1999-2000) 77
Donnelly & Borland (2002) 46
Gallagher & Allen (2000) 73, 94
Gordan, Habley, & Associates (2000) 74
Hunter, McCalla-Wriggins, & White (Eds.) (2007) 74
Johnson (2000-01) 63, 132
Keeling (2003) 12, 75
King & Kerr (2005) 75
Kuh, Kinzie, Schuh, Whitt, & Associates (2005) 80
Mastrodicasa (2001) 75, 114
Sams, Brown, Hussey, & Leonard (2003) 76
Smith (2002) 76, 94
Training
King & Kerr (2005) 75
Affairs (see collaboration)
Aspirations
Weissman, Bulakowski, & Jumisko (1998) 28, 113
Integration
Nagda, Gregerman, Jonides, von
Hippel, & Lerner (1998) 92
Perry, Cabrera, & Vogt (1999) 81
Motivation
Hodges, Dochen, & Joy (2001) 71
Stage & Hossler (2000) 121
Performance
Barrows & Goodfellow (2005) 59
Braunstein, McGrath, & Pescatrice (2000-01) 129, 141
Charles, Dinwiddie, & Massey (2004) 15, 22
Chemers, Hu, & Garcia (2001) 119
Dahlgren, Wille, Finkel, & Burger (2005) 51
Furr & Elling (2002) 22
Kubey, Lavin, & Barrows (2001) 87
Pike & Staupe (2002) 134, 144
Potts, Schultz, & Foust (2003-4) 66, 102
Schwartz & Washington (2002) 27, 115, 135
Somers, Woodhouse, & Cofer (2004) 32
Zhao & Kuh (2004) 67
Planning
Sams, Brown, Hussey, & Leonard (2003) 76
Preparation
Cabrera, & La Nasa (2001) 107
Chenoweth (1998) 108
Jones (2005) 23

Success (see student success)
Support
Bryson, Smith, & Vineyard (2002) 21, 42
Commander, Valeri-Gold, & Darnell (2004) 60
Cuseo (2003) 77
Dillon (2003) 61, 83
Rendón, García, & Person (2004) 26
Access to Higher Education
Black & Amir (2002) 135
Heller (2001) 108
Kim (2004) 109
Lumina Foundation for Education (2005) 137
McLure & Child (1999) 38
Mortenson (2004) 137
Mortenson (2005, August) 137
Mortenson (2005, September) 109, 138
St. John, Chung, Musoba, Simmons,
Wooden, & Mendez (2004) 110
St. John, Gross, Musoba, & Chung (2005) 110, 139
St. John, Musoba, Simmons, & Choong-Geun (2002) 138
Tsao (2005) 28, 112
Wallace, Abel, & Ropers-Huilman (2000) 42
White (2005) 29
Active Learning
Braxton, Milem, & Sullivan (2000) 51, 129
Dahlgren, Wille, Finkel, & Burger (2005) 51
Admissions
Young & Johnson (2004) 111
Early Notification Programs
Reingold (2004) 44
Selective Admissions
Reingold (2004) 44
St. John, Hu, Simmons, & Musoba (2001) 44
Standards
Bryson, Smith, & Vineyard (2002) 21, 42
Freer-Weiss (2004-5) 43, 112
Tam & Sukhatme (2004) 44
Adult Learners
Haulmark & Williams (2004) 47
Advocacy
Anttonen & Chaskes (2002) 93
African American Students (see also students of color)
Chenoweth (1998) 108
Furr & Elling (2002) 22
Schwartz & Washington (2002) 27, 114, 134
Weissman, Bulakowski, & Jumisko (1998) 28, 113
Anticipatory Socialization
Hossler, Kuh, & Olsen (2001) 125
Assessment
Barefoot (2004) 140
Blackhurst, Akey, & Bobilya (2003) 59, 82
Braxton, Bray, & Berger (2000) 89
Braxton, Milem, & Sullivan (2000) 51, 129
Boulter (2002) 89

Busby, Gammel, & Jeffcoat (2002) 45
Charles, Dinwiddie, & Massey (2004) 15, 22
Coffman & Gilligan (2002) 99, 120
Crissman Ishler & Upcraft (2001) 45, 141
Dooris & Blood (2001) 53, 142
Evenbeck & Borden (2001) 142
Flowers, Pascarella, & Pierson (2000) 87
Gordan, Habley, & Associates (2000) 74
Gordon & Steele (2003) 11
Greiner & Westbrook (2002) 90
Henscheid (2004) 54, 62
Hickman, Bartholomae, & McKenry (2000) 97
Hickman & Crossland (2004-5) 96
Hodges, Dochen, & Joy (2001) 71
Hoffman, Richmond, Morrow, &
    Salomone (2002-3) 62, 90, 100
Inkelas & Weisman (2003) 83
Ishitani (2003) 143
Kaya (2004) 83
King & Kerr (2005) 75
Kuh, Kinzie, Schuh, Whitt, & Associates (2005) 80
Logan, Salisbury-Glennon, & Spence (2000) 64
Mandel & Evans (2003) 58, 126
Martin & Hurley (2005) 72
Martin, Swartz-Kulstad, & Madson (1999) 80
Murie & Thomson (2001) 72
Oates & Leavitt (2003) 65, 69
Pike & Staupe (2002) 134, 144
Sax, Gilmartin, & Bryant (2003) 145
Schroeder (2003) 127
Schuh (2005) 145
Skipper (2005) 14
Smith (2002) 76, 94
Swing (2004a) 122, 145
Swing (2004b) 146
Swing & Upcraft (2005) 146
Ting, Grant, & Pienert (2000) 82
Tobolowsky, Cox, & Wagner (2005) 56
Upcraft (2005) 147

Measures
Bauer & Liang (2003) 9, 128
Boyd, Hunt, Kandell, & Lucas (2003) 119
Bryson, Smith, & Vineyard (2002) 21, 42
Carini, Hayek, Kuh, Kennedy, & Ouimet (2003) 141
Hagedorn, Siadet, Fogel, Nora, & Pascarella (1999) 70, 131
Hayek & Kuh (2004) 143
Helland, Stallings, & Braxton (2001-2) 39
Hoover (2003) 12, 132
Hicks (2003) 40
Kahn & Nauta (2001) 133, 144
Keup (2004) 144
Logan, Salisbury-Glennon, & Spence (2000) 37
Longerbeam & Sedlacek (2006) 24, 64
Schlosser & Sedlacek (2001) 121
Schwartz & Washington (2002) 27, 114, 134
Smith, English, & Vasek (2002) 31
Struthers, Perry, & Menec (2000) 19
Swing (2004a) 122, 145
Swing & Upcraft (2005) 146
Wasburn & Miller (2004) 28

Longitudinal
Nadler, Miller, & Dyer (2004) 48
At-Risk Students
Bryson, Smith, & Vineyard (2002) 19
Colton, Connor, Schultz, & Easter (1999-2000) 77
Engle, Reilly, & Levine (2003-4) 78
Freer-Weiss (2004-5) 43, 112
Horn & Carroll (2004) 136
Johnson (2000-01) 63, 132
Santos & Reigadas (2004-5) 93
Attachment
Perrine (2001) 17, 81
Campus Climate
Hurtado & Carter (1997) 23
Jones (2005) 23
Wasburn & Miller (2004) 28
Career Development
Gore (2005) 74
Perry, Cabrera, & Vogt (1999) 81
CAS Standards
Fabich (2004) 46, 111
Gordan, Habley, & Associates (2000) 74
Miller, Dyer, & Nadler (2002) 47
Nadler, Miller, & Dyer (2004) 48
Case Studies
Barefoot, et al. (2005) 124
Henscheid (2004) 54, 62
Kuh, Kinzie, Schuh, Whitt, & Associates (2005) 125
Zlotkowski (2002) 69
Clustered/Linked Courses (see also learning communities)
Crissman Ishler (2001) 60
Kutnowski (2005) 63, 112
Logan, Salisbury-Glennon, & Spence (2000) 37, 64
Stassen (2003) 66
Cocurricular
Activities
Kuh, Palmer, & Kish (2003) 84
Terenzini, Pascarella, & Blimling (1999) 85, 122
Involvement
Keup & Barefoot (2005) 54
Cognitive
Development (see also student development)
Terenzini, Pascarella, & Blimling (1999) 85, 122
Walker (2003) 67, 115
Measures
Swing (2004a) 122, 145
Cohorts
Maher (2004) 65, 101
Collaboration, Academic Affairs and Student Affairs
Hossler, Kuh, & Olsen (2001) 125
Kuh, Kinzie, Schuh, Whitt, & Associates (2005) 94
Mandel & Evans (2003) 58, 126
Schroeder (2003) 127
College
Adjustment
Blackhurst, Akey, & Bobilya (2003) 59, 82
Boulter (2002) 89
Brissette, Scheier, & Carver (2002) 98
Chemers, Hu, & Garcia (2001) 119
Clark (2005) 29, 130

Crissman Ishler (2002) 99
Grant-Vallone, Reid, Umali, & Pohlert (2003-4) 32, 79
Hickman, Bartholomae, & McKenry (2000) 97
Hickman & Crossland (2004-5) 96
Hickman, Toews, & Andrews (2001) 96
Jackson, Pancer, Pratt, & Hunsberger (2000) 40
Kaya (2004) 83
Keup & Barefoot (2005) 54
Logan, Salisbury-Glennon, & Spence (2000) 37, 64
Martin, Swartz-Kulstad, & Madson (1999) 80
Miller, Bender, & Schuh (2005) 40
Paul & Brier (2001) 101
Paul, Manetas, Grady, & Vivona (2001) 38
Schilling & Schilling (2005) 41
Schwartz & Buboltz (2004) 98
Schwartz & Washington (2002) 27, 115, 134
Wolf-Wendel, Tuttle, & Keller-Wolff (1999) 39
Choice
Kim (2004) 109
Stage & Hossler (2000) 121
Costs
Heller (2001) 108
Lumina Foundation for Education (2005) 137
Outcomes
Kuh, Palmer, & Kish (2003) 84
Pascarella & Terenzini (2001) 92
Pascarella & Terenzini (2005) 13, 126
Community Colleges (see two-year institutions)
Commuter Students
Clark (2005) 30
Jacoby & Garland (2004) 30
Sessa (2005) 19, 30, 98
Counseling
Colton, Connor, Schultz, & Easter (1999-2000) 77
Engle, Reilly, & Levine (2003-4) 78
Services
Kitzrow (2003) 16
Martin, Swartz-Kulstad, & Madson (1999) 80
Curriculum Reform
Andrade (2001) 139
Degree Attainment (see also graduation rates)
Arredondo & Knight (2005) 128, 139
Demographics
Chen & Carroll (2005) 135
Harvey & Anderson (2005) 136
Developmental Education
Hagedorn, Siadet, Fogel, Nora, & Pascarella (1999) 70, 132
Higbee (2005) 71
Murie & Thomson (2001) 72
Diversity
Crissman Ishler (2005) 10
Fabich (2004) 46, 111
Jones (2005) 23
King & Kerr (2005) 75
Light (2001) 85, 126
Longerbeam & Sedlacek (2006) 24, 64
Malaney & Berger (2005) 25
McLure & Child (1999) 38
Perna (2002) 38
St. John, Hu, Simmons, & Musoba (2001) 44

Wallace, Abel, & Ropers-Huilman (2000) 42
Education
Laar, Levin, Sinclair, & Sidanius (2005) 24, 84
Diverse Student Groups
Gordan, Habley, & Associates (2000) 74
Hunter, McCalla-Wriggins, & White (2007) 75
Early Warning Systems
Beck & Davidson (2001) 77
Johnson (2000-2001) 63, 132
Kuh, Kinzie, Schuh, Whitt, & Associates (2005) 80
Eating Disorders
Schwitzer & Rodriguez (2002) 19
Emotional Intelligence
Parker, Duffy, Wood, Bond, & Hogan (2005) 120, 134
Engagement
Barefoot (2000) 54, 56, 124
Hayek & Kuh (2004) 143
Keup & Barefoot (2005) 54
Kuh, Kinzie, Schuh, Whitt, & Associates
(2005) 80, 91, 94, 125
Terenzini, Pascarella, & Blimling (1999) 85, 122
Zhao & Kuh (2004) 67
English Composition
Hafer (2001) 70
Tsao (2005) 28, 112
Enrollment
King & Wessell (2004) 43
Data
Chen & Carroll (2005) 135
Harvey & Anderson (2005) 136
National Center for Education Statistics (2005) 12, 138
U. S. Census Bureau (2005) 13, 110
Management
Hutto & Fenwick (2002) 79, 114
Ethics
Upcraft (2005) 147
ESL Instruction
Murie & Thomson (2001) 72
Faculty
Braxton, Bray, & Berger (2000) 89
Golde & Pribbenow (2000) 61
Greiner & Westbrook (2002) 90
Lundquist, Spalding, & Landrum (2002-3) 92
Nora (2001) 97
Support
Martin, Swartz-Kulstad, & Madson (1999) 80
Female Students
Gold, Miller, & Rutholz (2001) 15, 78
Packard, Walsh, & Seidenberg (2004) 26
Wasburn & Miller (2004) 28
Financial Aid
Ackerman, Young, & Young (2005) 107
Braunstein, McGrath, & Pescatrice (2000-01) 129, 141
Fenske, Porter, & DuBrock (2000) 142
Hu & Hossler (2000) 108
Hutto & Fenwick (2002) 79, 114
Kim (2004) 109
McLure & Child (1999) 38
First-Generation Students
Chen & Carroll (2005) 135

Grant-Vallone, Reid, Umali, & Pohlert (2003-4) 32, 79
Hicks (2003) 40
Ishitani (2003) 143
Perna (2002) 38
Somers, Woodhouse & Cofer (2004) 32
White (2005) 29

First-Year Experience
Upcraft, Gardner, Barefoot, & Associates (2004) 128
Comprehensive Initiatives
Barefoot, et al. 124
Mandel & Evans (2003) 58,126
Program Standards
Barefoot (2004) 140
Seminars
Barrows & Goodfellow (2005) 59
Cavote & Kopera-Frye (2004) 53
Crissman Ishler (2001) 60
Crissman Ishler (2002) 99
Cuseo (2003) 77
Donahue (2004) 89, 100
Dooris & Blood (2001) 53, 142
First-year experience to help students
    succeed (2005) 22, 114
Gore (2005) 74
Haulmark & Williams (2004) 47
Henscheid (2004) 54, 62
Hodges & White (2001) 71
Hoffman, Richmond, Morrow, &
    Salomone (2002-3) 62, 90, 100
Hunter & Linder (2005) 54
Keup (2005) 57
Keup & Barefoot (2005) 54
Parang, Raine, & Stevenson (2000) 68
Potts, Schultz, & Foust (2003-4) 66, 102
Schnell & Doetkott (2002-3) 55
Starke, Harth, & Sirianni (2001) 55
Thomson & Stringer (2000) 55, 88
Tobolowsky (2005) 56
Tobolowsky, Cox, & Wagner (2005) 56

Focus Groups
Weissman, Bulakowski, & Jumisko (1998) 28, 113
"Freshman Myth"
Jackson, Pancer, Pratt, & Hunsberger (2000) 40
Schilling & Schilling (2005) 41
Smith & Wertlieb (2005) 42, 109
Friendship/ Friends
Crissman Ishler (2002) 99
Paul & Brier (2001) 101
Gateway Courses
Smith (2003) 127
Gender
Arredondo & Knight (2005) 128, 139
Hagedorn, Siadet, Fogel, Nora, & Pascarella (1999) 70, 131
Differences
Baker, Meyer, & Hunt (2005) 59
Dadonna & Cooper (2002) 46
Hickman, Toews, & Andrews (2001) 96
Lowery, et al. (2005) 16
Sax, Bryant, & Gilmartin (2004) 18

General Education
Dooris & Blood (2001) 53, 142
Goal Commitment
Perry, Cabrera, & Vogt (1999) 81
Graduation Rates (see also degree attainment)
Chen and Carroll (2005) 135
Fenske, Porter, & DuBrock (2000) 142
Harvey & Anderson (2005) 136
Horn & Carroll (2004) 136
Tam & Sukhatme (2004) 44
Grief Experiences
Gold, Miller, & Rutholz (2001) 15, 78
Group Development
Maher (2004) 65, 101
HBCUs
Hutto & Fenwick (2002) 79, 114
Honors Programs
Glennen, Martin, & Walden (2000) 37
Humor
Hickman & Crossland (2004-5) 96
Identity Development
Boyd, Hunt, Kandell, & Lucas (2003) 119
Information Literacy
Hardesty (2007) 68
Nugent & Myers (2000) 68
Parang, Raine, & Stevenson (2000) 68
Institutional
Commitment
Perry, Cabrera, & Vogt (1999) 81
Identity
Helland, Stallings, & Braxton (2001-2) 39
Mission
King & Kerr (2005) 75
Instruments (see assessment measures)
Interdisciplinary Education
Smith & McCann (2001) 53
Intergroup Relations
Rendón, García, & Person (2004) 26
Internet Addiction
Kubey, Lavin, & Barrows (2001) 87
Intervention Strategies
Bergen-Cico (2000) 14
Pike & Staupe (2002) 134, 144
Schwitzer & Rodriguez (2002) 19
Involvement
Barefoot (2000) 56
Bauer & Liang (2003) 9, 128
Kuh, Palmer, & Kish (2003) 84
Light (2001) 85, 126
Schilling & Schilling (1999) 41
Terenzini, Pascarella, & Blimling (1999) 85, 122
Latino Students (see also students of color)
Chenoweth (1998) 108
Hernandez & Lopez (2004) 23
Hurtado & Carter (1997) 23
Longerbeam, Sedlacek, & Alatorre (2004) 26
Torres (2004) 27, 98
Weissman, Bulakowski, & Jumisko (1998) 28, 113
Zurita (2005) 29

Leadership
    Anttonen & Chaskes (2002) 93
Learning
    Donahue (2004) 89, 100
    Erickson & Strommer (2005) 51
    Hunter (2006) 57
    Schroeder (2003) 127
    Smith & McCann (2001) 53
    Tuckman (2003) 123
    Outcomes-based
        Belcher (2005) 140
    Strategies
        Ting, Grant, & Pienert (2000) 82
Learning Communities
    Baker, Meyer, & Hunt (2005) 59
    Barrows & Goodfellow (2005) 59
    Blackhurst, Akey, & Bobilya (2003) 59, 82
    Commander, Valeri-Gold, & Darnell (2004) 60
    Crissman Ishler (2001) 60
    Cutright (2002) 57, 78, 113, 125
    Franklin (2000) 61
    Golde & Pribbenow (2000) 61
    Henscheid (2004) 54, 62
    Hoffman, Richmond, Morrow, &
        Salomone (2002-3) 62, 90, 100
    Johnson (2000-01) 63, 132
    Keup (2005) 57
    Kutnowski (2005) 63, 112
    Laufgraben (2005) 64
    MacGregor & Smith (2005) 65
    Maher (2004) 65, 101
    Mangold, Bean, Adams, Schwab, & Lynch (2002-3) 80
    Oates & Leavitt (2003) 65, 69
    Potts, Schultz, & Foust (2003-4) 66, 102
    Smith & McCann (2001) 53
    Tinto (2000) 66
    Tobolowsky (2005) 56
    Tobolowsky, Cox, & Wagner (2005) 56
    Walker (2003) 67, 115
    Zhao & Kuh (2004) 67
    Residential
        Blackhurst, Akey, & Bobilya (2003) 59, 82
        Cuseo (2003) 77
        Dillon (2003) 61, 83
        Golde & Pribbenow (2000) 61
        Inkelas & Weisman (2003) 83
        Longerbeam & Sedlacek (2006) 24, 64
        Pascarella & Terenzini (2001) 92
        Stassen (2003) 66
        Zheng, Saunders, Shelley, & Whelan (2002) 86
Learning Disabilities
    Smith, English, & Vasek (2002) 31
Lesbian/ Gay/ Bisexual/ Transgendered Students
    Sanlo (2005) 27
Library Instruction
    Hardesty (2007) 68
    Nugent & Myers (2000) 68
    Parang, Raine, & Stevenson (2000) 68
Living Environments
    Charles, Dinwiddie, & Massey (2004) 15, 22

Living-Learning Communities (see learning communities)
Locus of Control
    Bean & Eaton (2000) 119
    Clark (2005) 29, 130
    Hoover (2003) 120, 132
Low-Income Students
    Black & Amir (2002) 135
    Mortenson (2004) 137
    Mortenson (2005, September) 109, 138
    St. John, Chung, Musoba, Simmons,
        Wooden, & Mendez (2004) 110
    St. John, Gross, Musoba, & Chung (2005) 110, 139
    St. John, Musoba, Simmons, & Choong-Geun (2002) 138
Mental Health
    Bray & Born (2004) 15
    Kitzrow (2003) 16
    Lenz (2004) 16
    Pritchard & Wilson (2003) 17, 121
    Sax, Bryant, & Gilmartin (2004) 18
    Schwitzer & Rodriguez (2002) 19
Mentoring (see also students of color)
    Colton, Connor, Schultz, & Easter (1999-2000) 77
    Cuseo (2003) 77
    Hrabowski (2005) 23
    Kuh, Kinzie, Schuh, Whitt, & Associates (2005) 80
    Mangold, Bean, Adams, Schwab, & Lynch (2002-3) 80
    Packard, Walsh, & Seidenberg (2004) 26
    Santos & Reigadas (2004-5) 93
    Walker & Taub (2001) 103
Millennial Students
    Brooks (2001) 10
    Coomes & DeBard (2004) 10
    Crissman Ishler (2005) 10
    Horn, Peter, & Rooney (2002) 11
    Howe & Strauss (2000) 11
    Keeling (2003) 12, 75
    Newton (2000) 12
Motivation
    Bean & Eaton (2000) 119
    Stage & Hossler (2000) 121
    Struthers, Perry, & Menec (2000) 19
    Gordon & Steele (2003) 11
    Tuckman (2003) 123
National Data Sets
    Astin, Oseguera, Sax, & Korn (2002) 9
    Horn, Peter, & Rooney (2002) 11
    Keup & Stolzenberg (2004) 84
    National Center for Education Statistics (2005) 12, 138
    Pryor, Hurtado, Saenz, Lindholm,
        Korn, & Mahoney (2005) 12
    U. S. Census Bureau (2005) 13, 110
    Zhao & Kuh (2004) 67
National Survey Findings
    Hunter & Linder (2005) 54
    Keup (2005) 57
    Kuh & Hu (2001) 90
    Zheng, Saunders, Shelley, & Whelan (2002) 86
National Trends
    MacGregor & Smith (2005) 65

Native American Students (see also students of color)
  First-year experience to help students
    succeed (2005) 22, 114
  Ness (2002) 26, 115
Online Learning
  Haulmark & Williams (2004) 47
Optimism
  Chemers, Hu, & Garcia (2001) 119
Orientation
  Busby, Gammel, & Jeffcoat (2002) 45
  Crissman Ishler & Upcraft (2001) 45, 141
  Dadonna & Cooper (2002) 46
  Daniel & Scott (2001) 95
  Donnelly & Borland (2002) 46
  Fabich (2004) 46, 111
  Haulmark & Williams (2004) 47
  Keppler, Mullendore, & Carey (2005) 47, 97
  King & Wessel (2004) 43
  Mastrodicasa (2001) 75, 114
  Miller, Dyer, & Nadler (2002) 47
  Nadler, Miller, & Dyer (2004) 48
  Paul, Manetas, Grady, & Vivona (2001) 38
  Smith (2003) 127
  Twale & Schaller (2003) 48
Outreach Programs
  Paul, Manetas, Grady, & Vivona (2001) 38
  Perna (2002) 38
Parental Involvement
  Cabrera, & LaNasa (2001) 107
  Elkins, Braxton, & James (2000) 31, 95, 131
  Hickman, Toews, & Andrews (2001) 96
  Keppler, Mullendore, & Carey (2005) 47
  Paul, Manetas, Grady, & Vivona (2001) 38
  Sessa (2005) 19, 30, 98
  Smith, English, & Vasek (2002) 31
Parents
  Daniel & Scott (2001) 95
  Hickman & Crossland (2004-5) 96
  Hickman, Bartholomae, & McKenry (2000) 97
  Keppler, Mullendore, & Carey (2005) 97
  Schwartz & Buboltz (2004) 98
Pedagogy (See teaching strategies)
Peer Support
  Brissette, Scheier, & Carver (2002) 99
  Donahue (2004) 89, 100
  Hoffman, Richmond, Morrow, &
    Salomone (2002-3) 62, 90, 100
  Kuh, Kinzie, Schuh, Whitt, & Associates (2005) 80
  Martin, Swartz-Kulstad, & Madson (1999) 80
  Thomas (2000) 102
Performance Indicators
  Belcher (2005) 140
Persistence (see also retention)
  Braxton, Milem, & Sullivan (2000) 51, 129
  Braunstein, McGrath, & Pescatrice (2000-01) 129, 141
  Daempfle (2003-04) 131
  Dahlgren, Wille, Finkel, & Burger (2005) 51
  Fenske, Porter, & DuBrock (2000) 142
  Gold, Miller, & Rutholz (2001) 15, 78
  Hickman & Crossland (2004-5) 96

Ishitani (2003) 143
Kahn & Nauta (2001) 133, 144
King & Wessel (2004) 43
Lounsbury, Saudargas, & Gibson (2004) 133
Perrine (2001) 17, 81
Pritchard & Wilson (2001) 17, 121
Somers, Woodhouse, & Cofer (2004) 32
St. John, Hu, Simmons, & Musoba (2001) 44
Physical Health
  Bray & Born (2004) 15
  Lenz (2004) 16
  Lowery et al. (2005) 16
  Racette, Deusinger, Strube, Highsteing,
    & Deusinger (2005) 17
  Schwitzer & Rodriguez (2002) 19
Policy
  Heller (2001) 108
Prejudice
  Laar, Levin, Sinclair, & Sidanius (2005) 24, 84
Pre-enrollment Programs
  King & Wessel (2004) 43
Private Institutions
  Hu & Hossler (2000) 108
Program Evaluation (see also assessment)
  Evenbeck & Borden (2001) 142
Race/Ethnicity (see also students of color)
  Black & Amir (2002) 135
  Harvey & Anderson (2005) 136
  Tsao (2005) 28, 112
  Racial/Ethnic Identity Development
    Torres (2004) 27, 98
Religion (see spirituality)
Research
  Design
    Keup (2004) 144
    Swing & Upcraft (2005) 146
  Studies
    Bailey & Alfonso (2005) 58, 111
    Fenske, Porter, & DuBrock (2000) 142
    Horn & Carroll (2004) 136
    Light (2001) 85, 126
    Ness (2002) 26, 115
    Swing & Upcraft (2005) 146
  Universities
    Cutright (2002) 57, 78, 113, 125
Residence Life
  Inkelas & Weisman (2003) 83
  Kaya (2004) 83
  Laar, Levin, Sinclair, & Sidanius (2005) 24, 84
  Pascarella & Terenzini (2001) 92
Residential Learning Communities (see learning communities)
Response Rates
  Sax, Gilmartin, & Bryant (2003) 145
Retention (see also persistence)
  Arredondo & Knight (2005) 128, 139
  Bailey & Alfonso (2005) 58, 111
  Bean & Eaton (2000) 119
  Belch (2005) 131
  Bergen-Cico (2000) 14
  Boyd, Hunt, Kandell, & Lucas (2003) 119

Braxton, Bray, & Berger (2000) 89
Braxton & McClendon (2001-2) 124, 130
Braxton, Milem, & Sullivan (2000) 51, 129
Cavote & Kopera-Frye (2004) 53
Chen & Carroll (2005) 135
Colton, Connor, Schultz, & Easter (1999-2000) 77
Daempfle (2003-04) 131
Dillon (2003) 61, 83
Donnelly & Borland (2002) 46
Engle, Reilly, & Levine (2003-4) 78
Fenske, Porter, & DuBrock (2000) 142
Furr & Elling (2002) 22
Harvey & Anderson (2005) 136
Helland, Stallings, & Braxton (2001-2) 39
Hernandez & Lopez (2004) 23
Horn & Carroll (2004) 136
Hrabowski (2005) 23
Hunter (2006) 57
Hurtado & Carter (1997) 23
Hutto & Fenwick (2002) 79, 114
Johnson (2000-01) 63, 132
Keup (2005) 57
Logan, Salisbury-Glennon, & Spence (2000) 37, 64
Longerbeam, Sedlacek, & Alatorre (2004) 25
Lumina Foundation for Education (2004) 136
Lundquist, Spalding, & Landrum (2002-3) 92
Mangold, Bean, Adams, Schwab, & Lynch (2002-3) 80
Murie & Thomson (2001) 73
Murtaugh, Burns, & Schuster (1999) 133
Nagda, Gregerman, Jonides, von
    Hippel, & Lerner (1998) 92
Ness (2002) 26, 115
Nora (2001) 97
Packard, Walsh, & Seidenberg (2004) 26
Perry, Cabrera, & Vogt (1999) 81
Potts, Schultz, & Foust (2003-4) 66, 102
Schnell & Doetkott (2002-3) 55
Smith (2003) 127
Stage & Hossler (2000) 121
Starke, Harth, & Sirianni (2001) 55
Thomas (2000) 102
Tinto (2000) 66
Upcraft, Gardner, Barefoot, & Associates (2004) 128
Wasburn & Miller (2004) 28
Wolf-Wendel, Tuttle, & Keller-Wolff (1999) 39
Zurita (2005) 29
    Theory
        Belch (2005) 31
        Braxton (2000) 129
        Elkins, Braxton, & James (2000) 31, 95, 131
        Hernandez & Lopez (2004) 23
        Hurtado & Carter (1997) 23
Scholarship Programs
    Ackerman, Young, & Young (2005) 107
    St. John, Gross, Musoba, & Chung (2005) 110, 139
Self-Advocacy
    Smith, English, & Vasek (2002) 31
Self-Efficacy
    Bean & Eaton (2000) 119
    Boyd, Hunt, Kandell, & Lucas (2003) 119

Chemers, Hu, & Garcia (2001) 119
Coffman & Gilligan (2002) 99, 120
Engle, Reilly, & Levine (2003-4) 78
Hoover (2003) 120, 132
Kahn & Nauta (2001) 133, 144
Stage & Hossler (2000) 121
Wolf-Wendel, Tuttle, & Keller-Wolff (1999) 39
Zajacova, Lynch, & Espenshade (2005) 20, 123
Self-Esteem
    Engle, Reilly, & Levine (2003-4) 78
    Schwartz & Washington (2002) 27, 115, 134
Self-Image/Concept
    Boulter (2002) 89
    Bryson, Smith, & Vineyard (2002) 21, 42
    Lowery et al. (2005) 16
    Schlosser & Sedlacek (2001) 121
Sense of Belonging
    Donahue (2004) 89, 100
    Hoffman, Richmond, Morrow, &
        Salomone (2002-3) 62, 90, 100
Service-Learning
    Keup (2005) 57
    Oates & Leavitt (2003) 65, 69
    Smith & McCann (2001) 53
    Tobolowsky (2005) 56
    Zlotkowski (2002) 69
    Zlotkowski (2005) 70
Social Integration
    Braxton, Bray, & Berger (2000) 89
    Braxton & McClendon (2001-2) 124, 130
    Nagda, Gregerman, Jonides, von
        Hippel, & Lerner (1998) 92
    Thomas (2000) 102
Social Support
    Coffman & Gilligan (2002) 99, 120
    Colton, Connor, Schultz, & Easter (1999-2000) 77
    Elkins, Braxton, & James (2000) 31, 95, 131
    Paul & Brier (2001) 101
    Perrine (2001) 17, 81
    Pritchard & Wilson (2003) 17, 121
    Perry, Cabrera, & Vogt (1999) 81
Socioeconomic Status
    Braunstein, McGrath, & Pescatrice (2000-01) 129, 141
    Cabrera, & LaNasa (2001) 107
    Jones (2005) 23
    Young & Johnson (2004) 111
Spirituality
    Bryant, Choi, & Yasuno (2003) 20
    Higher Education Research Institute (2005) 21
Standardized Tests
    Chenoweth (1998) 108
STEM Disciplines
    Andrade (2001) 139
    Barrows & Goodfellow (2005) 59
    Bauer & Liang (2003) 9, 128
    Daempfle (2003-04) 131
    Fenske, Porter, & DuBrock (2000) 142
    Hagedorn, Siadet, Fogel, Nora, & Pascarella (1999) 70, 131
    Wasburn & Miller (2004) 28

Stress

Charles, Dinwiddie, & Massey (2004) 15, 22

Chemers, Hu, & Garcia (2001) 119

Hickman & Crossland (2004-5) 96

Perrine (2001) 17, 81

Struthers, Perry, & Menec (2000) 19

Coping with

Struthers, Perry, & Menec (2000) 19

Effects of

Zajacova, Lynch, & Espenshade (2005) 20, 123

Management

Parker, Duffy, Wood, Bond, & Hogan (2005) 120, 134

Student

Affairs Practice

Coomes & DeBard (2004) 10

Crissman Ishler & Upcraft (2001) 45, 141

Characteristics

Astin, Oseguera, Sax, & Korn (2002) 9

Bauer & Liang (2003) 9, 128

Crissman Ishler (2005) 10

Horn, Peter, & Rooney (2002) 11

Howe & Strauss (2000) 11

Keeling (2003) 12, 75

Keup & Stolzenberg (2004) 84

Lounsbury, Saudargas, & Gibson (2004) 133

Murtaugh, Burns, & Schuster (1999) 133

Newton (2000) 12

Pryor, Hurtado, Saenz, Lindholm,
    Korn, & Mahoney (2005) 12

Pascarella & Terenzini (2005) 13, 126

Higher Education Research Institute (2005) 21

Development (see also cognitive development)

Bryant, Choi, & Yasuno (2003) 20

Jones (2005) 23

Kuh & Hu (2001) 91

Zhao & Kuh (2004) 67

Development Theory

Higbee (2005) 71

Pascarella & Terenzini (2005) 13, 126

Skipper (2005) 12

Ting, Grant, & Pienert (2000) 82

Expectations

Daempfle (2003-04) 131

Gallagher & Allen (2000) 73, 94

Gordon & Steele (2003) 11

Helland, Stallings, & Braxton (2001-2) 39

Hicks (2003) 40

Jackson, Pancer, Pratt, & Hunsberger (2000) 40

Longerbeam, Sedlacek, & Alatorre (2004) 25

Paul, Manetas, Grady, & Vivona (2001) 38

Schilling & Schilling (2005) 41

Schilling & Schilling (1999) 41

Schwartz & Washington (2002) 27, 115, 134

Needs

Dadonna & Cooper (2002) 46

Optimism

Brissette, Scheier, & Carver (2002) 99

Satisfaction

Coffman & Gilligan (2002) 99, 120

Gallagher & Allen (2000) 73, 94

Hutto & Fenwick (2002) 79, 114

Kuh & Hu (2001) 91

Mastrodicasa (2001) 75, 114

Walker & Taub (2001) 103

Services

Daniel & Scott (2001) 95

Grant-Vallone, Reid, Umali, & Pohlert (2003-4) 32, 79

Hossler, Kuh, & Olsen (2001) 125

Success

Barefoot (2000) 56, 124

Barefoot et al. (2005) 124

Bean & Eaton (2000) 119

Boyd, Hunt, Kandell, & Lucas (2003) 119

Busby, Gammel, & Jeffcoat (2002) 45

Clark (2005) 29, 130

Dillon (2003) 61, 83

Engle, Reilly, & Levine (2003-4) 78

Hossler, Kuh, & Olsen (2001) 125

Hunter (2006) 57

Jacoby & Garland (2004) 30

Kuh, Kinzie, Schuh, Whitt, &
    Associates (2005) 91, 94, 125

Lumina Foundation for Education (2004, Spring) 136

McLure & Child (1999) 38

Miller, Bender, & Schuh (2005) 40

Parker, Duffy, Wood, Bond, & Hogan (2005) 120, 134

Pritchard & Wilson (2003) 17, 121

Schilling & Schilling (2005) 41

Schlosser & Sedlacek (2001) 121

Ting, Grant, & Pienert (2000) 82

Tuckman (2003) 123

Academic Success

Bauer & Liang (2003) 9, 128

Bryson, Smith, & Vineyard (2002) 21, 42

Cavote & Kopera-Frye (2004) 53

Commander, Valeri-Gold, & Darnell (2004) 60

Freer-Weiss (2004-5) 43, 112

Glennen, Martin, & Walden (2000) 37

Hoover (2003) 120, 132

Hrabowski (2005) 23

Martin & Walden (2000) 37

Schilling & Schilling (1999) 41

Starke, Harth, & Sirianni (2001) 55

Upcraft, Gardner, Barefoot, & Associates (2004) 128

Zajacova, Lynch, & Espenshade (2005) 20, 123

Support

Bergen-Cico (2000) 14

Kuh, Kinzie, Schuh, Whitt, & Associates (2005) 80

Trends

Astin, Oseguera, Sax, & Korn (2002) 9

Pryor, Hurtado, Saenz, Lindholm,
    Korn, & Mahoney (2005) 12

Students of Color

Arredondo & Knight (2005) 128, 139

Black & Amir (2002) 135

Bryson, Smith, & Vineyard (2002) 21, 42

Charles, Dinwiddie, & Massey (2004) 15, 22

Dadonna & Cooper (2002) 46

Harvey & Anderson (2005) 136

Hernandez & Lopez (2004) 23

Hrabowski (2005) 23
Hurtado & Carter (1997) 23
Hutto & Fenwick (2002) 79, 114
Kim (2004) 109
Mangold, Bean, Adams, Schwab, & Lynch (2002-3) 80
Mortenson (2005, August) 137
Nagda, Gregerman, Jonides, von
    Hippel, & Lerner (1998) 92
Perna (2002) 38
Rendón, García, & Person (2004) 26
Santos & Reigadas (2004-5) 93
Starke, Harth, & Sirianni (2001) 55
St. John, Hu, Simmons, & Musoba (2001) 44
Weissman, Bulakowski, & Jumisko (1998) 28, 113
White (2005) 29
Zurita (2005) 29
 Mentoring
Wallace, Abel, & Ropers-Huilman (2000) 42
Students with Disabilities
Belch (2005) 31
Smith, English, & Vasek (2002) 31
Student-Faculty Interaction
Baker, Meyer, & Hunt (2005) 59
Boulter (2002) 89
Colton, Connor, Schultz, & Easter (1999-2000) 77
Dillon (2003) 61, 83
Donahue (2004) 89, 100
Kuh & Hu (2001) 91
Kuh, Kinzie, Schuh, Whitt, & Associates (2005) 91
Light (2001) 85, 126
Mastrodicasa (2001) 75, 114
Perry, Cabrera, & Vogt (1999) 81
Santos & Reigadas (2004-5) 93
Study Skills
Ting, Grant, & Pienert (2000) 82
Substance Abuse
Bergen-Cico (2000) 14
Lenz (2004) 16
Reifman & Watson (2003) 18
Sessa (2005) 19, 30, 98
Summer Bridge Programs
Cuseo (2003) 77
Glennen, Martin, & Walden (2000) 37
Logan, Salisbury-Glennon, & Spence (2000) 37, 64
Wolf-Wendel, Tuttle, & Keller-Wolff (1999) 39
Supplemental Instruction
Hafer (2001) 70
Hodges, Dochen, & Joy (2001) 71
Hodges & White (2001) 71
Martin & Hurley (2005) 72
Teaching
Braxton, Bray, & Berger (2000) 89
Greiner & Westbrook (2002) 90
 Strategies
Erickson & Strommer (2005) 51
Smith & McCann (2001) 53
Zlotkowski (2002) 69
Technology
Barone & Hagner (2001) 86
Fabich (2004) 46, 111

Gordan, Habley, & Associates (2000) 74
Haulmark & Williams (2004) 47
King & Kerr (2005) 75
Kubey, Lavin, & Barrows (2001) 87
Kuh, Kinzie, Schuh, Whitt, & Associates (2005) 91
Logan, Salisbury-Glennon, & Spence (2000) 37, 64
Twale & Schaller (2003) 48
 ...and Learning
Shuell & Farber (2001) 88
 ...and Teaching
Barone & Hagner (2001) 86
Flowers, Pascarella, & Pierson (2000) 87
Junco (2005) 52, 87
Parang, Raine, & Stevenson (2000) 68
Thomson & Stringer (2000) 55, 88
Transition to College (see also college adjustment)
Belcher (2005) 140
Bray & Born (2004) 15
Gold, Miller, & Rutholz (2001) 15, 78
Miller, Dyer, & Nadler (2002) 47
National Center for Education Statistics (2005) 12, 138
Nora (2001) 97
Rendón, García, & Person (2004) 26
Schwartz & Buboltz (2004) 98
U. S. Census Bureau (2005) 13, 110
Weissman, Bulakowski, & Jumisko (1998) 28, 113
Tribal Colleges
First-year experience to help students
    succeed (2005) 22, 114
Ness (2002) 26, 115
TRIO Programs
Colton, Connor, Schultz, & Easter (1999-2000) 77
Tutoring
Cuseo (2003) 77
Hodges & White (2001) 71
Perrine & Wilkins (2001) 73, 81
Two-Year Institutions
Bailey & Alfonso (2005) 58, 111
Fabich (2004) 46, 111
Freer-Weiss (2004-5) 43, 111
Mortenson (2005, September) 109, 138
National Center for Education Statistics (2005) 12, 138
Tobolowsky (2005) 56
Undecided Students
Donnelly & Borland (2002) 46
Gordon & Steele (2003) 11
Sams, Brown, Hussey, & Leonard (2003) 76
Undergraduate Research
Nagda, Gregerman, Jonides, von
    Hippel, & Lerner (1998) 92
Underprepared Students
Martin & Hurley (2005) 72
Web-based
 Instruction (see technology and teaching)
 Surveys
Carini, Hayek, Kuh, Kennedy, & Ouimet (2003) 141
Sax, Gilmartin, & Bryant (2003) 145